# DESIGNING and DELIVERING

# SUPERIOR CUSTOMER VALUE

## Concepts, Cases, and Applications

Art Weinstein
William C. Johnson

$S^t_L$

St. Lucie Press
Boca Raton   London   New York   Washington, D.C.

**Library of Congress Cataloging-in-Publication Data**

Weinstein, Art
  Designing and delivering superior customer value: concepts, cases, and applications /
by Art Weinstein and William C. Johnson.
    p. cm.
  Includes bibliographical references and index.
  ISBN 1-57444-240-6 (alk. paper)
    1. Customer services—Management. 2. Customer satisfaction.
  I. Johnson, William C. (William Charles), 1954–. II. Title.
  HF5415.5.J6393  1999
  658.8′12—dc21
                            99-29151
                               CIP

No claim to original U.S. Government works
International Standard Book Number 1-57444-240-6
Library of Congress Card Number 99-29151
Printed in the United States of America 1 2 3 4 5 6 7 8 9 0
Printed on acid-free paper

# Preface

Designing and delivering superior customer value are the keys to successful business strategy in the 21st century. Value reigns supreme in today's marketplace, where customers are no longer willing to pay more than a good or service is worth. Consider the remarkable success of service organizations such as Amazon.com, Dell Computer, General Electric, Hewlett-Packard, Lexus, Motorola, Nordstrom, Rubbermaid, Southwest Airlines, and Wal-Mart — these companies truly know how to maximize value for their customers.

According to the Marketing Science Institute, customer value issues dealing with marketing metrics (the value of a customer, the value of loyalty, and lifetime value) and understanding the customer experience (value from the customer's perspective) are research priorities one and two — out of 14 sets of pressing marketing issues — for the new millennium.[1] Market-focused management posits that organizations should provide outstanding value to customers, as they are the most important organizational stakeholder. A recent study of chief marketing officers (CMOs) and chief financial officers (CFOs) in *Fortune* 1000 firms affirmed this proposition. Of 16 organizational goals mentioned, both groups of top executives ranked customer satisfaction as the primary business goal. The CMOs rated customer value creation second,

---

[1] Anon. (1998) *Research Priorities 1998–2000,* Cambridge, MA: Marketing Science Institute.

---

[2] Hall, P.L. and Williams, T.G. (1998) Marketing/finance executives' personal and business value perspectives: implications for market-focused management, *International Journal of Value-Based Management,* 95, pp. 125–157.

while the CFOs listed this third (long-term profit was cited second for CFOs and third for CMOs).[2]

We have been researching, writing, and speaking about customer value in service markets for more than 3 years. In addition, we have developed and teach the definitive MBA course on the subject, "Delivering Superior Customer Value." We are truly convinced that developing the right value proposition (combining quality, service, price, image, innovation, and intangibles) must be the top priority for management. A customer-driven business culture that stresses service management, continuous quality improvement, and product innovation provides focus and direction for the organization and ensures that outstanding value will be offered to customers; this, in turn, results in enhanced market performance. Unfortunately, when they are caught up in the daily pressures of running complex organizations, many managers lose sight of customers' needs and wants. As a result, the delivered experience often falls short of customer expectations. Great companies consistently meet and exceed customer desires.

*Superior Customer Value* is assembled from the latest thinking in the business and academic communities. It summarizes and extends leading marketing/management work in this crucial area. Building on a three-pronged approach to the study of customer value — concepts, cases, and applications — the book provides a comprehensive and highly practical marketing management resource. It explores important marketing planning and strategy issues which emphasize relationship management strategies to keep customers satisfied, as well as "best practices" in customer service, organizational responsiveness, and market orientation which impact value-creating managers in fast-changing, highly competitive global service industries.

*Superior Customer Value* was written to provide marketing practitioners, managers and executives, and scholars (professors and graduate students) with an informative, state-of-the-art guide to designing, implementing, and evaluating a customer value strategy in service organizations. Most of the material appearing in the book has been discussed at length in our MBA course, "Delivering Superior Customer Value." In addition to the thousands of MBA students who have been exposed to these ideas, hundreds of managers have benefited from our interpreta-

---

[3] See Weinstein, A. (1998) How to create an innovative MBA course, *Marketing Educator*, Spring, p. 6, for further discussion regarding the development and acceptance of the MBA course "Delivering Superior Customer Value."

tion of the new customer value paradigm via executive seminars and marketing doctoral courses.[3]

*Superior Customer Value* is organized into five parts. *Part 1: Customer Value Concepts* is the foundation material, Chapters 1 through 9. This text component examines critical business issues such as the importance of creating value for customers, customer orientation, value-creating processes and operations, value propositions, quality service, pricing, strategies for adding and promoting value, customer retention approaches, and relationship marketing. Each chapter includes useful figures, tables, checklists, end-of-chapter discussion questions, and additional reference material.

*Part 2: Customer Value Cases* provides 19 detailed, "hands-on" examples of how successful organizations create value for their customers. This section opens with a framework for analyzing business cases called the Customer Value Funnel Approach. Cases about leading companies such as AAA Motor Club, Ethyl Corporation, Glaxo, Harrah's Entertainment, Motorola, Pizza Hut, Publix Super Markets, Southwest Airlines, and others are presented. Each case provides an in-depth look at a dominant customer value theme (e.g., responding to change, being customer oriented, achieving customer loyalty, etc.) and offers end-of-case questions to guide the analyses. The cases provide learning opportunities to model effective customer value practices.

Parts 3, 4, and 5 consist of abstracts, exercises, and a customer value audit. Twenty recent articles on customer value topics have been condensed for interested readers. Each abstract includes a contribution of the work, a summary of major findings, and the customer value implication(s). Eight field-tested learning exercises follow. These discussion-generating activities are ideal for small group classes or seminars. Finally, the Customer Value Assessment Tool (CVAT), a self-evaluation tool, helps organizations diagnose their value proposition.

We look forward to learning more about your customer value marketing experiences. Feel free to contact us to discuss any of the material in our text further (School of Business and Entrepreneurship; Nova Southeastern University; 3100 SW 9th Avenue; Ft. Lauderdale, FL 33315; 1-800-672-7223 [phone]; 954-262-3965 [fax]; art@sbe.nova.edu; billyboy@sbe.nova.edu).

Art Weinstein
Bill Johnson

# Acknowledgments

Many individuals provided valuable input toward the preparation of *Superior Customer Value*. First and foremost, we thank our Nova Southeastern University associates. In particular, Randy Pohlman, Dean of the School of Business and Entrepreneurship, re-energized us to think about customer value in marketing in a new light. Norapol (Paul) Chinuntdej did a stellar job as our research assistant by locating important scholarly references, drafting the article abstracts, and writing the Amazon.com vignette in Chapter 7. Isabell Layer provided computer graphics support for several key figures and exhibits. Professor Cathy Goodwin's insights were invaluable while editing some of our material. Sylvia Lanski word processed some of the case studies. Over the past 3 years, the thousands of MBA students that have benefited from taking "Delivering Superior Customer Value" and dozens of executive seminar participants in marketing provided us with a tremendous learning laboratory in which to sculpt and fine tune our new marketing philosophy.

Second, we acknowledge the following people for generously sharing their outstanding case studies and other contributions. In alphabetical order, thank you to Barry Barnes, Hilton Barrett, Eldon H. Bernstein, Samir Chacour, Richard J. Chvala, John Feather, Les Feldman, Brett A. Gordon, Pam A. Gordon, Bob Green, Pam Hillery, Donald J. King, Bill McDonald, Jim Moylan, Dean Mujtaba, Linda Burke Rutherford, Ed Schwerin, Alan Seidman, Wolfgang Ulaga, and Miles J. Volin.

Last but not least, we especially thank you for reading *Superior Customer Value*!

# The Authors

**Art Weinstein** earned his Ph.D. in 1991 from Florida International University and is a Professor of Marketing at Nova Southeastern University, Fort Lauderdale, FL. Dr. Weinstein is the author of *Defining Your Market* (Haworth Press, 1998) and *Market Segmentation* (Irwin Publishing, 1994) and more than 40 scholarly articles and papers on customer-focused topics and marketing strategy issues. He is the founder/editor of the *Journal of Segmentation in Marketing*. Dr. Weinstein has consulted for many high-tech and service firms.

**William C. Johnson** earned his Ph.D. in 1985 from Arizona State University and is a Professor of Marketing at Nova Southeastern University, Fort Lauderdale, FL. Dr. Johnson is the co-author of *Total Quality in Marketing* (St. Lucie Press, 1996) and has published widely in marketing journals and trade publications. He has consulted for companies in the healthcare, industrial chemical, and soft-drink industries, as well as for small businesses.

# Contents

# Dedication

**AW:** *As always, with love to Sandee, my number one fan, and to our new blessing, Trevor.*

**WCJ:** *To my mother, who understood value when she gave unselfishly through the years.*

# Part 1. Customer Value Concepts

# 1 Customers Want Top Value

"The 1990s have become the 'value decade' … your challenge is to give customers all of what they want, and none of what they do not." (William A. Band, Vice President of Rand & Strong, Inc.)

Consider the remarkable success of companies such as Amazon.com, America Online, CarMax, Dell Computer, Kinko's, Starbuck's, and Yahoo!. These business pioneers have found better ways to create value for customers with changing needs and wants. Adaptable giants such as American Express, AT&T, Hertz, McDonald's, Marriott, Microsoft, and Wal-Mart have also benefited from customer value thinking. It has helped them design winning marketing strategies to maintain leadership positions in highly competitive markets.

In the 1980s, the battle for customers was won or lost based on quality. As Total Quality Management (TQM) became the rage in business, quality gaps diminished, and companies focused on customer service. Enhanced customer value synthesizes and extends the quality and customer service movements and has emerged as the dominant theme for business success for 21st century companies.[1]

Managing customer value will be even more critical to progressive organizations in our service- and information-based economy. Innovative companies that create maximum value for their customers will survive and thrive; they will carve sustainable competitive advantages in the marketplace. Other firms, those not providing adequate value, will struggle or disappear.

By examining relevant customer value, marketing, and services concepts and applications, this opening chapter accomplishes four objectives. First, we explain why customer value must be the overall basis for
business strategy. Second, we review the size and scope of the service
sector and show how service products create value for customers. Third,
we offer several key customer value implications for forward-thinking
managers. We conclude the chapter by discussing the attributes of
value-creating organizations.

## The Importance of Customer Value

Great companies do not just satisfy customers; they strive to delight and
"wow" them. Superior customer value means continually creating business experiences that exceed customer expectations. Value is the strategic driver that multinational companies, as well as entrepreneurial firms,
utilize to differentiate themselves from the pack in the minds of customers.

How is it that Lexus can sell sport utility vehicles for $60,000 and
Taco Bell can offer meal combinations for less than $4.00, and both are
considered good values? Value is the answer — and value is defined by
your customers. Companies that offer outstanding value turn buyers
("tryers") into lifetime customers.

### What Does Value Really Mean?

The concept of customer value is as old as ancient trade practices. In
early barter transactions, buyers carefully evaluated sellers' offerings;
they agreed to do business only if the benefits (products received)
relative to the cost (items traded) were perceived as being a fair (or
better) value. Hence, value is "the satisfaction of customer requirements
at the lowest total cost of acquisition, ownership, and use."[2] As an area
of formal marketing study, value-based thinking has evolved over a half
century; it originated at the General Electric Company in 1947.

According to a dictionary definition, *value* means relative worth or
importance. Furthermore, value implies excellence based on desirability
or usefulness and is represented as a magnitude or quantity. On the
other hand, *values* are the abstract concepts of what is right, worthwhile,
or desirable.[3] Management's values impact how an organization creates
value and, ultimately, its success. The legends about the Frito-Lay sales
rep stocking a small grocery store's potato chip rack in a blizzard and Art

Fry's intrapreneurial initiative that brought the Post-It to 3M reinforce organizational cultures.

A value-driven marketing strategy helps organizations in ten areas: (1) understanding customer choices, (2) identifying customer segments, (3) increasing competitive options (for example, offering more products), (4) avoiding price wars, (5) improving service quality, (6) strengthening communications, (7) focusing on what is meaningful to customers, (8) building customer loyalty, (9) improving brand success, and (10) developing strong customer relationships.[4]

According to Woodruff and Gardial,[5] a three-stage value hierarchy exists which consists of attributes, consequences, and desired end-states. These levels of abstraction describe the product/service, the user/product interaction, and the goals of the buyer (person or organization), respectively. For example, a new-car buyer may seek attributes such as comfortable seating, an easy-to-read instrumental panel, smooth shifting, a *Consumer Reports* endorsement, no pressure sales tactics, and a good service/warranty program. At higher levels of abstraction, buyers may want driving ease, no hassles, and reliability (consequences), and ultimately peace of mind (desired end-state).

## The Heart of Value: Product Quality, Service, and Price

Customer value can be expressed in many ways and is reviewed next. The approach known as QSP states that value is primarily a combination of quality, service, and price.[6] This set of three core ingredients — product quality, service quality, and value-based prices — is called the *customer value triad*. The triad provides a solid springboard for formulating an initial business strategy.[7]

Designing and delivering superior customer value has become a mandate for management. In choice-filled arenas, the balance of power has shifted from companies to value-seeking customers. Value-creating enterprises often differentiate themselves on one key attribute but must meet acceptable threshold levels with respect to quality, pricing, and service; competition provides little room for weakness in any area.

For example, Hewlett-Packard (H-P) is obsessed with new product development and product quality, Nordstrom is renowned for unparalleled customer service, and Wal-Mart stresses "Everyday Low Prices". While H-P, Nordstrom, and Wal-Mart have each created reputations due to a singular attribute, successful retailers such as Barnes and Noble,

Home Depot, and Victoria's Secret know that price is only part of the value equation — value is the total shopping experience. This includes such customer benefits as dominant product assortment, respect for customers, time and energy savings, and fun, as well as fair prices.[8]

American Airlines attempts to provide relatively high levels of both product quality and service quality. Because tradeoffs exist among the triad elements, companies cannot expect to be market leaders in all three areas. The cost of developing and sustaining a three-dimensional leadership position would be overwhelming.

Building on this idea, value is delivered to customers in one of three ways: (1) companies can opt to have the best product (product leadership), such as Johnson & Johnson, Motorola, and Nike; (2) best total cost (operational excellence), such as Dell Computer, Southwest Airlines, and Target Stores; or (3) best total solution (customer intimacy), such as Airborne Express, Frito-Lay, and Nordstrom. The core capabilities required to implement these strategies successfully are innovation (product leadership), process efficiency (operational excellence), and relationship building (customer intimacy).[9]

Value may be best defined from the customer's perspective as a tradeoff between the benefits received vs. the price paid. Value is created when product and user come together within a particular use situation. Thus, each transaction is evaluated as to a dissatisfaction, satisfaction, or high satisfaction experience, in terms of the value received. These service encounters impact customer decisions to form long-term relationships with organizations.

Clearly, we can see that value is a much richer concept than just a fair price. While low cost, top quality, and superb service are valued by specific target markets, value is really a multidimensional attribute. Varying emphases on quality, service, or price (the core elements) plus consideration of the firm's image and intangible factors define a company's value proposition (see Chapter 4).

## How Service Firms Create Value

Service opportunities create value in business and consumer markets. In addition, services affect all aspects of our lives and drive advanced economies. Many experts feel that the next economic wave is imminent — a transition into an information-led economy. Nicholas Negroponte, author of *Being Digital,* explains it best. He said that in the future, when we talk about products, we will be more likely to be talking about bits than atoms.[10]

Internet-housed companies such as Amazon.com, CDnow, and Virtual Vineyards have clearly demonstrated the rewards of competing in *market-space* as opposed to the *marketplace*. Today, a website presence is becoming as common as a listing in the Yellow Pages.

## The Significance of the Service Sector

The service sector now accounts for the majority of the gross domestic product (GDP) and jobs in the U.S. and in Australia, Canada, the European Union, Japan, and other industrialized nations. The U.S. service sector is comprised of five major subsectors: transportation and utilities; wholesale trade; retail trade; finance, insurance, and real estate (FIRE); and other consumer and business services. Recently, fast-growing services have included air transportation, commodity brokers, insurance carriers, security, and wholesaling. Overall, services-producing industries accounted for nearly $5 trillion in 1996. This sector represents more than 63% of the GDP. In contrast, goods-producing industries (manufacturing, construction, mining, and agricultural/forestry/fishing) accounted for less than $2 trillion, or less than 25% of the GDP. Because most output in the government sector (about $1 billion and 13% of GDP) is services oriented, in actuality the service sector accounts for nearly three quarters of the U.S. economic value (see Table 1.1).[11]

In 1950, more than 40% of U.S. payroll was found in goods-producing industries.[12] In the 23 most advanced countries, employment in manufacturing fell from 28% of the workforce in 1970 to 18% by 1995.[13] Today, the American and Canadian service sectors represent about 80% of employment.[11,14] Of the projected job growth in the U.S. through the year 2006, 87% will be in the service sector.[15] Table 1.2 lists jobs that are hot and not so hot for the new millennium.

## What Is a Service?

Products can be defined as goods, services, and ideas. Today, there are very few pure goods. Almost all consumer and business products (for example, cars, cell phones, computers, etc.) are packaged with strong service components. This can include a service warranty, monthly rate

**Table 1.1. The Importance of the Service Sector in the U.S. Economy**

| Industries | 1996 GDP (billions of dollars) | Percent of 1996 GDP (%) |
|---|---|---|
| Transportation, utilities | 645 | 8.5 |
| Wholesale trade | 517 | 6.8 |
| Retail trade | 668 | 8.7 |
| Finance, insurance, real estate | 1448 | 19.0 |
| Services | 1539 | 20.2 |
| Services-producing, private | 4818 | 63.1 |
| Government | 996 | 13.0 |
| Goods-producing, private | 1882 | 24.6 |
| Gross domestic product | 7636 | 100.0 |

*Note:* A rounding/statistical discrepancy of less than 1% is included in GDP total.

*Source:* Adapted from Lum, S.K.S. and Yuskavage, R.E. (1997) Gross product industry, 1947–1996, *Survey of Current Business,* Nov., Table 3.

plan, 24-hour access to technical support, and other service options. In the majority of cases, companies market blended products. A fast-food meal is the classic example — while the burger, fries, and Coke are the goods, the service experience (speed, brand image, atmospherics, etc.) is often more highly valued by consumers.

**Table 1.2. Job Creation in the Service Sector: 13 Winners and Losers**

| Fast Growth Jobs | Slow/No Growth Jobs |
|---|---|
| Business | Bookkeeper |
| Child care | Data processor |
| Computer graphics and science | Directory assistance operator |
| Consulting | Forester |
| Engineers | Jewelry repairer |
| Health services | Miner |
| Human resources | Petroleum worker |
| Information technology | Railroad worker |
| Media | Statistical clerk |
| Optical technologists | Stenographer |
| Residential care | Textile worker |
| Retail | Tobacco farmer |
| Temporary personnel services | Typesetter |

*Source:* Adapted from a Web article by Kleiman, C. (1997) Top jobs for the next century, *Chicago Tribune Media Services.*

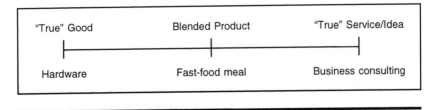

**Figure 1.1. Three Types of Products**

Pure services such as insurance are highly intangible and present unique challenges to marketers. Management consulting is an example of an idea (selling a client a feasibility study or reengineering plan). As Figure 1.1 illustrates, a continuum exists based on the degree of product tangibility. Effective service marketers must be able to make tangible the intangible (this service quality issue is discussed in Chapter 5).

To shed further light on business opportunities in the service sector, a 2 × 2 services classification matrix — consisting of four cells and four examples of organizations in each category — is presented in Figure 1.2. Two caveats are called for. First, some companies compete in more than one cell (banks, CPAs, insurance agents, etc.). Second, professionalism is a critical success factor for all organizations. The automotive detailer that takes two days to return telephone calls, shows up an hour late for scheduled appointments, or fails to make your car "shine" appropriately will not stay in business for long. The term *professional* used in the context of the matrix is to distinguish firms that have specialized knowledge and advanced education or training.

| Type of Service | Business | Consumer |
|-----------------|----------|----------|
| Professional | Accounting, legal, marketing research, and management consulting | Attorneys, dentists, financial planners, and physicians |
| Other | Logistics, janitorial, printers, and security | Fast food, hair stylists, lawn care, and pest control |

**Figure 1.2. Service Classification Matrix** (Adapted and expanded from Gronroos, C. (1979) An applied theory for marketing industrial services, *Industrial Marketing Management,* 8, pp. 45–50.)

## Customer Value: Marketing Management Implications

Maximizing customer value is an evolving challenge for service marketers. Visionary companies are responding to the new breed of smarter, more demanding customers by rethinking some of their traditional job functions, using customer value-based decision-making and stressing customer retention strategies. To adapt more effectively and efficiently to customers, new types of value providers (value adders) are often needed. While some changes may seem to be cosmetic, in reality they are sound strategic responses to the changing business environment and the need to deliver superior value to customers. Consider these four examples:

- Procter & Gamble, the quintessential consumer marketer, recently renamed its sales force the Customer Business Development (CBD) Group. Selling is now only a small part of the CBD representative's job function. More important marketing activities include assisting customers in reducing inventory, tailoring product and price offerings in each market, and creating suitable co-marketing promotional plans.[16]
- Merck, Xerox, and other *Fortune* 500 companies have created Market Segmentation Managers.
- The Differentiation Strategist of Micro Motion (a Colorado-based division of Emerson Electric that specializes in the production of mass flowmeters) is charged with the responsibility of enhancing the company's customer service activities.
- Vacation Break, a Fort Lauderdale travel provider and developer of vacation ownership resorts (recently acquired by Fairfield Communities), calls their front desk receptionist the Director of First Impressions.

A customer value decision-making framework offers management a unique and potentially superior way of understanding business problems and opportunities. For example, the Value Funnel (see "Analyzing Business Cases: The Customer Value Funnel Approach" in Part 2 of the book) is a systematic, multifaceted, integrated, and rich tool for making customer-focused marketing management decisions. Managers can consider value-based criteria such as economic values, relevant values of the various constituencies, maximizing value over time, value adders (or destroyers), value-based segments, and value tradeoffs to improve their

---

**Customer Value Checklist 1.**
**Guidelines for Creating Customer Value**

1. Do your goods and services really perform?
2. Do your company and its people give more than what is expected?
3. Does your firm stand behind its work with service warranties?
4. Are your pricing policies realistic?
5. Do your advertising and promotional materials give customers the necessary facts?
6. Do you use frequent-buyer programs, toll-free numbers, and membership clubs to build customer relationships?

(Adapted from Power, C. et al. (1991) Value marketing: quality, service, and fair pricing are the keys to selling in the '90s, *Business Week,* Nov. 11, pp. 132–140.)

---

business analyses. An initial list of six important customer value issues for managers to ponder is summarized in Customer Value Checklist 1.

The adoption of customer value in management's mission and vision statements means that customer retention (relationship management) becomes the primary vehicle for market success. Amazon.com's digital franchising concept links more than 40,000 websites and pays "associates" 5 to 15% of any revenues they generate. This clever cyber-based marketing strategy resulted in a 50% increase in new accounts, and repeat customers accounted for 60% of all orders.[17]

Enhanced customer value goes beyond isolated transactions and builds long-term bonds and partnerships in the marketplace. Strong customer/corporate ties change buyers to advocates. Increased customer loyalty results in increased usage frequency and variety. Perhaps more important, however, is the fact that delighted customers play an important word-of-mouth public relations role that creates new business opportunities via referrals. And, conversely, bad-mouthing by dissatisfied customers can be not only harmful but the very death knell to a company. Consider a case in point: one unhappy buyer at a computer superstore determined that the company lost $50,000 of his business (direct lifetime value) and another $350,000 (indirect lifetime value) due to negative word-of-mouth comments to his family and friends!

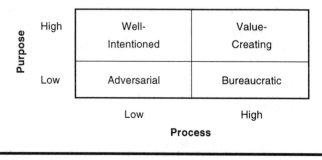

**Figure 1.3. The Value Matrix** (Adapted from Capowski, G. (1995) The force of value, *Management Review,* May, p. 34.)

## The Value-Creating Organization

Organizations should be viewed as value-creating entities. Customer-responsive organizations create value by solving individual customer problems. Delighted customers perceive a "high" value relative to the economic cost and hassle of obtaining a solution.[18] A strong competitive advantage can be gained through consistently providing superior customer value. As Figure 1.3 shows, value-creating firms such as Dell Computer score high in purpose (they understand their business and customers' desires) and high in process (they know how to utilize internal procedures to respond to customers effectively and efficiently).

Unfortunately, many organizations do not master both purpose (customer focus) and process (customer support) activities. The Internal Revenue Service (IRS) represents a bureaucratic organization. While the IRS does a reasonably good job processing tens of millions of tax packages annually, they rank relatively poorly on the purpose dimension. Recent developments in electronic filing, fax-on-demand tax forms and instructions, TeleTax phone service, and a website are all steps in the right direction. This government agency has a long way to go, however, in overcoming an unfavorable image. Most Americans perceive the tax system as overly complex, imprecise, time consuming, and at times unfair or even unnecessary.

Segmentation, targeting, and positioning (STP marketing) and product, price, promotion, and place (the 4P's) are focal points for value-creating actions in the firm. These strategic controllables have major implications for attracting (conquest marketing) and keeping (retention marketing) customers. Sometimes, companies may go too far in one direction at the expense of the latter. For example, America Online's solitary focus on the former cost the company millions of dollars in bad press; dealing with customer complaints, dissatisfaction, and defections; and legal fees. During this period of time, the company was viewed by their existing clients as adversarial (AOL's sales orientation during the mid-1990s is discussed further in Chapter 2). Recently, America Online has made tremendous improvements in both the purpose and process dimensions. To remain a market leader, AOL has committed itself to being a value-creating company.

Yet, there are some companies that try really hard, but just cannot seem to get it quite right — they are well intentioned. A foreign car repair specialist may do an excellent job of scheduling appointments with busy professionals only to find that the service technicians generally take longer than expected to fix cars or they routinely run out of stock on key auto parts.

The value matrix is a useful tool for management. Where would you place your company and your major competitors in the four quadrants? If your answer is anything other than value creating, then you clearly have some homework to do. As markets are dynamic, the status quo will not do; even value-creating organizations must constantly work at getting better to stay on top.

## Summary

To succeed in the new millennium, service organizations must do a great job of creating value for their customers. Developing strong bonds with customers creates loyalty which leads to high customer retention rates. Each firm must find the right mix of value ingredients to satisfy and delight their target markets. Creating and managing customer value is critical for business executives in today's highly changing and competitive markets. Next, we explore the two dimensions introduced in the value matrix. In Chapter 2, we explain what customer orientation means (purpose), and in Chapter 3 we review how to design and execute customer operations (processes) effectively.

## Customer Value Action Items

1. What is meant by customer value? In general, what do customers value?

2. How does your organization create value for customers? How are your competitors creating value? What can your organization do to offer superior value to customers?

3. Based on the QSP approach, objectively rate your company as above average, average, or below average on product quality, service, and pricing.

4. Using the value hierarchy (attributes, consequences, and end states), assess how well your organization fares with respect to customer value desires?

5. Identify three "best practices" from other industries that your company can adapt to provide better value to your customers.

6. How does your current service mix create value for customers? What new service products should be introduced that your company does not offer?

7. Are there new types of value providers (adders) that your firm should employ to do a better job of serving customers? Which existing management or staff positions should be restructured or eliminated because they add little or no value to customers?

8. Does your company stress conquest or retention marketing? What should they emphasize and why?

9. How can your organization improve with respect to purpose (customer focus) and process (customer support) activities?

# References

1. Fagiano, D. (1995) Fighting for customers on a new battlefield, *The American Salesman*, February, pp. 20–22.
2. DeRose, L.J. (1994) *The Value Network*, New York: AMACOM.
3. *Random House Webster's College Dictionary* (1992) New York: Random House.
4. MacStravic, S. (1997) Questions of value in health care, *Marketing Health Services*, Winter, pp. 50–53.
5. Woodruff, R.B. and Gardial, S.F. (1996) *Know Your Customer: New Approaches to Understanding Customer Value and Satisfaction*, Cambridge, MA: Blackwell Publishers.
6. Tucker, R.B. (1995) *Win the Value Revolution*, Franklin Lakes, NJ: Career Press.
7. Naumman, E. (1995) *Creating Customer Value*, Cincinnati, OH: Thompson Executive Press.
8. Berry, L. (1996) Retailers with a future, *Marketing Management*, Spring, pp. 39–46.
9. Treacy, M. and Wiersema, F. (1995) *The Discipline of Market Leaders*, Reading, MA: Addison-Wesley.
10. Negroponte, N. (1995) *Being Digital*, New York: Alfred A. Knopf.

11. Lum, S.K.S. and Yuskavage, R.E. (1997) Gross product by industry, 1947–96, *Survey of Current Business*, Nov., pp. 1–7.
12. Meisenheimer, J.R. (1998) Nonagricultural payroll and employment by industry, annual averages, 1939–97, in *U.S. Department of Labor, Current Employment Statistics Survey*, June 8, Washington, D.C.: Bureau of Labor Statistics, U.S. Government Printing Office.
13. Rowthorn, R. and Ramaswamy, R. (1997) Deindustrialization — its causes and implications, *Economic Issues*, No. 10, Washington, D.C.: International Monetary Fund, pp. 1–8.
14. Benjamin, T. (1998) MacJobs are a MacMyth, *The Labour Market Information Webzine for the Career Practitioner*, 1(6), April 24, pp. 1–2.
15. Franklin, J.C. (1997) Industry output and employment projections to 2006, *Monthly Labor Review*, Nov., pp. 39–57.
16. Conlon, G. (1997) Procter & Gamble, *Sales and Marketing Management*, Oct., p. 59.
17. Nakache, P. (1998) Secrets of the new brand builders, *Fortune*, June 22, pp. 167–170.
18. Davis, Jr., F.W. and Mandrodt, K.B. (1996) *Customer Responsive Management: The Flexible Advantage*, Cambridge, MA: Blackwell Business.

**Being Customer Oriented**

"Focus everything — all assets, all decisions — on your customers. They are the ultimate arbiters of success or failure." (Jack Smith, CEO of General Motors)

*et's get customer oriented!* Undoubtedly, you have heard this management mantra or a variation of this theme recently. Executives use phrases such as *customer driven, customer focused, market oriented,*[1] and so forth to motivate their people to do a better job serving the customer. While the idea is sound, too often it is just "lip service" or talk rather than a major investment for improving all facets of the organization and its business culture. A true customer-orientation basis creates and maximizes customer value which in turn leads to increased market performance.

This chapter explores how to implement a customer-focused marketing philosophy to impact long-term profitability favorably. First, we review examples of service companies that excel in this area. Next, we examine the changing marketing concept in business. Then, we compare a sales-oriented company to a marketing-driven firm. We conclude the chapter with practical managerial guidelines for creating a customer-oriented organization.

# Customer Commitment:
# How Market Leaders Do It

Great companies such as Dell Computer, FedEx, Nordstrom, and Southwest Airlines are extremely market oriented and are incredible at creating and delivering value to their highly satisfied, loyal customers. Here are three examples revealing how this key objective is accomplished: (1) Dell's customer-friendly website now generates more than $6 million a day in business; (2) Federal Express changed its name and repainted its trucks to read FedEx, as that is what customers called them ("let's FedEx this package to Omaha"); and (3) Nordstrom's sales associates have been known to buy products from a major competitor, Macy's, to satisfy an unfulfilled customer's request.

The spirit of Southwest Airlines is readily apparent. The Southwest culture creates customer value and lasting goodwill. On one entertaining flight from Baltimore to Fort Lauderdale, Southwest flight attendants played games with the passengers (for example, the passengers with the most credit cards, oldest penny, and best memory won cases of peanuts), joked about the captain's age, and encouraged passengers to smile and wave to passengers on the nearby American plane upon landing.

Greatness in marketing and customer service is a function of attitude, not resources. Consider the entrepreneurial tale of Hal and Sal. Hal, owner of a small diner/coffee shop, not only greets his regulars warmly by name (often with hugs and occasionally with kisses), but he also frequently sits with customers for a couple of minutes at their tables to show his genuine concern for how they are doing. Sal, a sidewalk newspaper vendor, gives his customers upbeat morning cheer, sports and news updates (including opinions), and even credit when they do not have the 35¢ in change that day.

Other companies do not do a very good job as marketers — you probably can identify several such firms. Consider when you have been put on hold endlessly when calling for technical support, when you have been ignored or treated indifferently when visiting a retail site, or when you have been sold inferior goods or services. While second-rate firms may survive in the short term, they will not last in the long run unless they change their philosophy and start creating superior value for their customers.

# The Marketing Concept Revisited

The marketing concept is that guiding business doctrine advocating a company-wide effort (interfunctional coordination) to satisfy both customers (customer orientation) and organizational objectives (in particular, profitability). The traditional marketing concept — summarized as customer satisfaction at a profit — has been the cornerstone of the marketing discipline for more than 40 years. This philosophy worked well in the 1980s and early 1990s, as most companies stressed conquest marketing (getting new business) over retention marketing (keeping customers).

In today's mature and highly competitive markets, a changing twofold objective exists: focus primarily on maintaining and upgrading customer relationships (this includes generating referral business), and secondarily grow the business by finding new customers. In many cases, this might mean investing 80% or more of the marketing budget on customer loyalty and retention programs; the balance would be directed to activities designed to win new customers (note that many companies currently have this ratio reversed).

Given the business environment of the late 1990s and beyond, we argue that a new marketing concept is called for. The revised marketing philosophy is that organizations must provide socially responsible business experiences that meet or exceed customer expectations while creating long-term value for all stakeholders (for example, owners, employees, customers, etc.).

# Sales vs. Marketing Oriented

Why do many companies fail to understand their customers' needs and wants? A major reason is that many organizations are not marketing oriented. Companies have different degrees of commitment to marketing. As Figure 2.1 illustrates, a four-stage continuum from production-driven to marketing-driven exists.

Production → Product → Sales → Marketing

**Figure 2.1. Business Orientations**

**Table 2.1. Becoming Marketing Oriented**

| Marketing Variables | Orientation | |
| --- | --- | --- |
| | Sales Oriented | Marketing Oriented |
| Starting point | Service organization | Target markets |
| Marketing focus | Service offerings | Customer needs |
| Customer focus | New business (attraction) | Existing customer base (retention) |
| Competitive edge | Lowest delivered cost | Superior quality or service |
| Product strategy | Generic product | Augmented product |
| Promotional strategy | Selling/advertising | Integrated marketing communications (IMC) |
| Pricing strategy | Maximizing profit margins | Profitable use of resources |
| Marketing objective | Sales volume | Customer satisfaction |
| Planning approach | Reactive | Proactive |
| Time perspective | Short term (tactical) | Medium and long term (strategic) |

Henry Ford pioneered the idea of mass production which led to mass marketing — remember "give them any car they want as long as it's a black Model-T"? Many medical clinics still practice such a production orientation nearly a century later. Other companies become enamored with their products (for example, many computer software firms) and employ a product orientation without carefully discerning customer problems. The selling orientation is widely used by automobile dealers, insurance firms, media companies, and network/multilevel marketers.

Let's review how a sales-oriented company differs from a marketing-oriented firm. As Table 2.1 shows, a sales-oriented firm bases market decisions on what the top executives think customers want. It often has a strong core product and/or an established, deep product line and spends heavily on advertising and selling to win new business. Attracting customers (conquest marketing) is the major objective of the firm.

America Online used a sales orientation to build a customer base exceeding 16 million subscribers in just a few short years. However, when AOL permitted unlimited access for a flat $19.95 monthly fee, it entered a logistical nightmare as the increased customer base took advantage of unprecedented levels of online service usage. Many existing customers became dissatisfied with the provider when they experienced log-on failure rates that at times were as high as 50%. In the bleakest period, AOL had customer turnover rates exceeding 20% a month. Finally, in an attempt to become market oriented, AOL added tens of thousands of new lines to deal effectively with the increased customer traffic generated.

As we can see, a marketing-oriented firm carefully researches and evaluates its target markets to provide products that satisfy or exceed customer needs. They invest in an integrated communications program (discussed further in Chapter 7) that allows them to grow, but its principal marketing objective is customer retention.

Customer retention is so critical because it directly impacts the bottom line. A 5% decrease in customer defections can lead to an increase in profitability of 25 to 50% (or more). While customer defection rates of 10 to 15% are common in many industries, Leo Burnett has done a stellar job in this area, having a remarkable 98% customer retention rate in one of the most hotly contested market sectors — advertising.[2]

Coca-Cola, General Electric, Procter & Gamble, and Sony are renowned for their marketing prowess (marketing orientation) which has been perfected over the years. Marketing is a relatively newer phenomena for many service organizations (banks, hospitals), professional service firms (accounting firms, attorneys, consulting organizations), information-based companies (high-tech companies, telecommunications firms, mailing list houses), and nonprofit organizations (museums, park and recreation departments, universities).

Regardless of the type of company you may work for, a market orientation provides the impetus for building an organizational culture which puts customers first, creates superior value for your customers, and leads to improved overall business performance. Employees of market-oriented companies become value adders; they know the importance of listening to and responding to customers. DuPont's "Adopt a Customer" program is one example of a successful customer-focused initiative. Workers visit customers monthly, learn the customer's needs, and are their representative on the factory floor.[3]

Customer orientation ascribes to Regis McKenna's philosophy that marketing is too important to be left to the marketing department. It is the responsibility of everyone in the organization. A customer orientation is a service organization practicing Japanese-style marketing — putting the customer first. In fact, the Japanese word *okyaku-sama* literally means "honored customer" or the "customer is God."[4] Is the customer really king in the U.S.? When leaving an American restaurant, sometimes one is barely acknowledged; in contrast, it is not uncommon at a Japanese dining establishment to have several parties graciously bow farewell in thanks for the customer's patronage.

## Market Orientation: Findings and Managerial Implications

Managers intuitively know that becoming market oriented favorably impacts business performance. Yet, there are relatively few studies of the consequences of a market orientation. According to Narver and Slater,[5] market orientation consists of three major components — customer orientation, competitor orientation, and interfunctional coordination. Their research showed a strong link between market orientation and business performance. Kohli and Jaworski[6] argued that the market orientation construct is comprised of intelligence generation, intelligence dissemination, and responsiveness; hence, market orientation involves learning about customers and competitors.

British Airways and Ford have a strong customer orientation; these organizations view themselves through their customers' eyes, know how to detect or predict underlying customer concerns, use formal customer-based performance measures, and have action-oriented implementation mechanisms in place.[7] Successful companies such as General Electric, Merck, and Sony are marketing driven but are equally adept at technological innovation. Preliminary evidence indicates that these balanced companies out-perform those stressing only marketing, selling, innovation, price, or production.[8] Yet, in another recent study, only 15% of a multinational sample of large businesses qualified as being truly market driven.[9] So, clearly, managers have their work cut out for them.

Firms operating in competitive industries are most likely to benefit from a market orientation. In a multistate study of hospital executives, "responsiveness to competition" was the only market-orientation issue that correlated with three hospital performance dimensions — financial performance, market/product development, and internal quality.[10] Also, market-orientation inputs are valuable for formulating an initial definition of one's market, as well as staying "in touch" with your customer base. A summary scale for market orientation is provided in Figure 2.2. Marketing managers can use this valuable tool to assess their current level of customer focus as well as to think about how their organization can improve in this critical area.

The statements below describe norms that operate in businesses. Indicate the extent of your agreement (SD = strongly disagree, D = disagree, N = neutral, A = agree, or SA = strongly agree) about how well the statements describe the actual norms in your strategic business unit.

| | SD | D | N | A | SA |
|---|---|---|---|---|---|
| 1. Our business objectives are driven primarily by customer satisfaction. | 1 | 2 | 3 | 4 | 5 |
| 2. We constantly monitor our level of commitment and orientation to serving customer needs. | 1 | 2 | 3 | 4 | 5 |
| 3. We freely communicate information about our successful and unsuccessful customer experiences across all business functions. | 1 | 2 | 3 | 4 | 5 |
| 4. Our strategy for competitive advantage is based on our understanding of customers' needs. | 1 | 2 | 3 | 4 | 5 |
| 5. We measure customer satisfaction systematically and regularly. | 1 | 2 | 3 | 4 | 5 |
| 6. We have routine or regular measures of customer service. | 1 | 2 | 3 | 4 | 5 |
| 7. We are more customer focused than our competitors. | 1 | 2 | 3 | 4 | 5 |
| 8. I believe this business exists primarily to serve customers. | 1 | 2 | 3 | 4 | 5 |
| 9. We poll end users at least once a year to assess the quality of our products and services. | 1 | 2 | 3 | 4 | 5 |
| 10. Data on customer satisfaction are disseminated at all levels in this business unit on a regular basis. | 1 | 2 | 3 | 4 | 5 |

**Figure 2.2. Market Orientation Scale** (Adapted from Deshpande, R. and Farley, J.U. (1996) *Understanding Market Orientation: A Prospectively Designed Meta-analysis of Three Market Orientation Scales,* Working Paper Report No. 96-125, December, Cambridge, MA: Marketing Science Institute.)

# Developing a Customer-Oriented Organization

How do companies become market oriented? It begins with the business culture — consider top management's values, employees, interdepartmental dynamics, organizational systems, and response to the environment. A dual emphasis on the customer (satisfy/delight the buyer) and on the competition (marketing has been likened to war) is needed, as well as a long-term view. The Japanese are known for long-term marketing plans (some span 25 to 100 years), which often will outlive the executives in the company sculpting the strategy.

Recognize that today's customers are quite smart and sophisticated, and they are looking for companies that: (1) create maximum value for them based on their needs and wants, and (2) demonstrate that they value their business. Road Runner Sports (which bills itself as your #1 running source) is a San Diego-based distributor of running shoes, running fashion accessories, and related running-oriented products. Using a direct mail catalog as their main marketing tool, Road Runner sells a complete line of specialized products to highly loyal customers (many of whom are members of the company's Run America Club) at very competitive prices.

John Naisbitt, author of *Megatrends*, noted that, "In today's Baskin-Robbin's society, everything comes in at least thirty-one varieties." The new value-seeking customers often possess the following attributes: they are choice seeking, demanding, and knowledgeable; they believe that loyalty must be earned; and they are price conscious, concerned about the environment, and convenience oriented (often times impoverished). Astute marketers recognize and respond to these issues when designing value propositions and marketing strategies. Furthermore, customer-oriented firms know how to use mass customization techniques, database/marketing information systems, research, integrated marketing communications (IMC), and the human touch (getting close to customers) to develop personalized marketing relationships which build long-term loyalty and ensure customer retention.

At times, excellent companies such as General Motors, IBM, Kodak, and Sears have become complacent. Management and employees lose their competitive edge and enthusiasm and become satisfied with the *status quo*. Fortunately for the market, strong rivals emerge, such as Toyota, Dell Computer, Fuji, and Wal-Mart; these companies provide a loud wake-up call to action and force once invincible giants to change or fade away.

Michael Dell, Chairman/CEO of the firm bearing his name, says it best: "There are only two types of companies: the quick and the dead." And, this incredibly successful young billionaire does not plan on dying young. To overcome complacency and stay relevant in the market, organizations must avoid marketing myopia, be creative in programs and processes, adapt and be flexible with respect to changing market conditions and tastes, and use a *kaizen* (continuous improvement) philosophy.

### Creating a Bias for Action

Great companies go beyond satisfying customers — they are able to predict customer needs and wants and practice anticipatory marketing. These organizations invest in research, get close to the customer, innovate, and

Nonresponsive → Reactive → Responsive → Proactive → Anticipatory

**Figure 2.3. The Bias for Action Continuum** (Adapted from Barrett, H. (1996) Ultimate goal is to anticipate the needs of market, *Marketing News,* Oct. 7, p. 4.)

accept reasonable business risks. According to Barrett, there is a 5-stage bias for action continuum (see Figure 2.3).[11]

At the nonresponsive level, there is limited awareness of external stimuli (for example, IBM initially ignored the PC market). At the reactive level, the firm is aware of the stimuli, but only after repeated prodding does it reply (e.g., Xerox was slow in developing competitive strategies to win back the low-end sector of the copier market from Canon in the 1980s).

Most companies are at the responsive level. Customers may force the firm to enter new product markets, sometimes reluctantly. Many companies will then take appropriate action, assuming the opportunity fits the present business mission and adequate resources are available.

Proactiveness is the fourth stage and implies that corporate entrepreneurism has surfaced in the organization. This means that larger companies simulate the innovation, flexibility, creativity, and speed to market of their smaller counterparts.

Anticipatory marketing is the aspirational level and is attained by relatively few firms (and then only infrequently). At this point, companies understand virtually all of the market nuances and treat their customers as business allies and partners. Kinko's Copy Centers have done a good job in this area by offering around-the-clock service and anticipating the desires of its customer base in its new product offerings. A strong market orientation and effective market definition can guide organizations through the continuum to, ultimately, the proactive and anticipatory stages.

## Customer Focus

Customer-oriented organizations build on the marketing concept (market orientation is the firm's implementation of the marketing concept), design customer-driven processes and programs, establish a strong marketing information system, segment and target markets, hire the best talent, stress operational efficiency, and continually measure and fine-tune their customer focus.

| | |
|---|---|
| 1. | Create customer focus throughout the business. |
| 2. | Listen to the customer. |
| 3. | Define and nurture your distinctive competence. |
| 4. | Define marketing as market intelligence. |
| 5. | Target customers precisely. |
| 6. | Manage for profitability, not sales volume. |
| 7. | Make customer value the guiding star. |
| 8. | Let the customer define quality. |
| 9. | Measure and manage customer expectations. |
| 10. | Build customer relationships and loyalty. |
| 11. | Define the business as a service business. |
| 12. | Commit to continuous improvement. |
| 13. | Manage culture along with strategy. |
| 14. | Grow with partners and alliances. |
| 15. | Destroy marketing bureaucracy. |

**Figure 2.4. Guidelines for the Market-Driven Manager** (Adapted from Webster, F.E., Jr. (1994) Executing the new marketing concept, *Marketing Management,* 3(1), pp. 8–16.)

ComUnity Lending is a medium-size regional lender in San Jose, CA. A three-part company credo helps them achieve their customer-driven focus. This action agenda is (1) think like the customer — comprehend his needs, (2) focus on the customer — anticipate his needs, and (3) work for the customer — exceed his needs.[12] Figure 2.4 and Customer Value Checklist 2 provide important planning and evaluative guidelines for market-driven managers.

Customer-oriented service organizations employ personnel that are value adders. Value can be created at three trigger points: company/customers (external marketing), company/employees (internal marketing), and employees/customers (interactive marketing). Traditionally, external marketing has been the focus for all customer-directed activities. Here, though, the four P's — product, price, promotion, and place — take center stage; however, in today's services-dominated economy, this view is limiting, and a fifth P — people — becomes paramount.

Internal marketing is used to develop customer-focused employees. Basic human resource management activities such as recruitment, training, motivating, compensating, and evaluation come into play in this

---

**Customer Value Checklist 2.**
**Guidelines for Customer Orientation**

1. Do you know the objectives of your customers (and their customers)?
2. Is your service offer designed with the customer in mind?
3. Are your internal systems (i.e., ordering, billing, shipping, computers, financial, etc.) geared toward how the customers prefer doing business with you?
4. Do you constantly measure customer satisfaction?
5. Do you continually meet with your customers to determine their needs today and tomorrow?
6. How is value created, delivered, monitored, and maximized in your organization?

---

area. Once the people are adequately prepared for their respective business challenges, interactive marketing (face-to-face and other customer contacts) takes over. Exceptional customer service differentiates market leaders from average companies.

Home Depot is known for its careful screening and selection process to find job applicants with a high social orientation (strong people skills). Home Depot's market leadership comes from the price and product mix expected of home improvement superstores coupled with the helpful advice and service provided by neighborhood hardware stores.[13]

## Summary

A firm that has a strong customer orientation fares well on the purpose dimension of the value matrix (introduced in Chapter 1). A market orientation builds the necessary business culture and customer-focused framework to enable service providers to deliver superior value to their target markets. In the next chapter, we will discuss how business processes can be used effectively by service organizations to create enhanced value for customers.

## Customer Value Action Items

1. How customer oriented is your organization? Comment on each of the following attributes:
   a. Customer focus — who are your customers and what do they value?
   b. Competitive focus — who are your competitors and what are their strengths and weaknesses?
   c. Interfunctional coordination — how is your company organized and how do the various departments interact?
   d. Market-driven objectives
   e. Market intelligence utilization
   f. Target marketing
   g. Performance measures
2. Discuss product-related factors that impact your market orientation (e.g., current product mix, new product development programs, perceived product and service quality, etc.).
3. Is top management committed to being market oriented? What changes does your company need to implement to become more customer driven? Discuss business culture and strategic issues in your response.
4. How does your firm's market orientation assist your firm in delivering superior customer value?
5. Are your company's marketing programs and processes non-responsive, reactive, responsive, proactive, or anticipatory? Provide anecdotal support for your view.
6. How good a job does your organization do with respect to internal, interactive, and external marketing? How can these areas be improved?

## References

1. Many writers have said that the terms *market oriented, market driven, customer focused, customer orientation,* and so forth are synonymous. For example, see Slater, S.F. and Narver, J.C (1995) Market orientation and the learning organization, *Journal of Marketing,* 59(July), p. 63; Nwankwo, S. (1995) Developing a customer orientation, *Journal of Consumer Marketing,* 12(5), p. 6; and Shapiro, B.P. (1988) What the hell is "market oriented"?, *Harvard Business Review,* Nov./Dec., p. 120.
2. Reichheld, F.F. (1996) *The Loyalty Effect,* Cambridge, MA: Harvard Business School Press.

3. Slater, S.F. and Narver, J.C. (1994) Market orientation, customer value, and superior performance, *Business Horizons*, March/April, pp. 22–28.

4. Adachi, Y. (1998) The effects of semantic difference on cross-cultural business negotiation: a Japanese and American case study, *The Journal of Language for International Business*, 9(1), pp. 43–52.

5. Narver, J.C. and Slater, S.F. (1990) The effect of a market orientation on business profitability, *Journal of Marketing*, 54(Oct.), pp. 20–35.

6. Kohli, A.K. and Jaworski, B.J. (1990), Market orientation: the construct, research propositions, and managerial implications, *Journal of Marketing*, 54(April), pp. 1–18.

7. Nwankwo, S. (1995) Developing a customer orientation, *Journal of Consumer Marketing*, 12(5), pp. 5–15.

8. Wong, V. and Saunders, S. (1993) Business orientations and corporate success, *Journal of Strategic Marketing*, 1, pp. 20–40.

9. Day, G.S. and Nedungadi, P. (1994) Managerial representations of competitive advantage, *Journal of Marketing*, 58(April), pp. 31–44.

10. Raju, P.S., Lonial, S.C., and Gupta, Y.P. (1995) Market orientation and performance in the hospital industry, *Journal of Health Care Marketing*, 15(Winter), pp. 34–41.

11. Barrett, H. (1996) Ultimate goal is to anticipate the needs of market, *Marketing News*, Oct. 7, p. 4.

12. Fry, W.D. (1995) The holy grail of customer contentment, *Mortgage Banking*, Oct., pp. 167–172.

13. Gubman, E.L. (1995) Aligning people strategies with customer value, *Compensation and Benefits Review*, Jan./Feb., pp. 15–22.

# 3 Process and Customer Value

"If you can't define what you do as a process, you don't know what your job is." (W. Edwards Deming)

## Introduction

As Chapter 2 explained, practicing a market orientation is fundamental to creating sustainable customer value. Exceeding customer expectations, knowing the competition — their strengths, weaknesses, and strategies — and encouraging cross-functional sharing and decision-making lead to superior business performance. This chapter focuses on designing business operations and processes that are value creating. That is, process design needs to follow a simple litmus test: Does the process create superior customer value? Moreover, value drives process design, as shown in Figure 3.1. Note that the goal of the organization is to maintain a fit between value and processes. Successful organizations recognize that value and process are "seamless" in the eyes of their customers. Ford recently announced that it was organizing its dealer service area around four key processes that create customer satisfaction. The prestigious Karolinska Hospital in Stockholm, Sweden, reorganized its key processes around patient flow, instead of allowing the patient to be bounced from department to department. What prompted these organizations to change their processes? In short, they desired to serve their customers better and in the process deliver greater value.

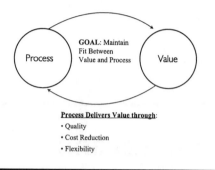

**Figure 3.1. Link Between Process and Value**

In fact, organizations that view themselves as a collection of processes that must be understood, managed, and improved are most likely to achieve this end. Thus, the focus needs to shift from managing departments to managing processes. We will examine key organizational processes, as well as the marketing cycle and its processes, and will assess process effectiveness, steps in process improvement, and process improvement tools.

## Key Organizational Processes

Before discussing key organizational processes, let's define what we mean by "process". A process is a specific group of activities and subordinate tasks which results in the performance of a service that is of value. Business process design involves the identification and sequencing of work activities, tasks, resources, decisions, and responsibilities across time and place, with a beginning and an end, along with clearly identified inputs and outputs. Processes must be able to be tracked as well, using cost, time, output quality, and satisfaction measurements. Businesses need to monitor, review, alter, and streamline processes continually in order to remain competitive. A process view of the organization differs from the traditional functional view, as presented in Table 3.1.

Processes are not simply obscure, back-room operations of the service concern, but instead are an integral part of delivering the value proposition. We maintain that processes and service are inseparable; that is, *the process is the service.* An effective process is results driven, deriving its form from customer requirements — how and when customers want to do business with you. Market-oriented companies ensure that the service encounter is positive by asking, "How can we make

**Table 3.1. Process View vs. Traditional Functional View**

| Process View | Functional View |
| --- | --- |
| Emphasis on improving on "how work is done" | Which products or services are delivered |
| Cross-functional coordination, teamwork stressed | Frequent "hand-offs" among functions, which remain largely uncoordinated |
| "Systems" view (i.e., entire process is managed) | Pieces of the process are managed |
| Customer orientation | Internal/company orientation |

our customers' lives easier?" General Electric (GE) asked that question and came up with the idea of GE's Answer Center, a fully staffed customer call center that operates 24 hours a day, offering repair tips and helping owners of GE appliances with their problems. We recommend that managers first take a "big picture" view of their company by looking at key processes in relationship to the marketing cycle.

Figure 3.2 shows the marketing cycle and how it relates to business processes and process indicators. You will note that the various market constituents such as customers, suppliers, and publics determine the

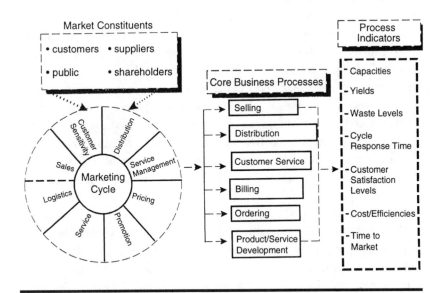

**Figure 3.2. Marketing Cycle and Process Model**

how and the extent to which marketing cycle elements are performed. Customers in particular determine the composition and nature of the marketing cycle and the subsequent core processes that are required to support these selected marketing cycle functions. For example, the customer service process is performed as part of the service management function of the marketing cycle. Customer service activities would include, but are not limited to, such activities as tracking and trending customer complaints, recovery from customer service failures, and establishing customer service standards. The process indicators represent the "metrics" for measuring the core processes. One of the process indicators for the customer service process is gauging customer satisfaction levels. Ford tracks customer retention as part of its service management process and has found that each additional percentage point in customer retention rates is worth $100 million in profits. It should also be pointed out that a synergy exists within the marketing cycle elements. That is, a process breakdown in one area, such as logistics, affects other areas such as distribution. The next section looks at some critical steps in assessing process effectiveness.

## Assessing Process Effectiveness

Dr. W. Edwards Deming pioneered the use of statistical tools and sampling methods for use in both product and process quality control. Much of Deming's work in these areas was applied during World War II to improve productivity for the U.S. war effort. Yet, after the war many of his applications disappeared from the American workplace, being considered by many companies as time consuming and unnecessary. However, Deming's work found wide acceptance in Japan, where he was asked to join the Japanese Union of Scientists and Engineers (JUSE) in the late 1940s. Eventually, he would conduct a series of statistical quality control seminars in Japan which would later accelerate the movement of Japanese industry into a statistical quality control phase of improvement.

Deming's quality philosophy finally resonated with corporate America in the mid-1980s, as the quality of U.S. products and services began to sag. Deming more broadly articulated his views on quality in his now famous "14 Points of Management" (also, see Chapter 5, Table 5.1, for a more detailed discussion of Demings's 14 Points).[1] One of Deming's recommendations in his 14 Points is for businesses to create a "constancy

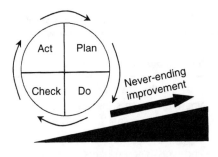

**Figure 3.3. The Deming Cycle**

of purpose" by continually improving products, services, and processes. *Kaizen*, or continuous improvement, is at the heart of Deming's quality philosophy, relying on both innovative and incremental changes to better satisfy customers. Deming argued that products, services, and processes should be continually redesigned and improved for quality.[1] Building on the early work of Shewhart, Deming introduced his PDCA (plan, do, check, act) approach to help organizations identify opportunities for process improvement and control. Figure 3.3 illustrates four separate but linked activities for stabilizing and improving processes.

The PDCA (or Deming) cycle is a continuous sequence of activities which, although deceptively simple, represents a powerful decision-making tool for effecting organizational change. Each of these four activities is held in equal balance and is equally important. That is, if you *plan* but never *do*, you will not improve. Moreover, the cycle indicates that the task of process improvement is never done, as past results drive future action.

## *Plan*

The first step in the process is planning, which involves examining how the type of value firms offer their customers affects their processes. An alignment between the value that customers want and the value the process generates indicates overall effectiveness. A useful tool for representing value attributes and core processes is the Value Deployment Matrix (see Part 4, Abstracts).[2] To ensure that a fit exists between value and process, a "value statement" should be developed that answers the question, "What do we do for our customers and why should they use us instead of our competition?"

### Table 3.2. Process Assessment

| Process Design Issues | Key Management Questions |
| --- | --- |
| What? | What are the customer requirements? |
| Where? | Where do process inefficiencies exist? |
| When? | When do processes start and end? |
| | When is each process activity performed? |
| Who? | Who is assigned process ownership? |
| Why? | Why does the process exist? |
| | Why organize around the process this way? |
| Would? | Would the customer be willing to pay for step(s) performed in the process? |
| Does? | Does the process (or steps in the process) bring you closer to delivering the service to the customer? |
| How? | How significant is the process? |
| | How does the process support the value? |

A firm's value statement should carry a strong, differentiated appeal to its customers about how its offer differs from those of its competitors in regard to price/performance characteristics. For example, Southwest Airlines' value statement communicates the concepts of fun, fast, and economy. The Circuit City value statement suggests not just low prices but exceptional service as well ("where service is state of the art"). The Simmons College Graduate School of Management value statement clearly limits what they do and who they serve: a graduate business program exclusively for women. Starbuck's value statement implies the reinvention of a commodity product as a high-quality, high-price beverage for image-conscious, upscale buyers. Finally, the Charles Schwab & Company value statement consists of delivering low price and convenient investment trading through highly automated systems. Other examples of value statements (also called value propositions) are reviewed in Chapter 4.

## Do

The second step in the Deming cycle is the "do" phase. Once a value statement is created or refined, processes need to be assessed according to their efficacy and congruence with the firm's value statement. A series of questions such as those provided in Table 3.2 can help determine where to direct process improvement efforts.

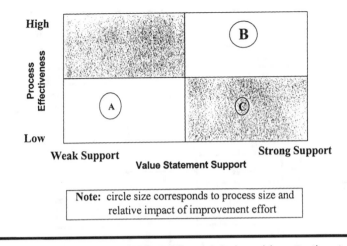

**Figure 3.4. Process Support of Value Statement** (Adapted from Feather, J. (1998) Using value analysis to target customer service process improvements, *IEE Solutions,* May, p. 34.)

Next processes should be examined to help identify and select those that have the greatest impact on creating customer value. John Feather, a partner with Corporate Renaissance, a management consulting group, suggests using a grid similar to Figure 3.4 which isolates those processes yielding the highest strategic gains.[3] For example, Process C, which directly supports the value statement, is ineffective in terms of process performance. Focusing on this process should be a priority, given its strategic importance relative to the value statement, and should produce significant performance gains if improved.

After examining processes for their fit with the firm's value statement, individual processes should be studied in order to determine their relevance and importance from the customer's perspective. A process flow diagram is a useful tool for defining the steps of a process and evaluating the importance of those steps in creating customer value. Blueprinting the steps of the process in this fashion helps visualize conceptually not only which steps are performed but also the timing and sequencing of relationships in the process. A process flow diagram also helps to identify "fail points" or steps in the process that are likely to go wrong.

Figure 3.5 shows an example of a flow diagram for a travel services firm. Flowcharting a process: [4]

■ Focuses on customers and their expectations and experiences

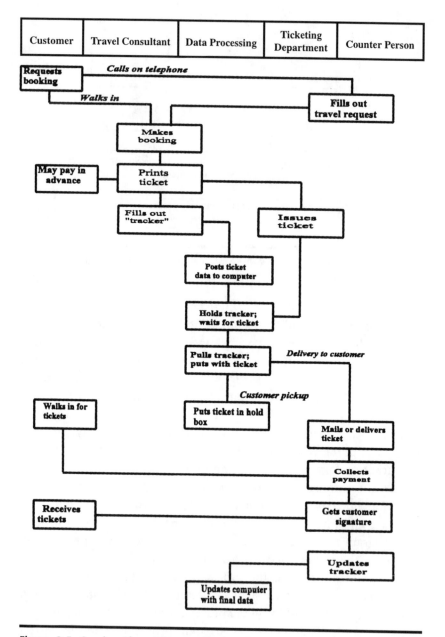

**Figure 3.5. Service Flow Diagram** (From Albrecht, K. (1990) *Service Within,* Homewood, IL: Irwin. With permission.)

- Shows how the technical procedures relate to administrative and relationship-building activities of product or service delivery
- Identifies those activities that can be proceduralized, as well as those that must be individualized and given special attention
- Identifies gaps in the market that should be addressed
- Shows staff members how their own activities relate to one another

MBNA Corp., the fourth largest credit-card issuer in the U.S., keeps its customers twice as long as the industry average by focusing on the critical items that it believes to be breakpoint issues to its customers, including answering every phone call within two rings and processing every credit-line increase request within an hour.

Finally, process measures should be developed. Measures are more relevant to management when they are tied to specific processes. The processes selected by the company will vary depending on the type of business, yet someone in the company needs to take ownership of the results.[5] Figure 3.6 shows business processes linked to customer needs for the General Business Systems Division of AT&T, along with appropriate metrics for each process. Realize that there must be a strong

| | Business Process | Customer Need | Internal Metric |
|---|---|---|---|
| | Product (30%) | Reliability (40%) | % repair calls |
| | | Easy to use (20%) | % calls for help |
| | | Features/functions (40%) | Function performance test |
| | Sales (30%) | Knowledge (30%) | Supervisor observations |
| | | Response (25%) | % proposals made on time |
| | | Follow-up (10%) | % follow-up made |
| Overall quality | Installation (10%) | Delivery interval (30%) | Average order interval |
| | | Does not break (30%) | % repair reports |
| | | Installed when promised (10%) | % installed on due date |
| | Repair (15%) | No repeat trouble (30%) | % repeat reports |
| | | Fixed quickly (25%) | Average speed of repair |
| | | Kept informed (10%) | % customers informed |
| | Billing (15%) | Accuracy, no surprises (45%) | % billing inquiries |
| | | Resolved on first call (35%) | % resolved first call |
| | | Easy to understand (10%) | % billing inquiries |

**Figure 3.6. Strategic Marketing Information Used To Focus Business Processes** (Adapted from Kordupleski, R. et al. (1993) *California Management Review,* 35(3), p. 89.)

## Table 3.3. Tools of Process Improvement

| Process Tool | Purpose |
|---|---|
| Benchmarking | Measure and compare process results to a standard of excellence (see Figure 3.7) |
| Data collection tools (surveys, sampling, checklists) | Document internal and external customer assumptions and perceptions about appropriateness and effectiveness of a process and reveal unstable processes |
| Control chart | Identify stability, capability, and central tendency of a process (see Figure 3.8) |
| Scatter diagram | Show graphically the relationship between process performance data and some overall performance measure, such as customer satisfaction or service quality (see Figure 3.9) |
| Pareto chart | Separate the "vital few" causes of process failures (see Figure 3.10) |
| Fishbone diagram | Show possible causes of process shortcomings or weaknesses (see Figure 3.11) |

linkage between customer needs and the internal metrics developed to assess the underlying process. Tracking these internal metrics is very useful and leads to process improvement and, more importantly, enhanced customer service quality.

## *Check*

The third step in the Deming cycle is to check. Once processes are evaluated for their value-creating effectiveness and measures are developed, then data-driven tools can be routinely used to monitor, inspect, and improve them. Table 3.3 lists some common tools for measuring, monitoring, controlling, and improving process quality.

Benchmarking is the most important tool for evaluating and improving processes. Benchmarking compares a company's own practices (processes or tasks) against similar practices of firms recognized as being superior in these areas. By comparing itself against the best possible practices, the benchmarking firm seeks to identify gaps between its current processes and the processes it should implement.

According to Camp,[6] benchmarking is a process of consistently researching new ideas for methods, practices, and processes; either adopting the practices or adapting the good features; and implementing them to obtain the "best of the best". When done continually for each company process, management can determine where improvements are possible and realistically assess how much improvement is possible. Benchmarking does not set hard goals for how much progress is possible, but it does provide a source of rich ideas for improvement that goes beyond internal experience. The upshot is that benchmarking facilitates the search for the practices that will lead to superior industry performance.

Besides uncovering industry-best practices, benchmarking offers others advantages as well. For example, benchmarking may help identify technological breakthroughs that might otherwise have gone unrecognized. While benchmarking traditionally focuses within an industry, many firms look outside the industry for breakthroughs in process redesign. For example, Xerox gained knowledge of warehousing and materials-handling operations technology by studying L.L. Bean.

Benchmarking also enables companies to more adequately meet customer requirements, leading to higher customer satisfaction. In addition, benchmarking helps firms determine true measures of productivity. Isolating the factors leading to higher productivity can facilitate process simplification and redesign. Finally, benchmarking helps firms attain a competitive position. While some organizations view benchmarking as a fad (28%), most companies clearly endorse the benchmarking concept. Seventy-nine percent of companies believe they must benchmark to survive, and 95% feel they do not know how to benchmark effectively.[7]

Which companies are worthy of being benchmarked? Of course, that depends on the particular core process. Table 3.4 reveals a list of companies that excel in applying quality practices in selected core processes and thus represent ideal candidates for process benchmarking. Companies considered ideal candidates for benchmarking should also be of similar size or attracting similar customers. For example, Northern Telecom , the Canadian telecommunications giant, benchmarked other high-tech companies, not just other telecommunication companies.

How is benchmarking conducted? In his book *Benchmarking: The Search for Industry Best Practices that Lead to Superior Performance,* Camp describes a benchmarking process which looks at business processes such as order fulfillment across a range of different industries (see Figure 3.7). It should be noted that the generic benchmarking process is divided into two parts: benchmark metrics and benchmark practices. Metrics represent the best

**Table 3.4. Exemplar Companies in Selected Service Marketing Areas**

| Core Processes To Be Benchmarked | Companies |
| --- | --- |
| Customer loyalty management | Xerox, Pizza Hut |
| Sales/service support | Maytag, IBM |
| Order fulfillment | L.L. Bean, Dell Computer |
| Logistics | Ryder, FedEx |
| Transaction processing | Amazon.com, Citibank |
| New service development | Disney, Charles Schwab |
| Customer database management | Blockbuster Entertainment, American Express |
| Procurement | Wal-Mart, General Electric |
| Customer service | Nordstrom, Ritz-Carlton |

practices in quantified form. Practices are the methods used to perform a process. Benchmarking should begin by investigating industry practices first. Once industry practices are understood, they can then be quantified to show their numeric effect. Benchmarking must also be understood by the organization in order to obtain the commitment necessary to take action. Management commits to benchmarking by communicating its

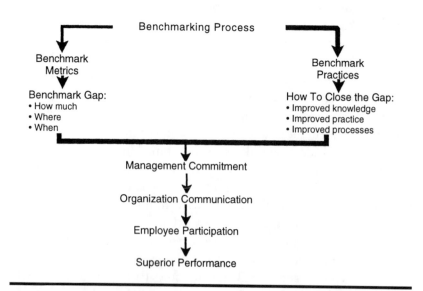

**Figure 3.7. Generic Benchmarking Process** (Adapted from Camp, R. (1989) *Benchmarking*, Milwaukee, WI: ASQC Quality Press. With permission.)

importance to employees and securing their participation, leading to the ultimate goal of benchmarking: superior business performance.

Perhaps the most difficult part of benchmarking is identifying what variables/issues are to be benchmarked. The key to determining what is to be benchmarked is to identify the result of the business process. For example, the marketing cycle function of logistics consists of several strategic deliverables, such as the level of customer satisfaction expected, the inventory level to be maintained, and the desired cost level to be achieved. These deliverables serve as a starting point for benchmarking, where each of these would require being broken down further into specific activities to be benchmarked. Customer satisfaction may be benchmarked by investigating the factors that are responsible for customer satisfaction, such as service response time and reliability, as well as professionalism, competence, and empathy of the service worker.

Finally, there are several common denominators in using the benchmarking process. First, you need to know your operations thoroughly, assessing the strengths and weaknesses of your internal processes. Second, you should know the industry leaders or competitors. Why are they better and how much better are they? What do they do that can be adopted by us? Third, learn from the industry leaders and emulate their strengths. For example, Southwest Airlines looked to Formula One Racing when it wanted to improve its refueling process. By adopting Formula One turnaround processes used during pit stops, Southwest can now refuel an airplane in 12 minutes. Fourth, use benchmarking as a proactive tool by looking not just at competitors, but at what customers value and how other practices meet those needs. Last, benchmarking must be continuous and institutionalized as part of the company culture.

While benchmarking is an important technique for improving business processes, other tools should also be employed (review Table 3.3). For example, data collection tools such as surveys or checklists can be extremely helpful in assessing customers' views of your business processes, especially the importance and relevance of specific activities and tasks. Typical information obtained from surveys or checklists include: (1) what happens; (2) how does it happen; (3) how often does it happen; (4) how long does it take; and (5) how important is this.

Control charts are useful for monitoring the performance of a process by reporting measurements that are predictable within a given process and those that are random in nature. Control charts usually show fluctuations within a process that occur within control limits.

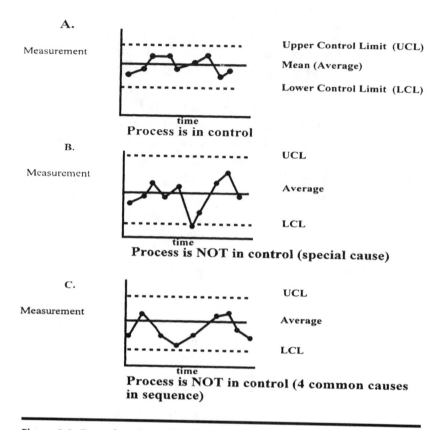

Figure 3.8. Examples of Control Charts

Points that fall outside the control limit range should be reported or investigated (see Figure 3.8).

A scatter diagram permits examining two variables at one time to determine the relationship that exists between them. The graphic display can help determine possible process "fail points" or measure the results of recently changed processes. For example, a direct-mail company might want to use a scatter diagram to understand better how order fulfillment time is related to customer retention (see Figure 3.9).

Pareto charts are used when there is a need to determine the relative importance of certain variables in process variation. They help isolate the "vital few" (as opposed to the trivial many) causes of process variation. For example, a hotel might be interested in learning which customer groups represent the highest source of guest complaints (see Figure 3.10).

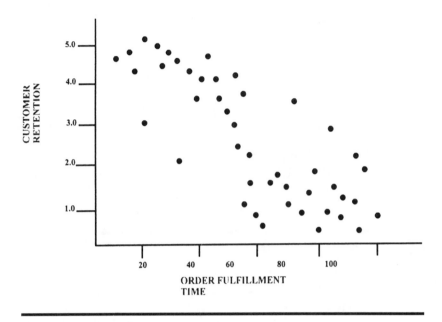

**Figure 3.9. Scatter Diagram**

The fishbone (or cause-and-effect) diagram is useful in process analysis and redesign by stimulating thinking about a process under investigation, helping to organize thoughts into a rationale whole. The fishbone diagram documents the level of understanding about a process and provides a framework for expanding an understanding of the "root cause" of the problem. A hospital experiencing delays in laboratory results could begin by first defining the effect (i.e., lab result delays) and then brainstorming the causes by diagraming the "bones" of the fish (i.e., equipment, policies, procedures, and people). Figure 3.11 provides a graphic representation of a problem and its potential causes.

## Act

The final step in the Deming cycle is to act. Based on data collected using the process improvement tools described, corrective actions should be taken to improve processes that fail to add value. Listed below are five ways to improve business processes:[8]

■ Eliminate tasks altogether if they have been determined to be unnecessary.

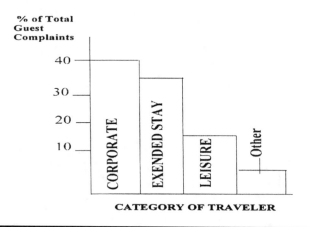

**Figure 3.10. Pareto Chart (Hotel)**

■ Simplify the work by eliminating all non-productive elements of a task.
■ Combine tasks, where appropriate.
■ Change the sequencing to improve the speed and execution.
■ Perform activities simultaneously.

Savin Corporation, a large copier company, conducted a careful analysis and found that call-backs were related to deficiencies in the

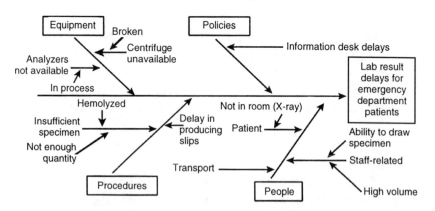

The Fishbone, or cause-and-effect, diagram (sometimes called an *Ishikawa* diagram after the Japanese quality control leader) is drawn during a brainstorming session. The central problem is visualized as the head of the fish, with the skeleton being divided into branches showing contributing causes of different parts of the problem.

**Figure 3.11. Fishbone Diagram**

training process (call-backs are when technicians are sent out on re-peated service calls). Pareto charts were prepared depicting those service engineers responsible for the largest number of call-backs. It was deter-mined that training just five engineers reduced call-backs by 19%. In most cases, the people who perform the processes are the ones most capable of determining how to improve or simplify the process. Man-agement has to create a culture that values employee input and rewards people for process innovation.

Once a process improvement has been made, the change must be measured and evaluated for effectiveness. Comparing before and after indicators would be useful here, as well as comparing results with the targeted performance. Also, efforts should be made to celebrate and reward those participating in the process improvement activity (see Customer Value Checklist 3, next page).

## Customer Value Action Items

1. Describe the relationship between process and value.
2. How does the process view differ from the functional view?
3. Explain how you would use the marketing cycle and process model to analyze your current business situation.
4. Explain the purpose of the Deming cycle for assessing process effectiveness.
5. What questions would you ask if your company was currently undergoing a review of its processes?
6. What is a value statement? See if you can describe your firm's value statement.
7. What is service blueprinting and when is it appropriate to use?
8. Suppose you are the manager of a quick-serve restaurant and you begin to notice that your lunch business is steadily declin-ing. Moreover, you notice that customers are queuing up longer at the drive-through window. Which of the process improve-ment tools would you consider using, and why?

## References

1. Deming, E. (1986) *Out of Crisis,* Cambridge, MA: MIT Center for Advanced Engineering Study.

**Customer Value Checklist 3.**
**Key Success Factors For Improving Business Processes**

The following represent some key factors in developing processes that are truly value added. Circle the response that most
closely fits your company's situation.

1. Does your company organize around value-added processes, not tasks? **Yes No**

2. Do those who use the output of the process perform the
   task (that is, are the people closest to the process the ones
   who actually perform the activity)? **Yes No**

3. Does your company forge links between functions and
   coordinate them while their activities are in process rather
   than after they have been completed? **Yes No**

4. Does your company put the decision point where the work
   is performed and build control into the process? **Yes No**

5. Does your company capture information once and at the
   source where it was created? **Yes No**

6. Does your company design processes in cooperation with
   customers? **Yes No**

7. Does your company "blueprint" the process cycle, defining not only the steps performed in the process, but also
   the timing and sequencing of relationships of those
   steps? **Yes No**

8. Is process simplification practiced regularly, removing
   unnecessary and bureaucratic procedures? **Yes No**

9. Does your company utilize appropriate process measurements (i.e., cycle response time, customer satisfaction,
   etc.)? **Yes No**

10. Does your company reward process improvement
    efforts? **Yes No**

2. Band, W. (1995) Customer-accelerated change, *Marketing Management,* 4(3), pp. 47–59.

3. Feather, J. (1998) Using value analysis to target customer service process improvements, *IIE Solutions,* May, pp. 33–39.

4. Congram, C. (1991) Focuses on the customer, in *The Handbook of Services Marketing,* New York: The American Management Association, pp. 479–490.

5. Kordupleski, R., Rust, R., and Zahorik, T. (1993) Why improving quality doesn't improve quality, *California Management Review,* Spring, pp. 82–95

6. Camp, R. (1989) *Benchmarking: The Search for Industry Best Practices That Lead to Superior Performance,* Milwaukee, WI: ASQC Quality Press.

7. Sprow, E. (1993) Benchmarking: it's time to stop tinkering with manufacturing and start clocking yourself against the best, *Manufacturing Engineering,* 111(3), p. 58.

8. Johnson, W. and Chvala, R. (1995) *Total Quality in Marketing,* Boca Raton, FL: St. Lucie Press.

# 4 Defining and Refining the Value Proposition

"It ain't that hard to be different." (Tom Peters)

One of the most critical challenges for service firms is to differentiate themselves from competitors. It is relatively easy to be like everyone else; great companies have their own unique identities and carefully conceived value propositions. It is important to realize that different is not always better, but better is always different. In this chapter, we explain what is meant by a value statement, explain how organizations must constantly work on getting better through rethinking and redesigning their value propositions, and discuss strategic implications for customer value managers.

## The Value Statement as the Basis for Competitive Strategy

McDonald's proven recipe for success is quality, service, cleanliness, and value — also known as QSCV. Superior customer value is achieved through low prices, good-tasting food, a trusted brand name, and emotional bonding with customers (primarily through advertising and promotions). The "food, folks, and fun" formula is designed to enhance the service experience and build worldwide customer loyalty. As the world's leading food service retailer, McDonald's is a $34 billion company doing

---

1. Does your value proposition take the customer's perspective?
2. Is it easy to understand?
3. Does it encapsulate the value you offer to your: people, the sales channel, the press, and your customers?
4. Is it strategically compatible with your business?
5. Is it acceptable given your organizational culture?
6. Is it honest?
7. Is it promotable? That is, is it logical, easily communicated, and solutions oriented? Does it have a headline or graphic with stopping power? Does it have different benefits for different buying influences? Is it original?

---

**Figure 4.1. Critiquing Your Value Proposition** (Adapted from Dovel, G.P. (1990) Stake it out: positioning success, step by step, *Business Marketing,* July, pp. 43–51.)

business in more than 100 nations and serving about 14 billion customer transactions annually. While about half of their 23,000 units are in the U.S., 23 other countries have more than 100 restaurants each (Australia, Brazil, Canada, England, France, Germany, and Japan each have more than 480 or more sites).[1]

According to Frederick Webster, the value proposition (VP) is a "verbal statement that matches up the firm's distinctive competencies with the needs and preferences of a carefully designed set of potential customers." He adds that the VP helps firms as a communications device and is a basis for creating a shared understanding between the company and its customers.[2]

Value propositions should be clear, concise, credible, and consistent over time. For example, the "Intel inside" personal computer campaign demonstrated that an industrial part (computer chips) could be differentiated in a manner similar to consumer products (such as potato chips). The overwhelming success of this program demonstrated that users valued Intel as a trusted component, the heart of the PC. In fact, the so-called "Wintel" standard (Microsoft Windows software, Intel microprocessors) has become more valued than the hardware manufacturer/assembler to many computer buyers.

Because customers rather than management set the true value agenda, value statements must assess customers' interpretation of value. How do we know if our value proposition or positioning statement is effective? Figure 4.1 lists several questions for management to address.

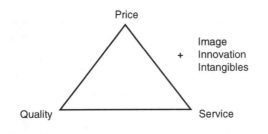

**Figure 4.2. Designing a Value Proposition**

## Building Your Value Proposition: QSP + 3I's

As noted in Chapter 1, the value triad of QSP consists of three components: product quality, service, and price. Extracting key differentiators from one or more of these core elements provides the basis of an organization's value proposition. QSP (the "big 3") establishes a solid business philosophy for the organization, guides all strategic decisions, and ultimately affects business performance.

A second set of variables, the 3I's, can also be used to augment and articulate a value proposition. These value adders are image, innovation, and intangibles (e.g., time, specialized knowledge, etc.). The value proposition concept is illustrated in Figure 4.2 (we discuss QSP in detail in Chapters 5 and 6).

Let's examine some examples of how firms successfully execute the value proposition as the basis of their business model. In the financial services arena, Charles Schwab competes via low price and convenient automated systems (lowest cost), while J.P. Morgan stresses hiring the best bankers to build flexibility and customer intimacy (best total solution), and the Morgan Stanley Group emphasizes innovation and new product offerings (world-class products).[3]

Virgin Enterprises has used a strong brand name and global image to create value for customers. Richard Branson's business empire extends into an airline, music production business, music retail stores, soft drinks, and other youth-oriented goods and services.

Broderbund Software has used innovative product offerings and niche marketing to succeed in the educational and gaming software markets. Value innovation can be fostered in companies by reducing investment in business units that are settlers (offer me-too products and services), increasing investment in migrators (businesses with value improvements), and using corporate entrepreneurship initiatives to create pioneers (businesses that represent value innovations). Research on the source of high growth in diverse organizations found that only 14% of new business initiatives were true value innovations; yet, these breakthrough concepts yielded 38% of total revenues and an impressive 61% of total profits.[4]

Many service companies compete successfully based on speed or time. Today, one-hour photo-finishing shops, 24-hour dry cleaners, and drive-through wedding chapels all respond to the customer need for convenience or immediate gratification.

FedEx built its reputation on a strong value proposition that guarantees package delivery by 10:30 a.m. the next morning. In contrast, the U.S. Post Office's priority mail service suffers some because of a much weaker value statement. While the flat-rate, two-pound envelope is a good deal at $3.00, its relatively slow 2- or 3-day delivery is a serious drawback. Many customers often send items priority mail because of image rather than speed — the red, white, and blue package looks more important than regular mail when it arrives on a client's desk. A 33% increase in price (to $4.00) to ensure 2-day delivery would greatly strengthen this product.

The American Productivity & Quality Center (APQC) has studied more than 100 companies and found that learning how to tap into and use knowledge can be an important source for creating customer value and obtaining a competitive advantage in the marketplace. Specifically, five knowledge-based routes to designing successful value propositions have been identified. These are (1) knowledge as a product — selling consulting services, databases, etc.; (2) knowledge transfer — adapting best practices from high-performing units of an organization; (3) customer-focused knowledge — data mining, using database information and customized responses to customer concerns, etc.; (4) personal responsibility for knowledge — empowering front-line service employees to have the necessary information and ability to act to solve customer problems; and (5) intellectual-asset management — use patents, licensing, and technology to generate value for the customer and the company.[5]

## The Value Proposition: Some Applications

Because all organizations are separate entities, ideally they should each have their own identities. This requires a careful analysis of all potential

Astra/Merck: *Customized healthcare solutions to deliver optimal patient care*
AT&T: *The right choice*
Dell Computer: *Custom computers sold direct to customers*
FedEx: *When it absolutely, positively has to get there overnight*
General Electric: *We bring good things to life*
Publix Super Markets: *Where shopping is a pleasure*
Snapple: *Natural beverages, made from the best stuff on Earth*
VISA: *It's everywhere you want to be*
Wal-Mart: *The customer is boss ... Everyday low prices ... Made in America*

**Figure 4.3. Examples of Value Propositions**

value proposition ingredients. The more unique the articulation of the core and augmented VP elements, the more memorable the message and more likely the success.

A good value proposition is difficult to imitate. While there are many online service providers, there is only one America Online, which has captured a huge customer base by offering an affordable, easy-to-use service with attractive graphics, excellent variety of content (information, entertainment, and communication features), solid infrastructure, and good advertising support. With this backdrop in place, Figure 4.3 lists several examples of strong value propositions (note that simple messages work best). Realize that a good VP is more than just a cute slogan; it is a corporate commitment to pursue a specific strategic direction. An expanded value proposition from a healthcare provider is summarized in Figure 4.4. The value equations clarify how consumers measure value in this context.

# Developing Unique Value Propositions

A major challenge for firms is to be perceived as different by the market — which requires the development of a unique value proposition. While the QSP + 3I's idea discussed earlier in this chapter may be sufficient, many 21st century companies find that the best path to creating value and setting themselves apart from the rest of the field is to change the rules of the game.

Airlines and hotels are two service industries (among many) that have created "artificial" resistance barriers for customers. For airlines, it is the Saturday night stay-over requirement, without which round-trip

1. VP = Benefits − Costs.
2. VP = (Quality + Service + Intangibles) − (Price + Nonmonetary Costs),
   where:
   a. Quality or outcome is the correct diagnosis and treatment, prevention of illness, etc.
   b. Service includes accessibility, compassion, dependability, employee knowledge, etc.
   c. Intangibles are the reputation of the provider, special services, long-term outcomes, use of latest technology, etc.
   d. Price is the consumer's expenditure for the service.
   e. Non-monetary costs include time, energy, and psychological stress.

**Figure 4.4. A Healthcare Consumer Value Equation** (Adapted from Ettinger, Jr., W.H. (1998) Consumer-perceived value: the key to a successful business strategy in the healthcare marketplace, *Journal of the American Geriatrics Society,* 46, pp. 111–113.)

fares can double or triple. Inconvenient hotel check-in (for example, by 4:00 p.m.) and check-out (for example, by 10:00 a.m.) policies mean that a day is not really a day. While the folly (or short-term profitability) of these unneccessary requirements is readily apparent, great companies do not take these industry "rules" as given; these companies design their own rules for the game. Southwest Airlines does not force their customers to spend a Saturday evening somewhere they choose not to be to get low fares. Crowne Plaza and Sheraton are some hotel chains that are experimenting with more equitable day rates for their valued guests.

Value Rental Car's now defunct 99¢ per hour pricing plan was widely embraced by customers as an innovative marketing strategy. Unfortunately, the accountants now had more work to do and the profitability of this tactic was not demonstrated. Regardless, as these travel industry examples illustrate, companies do not have to succumb to questionable industry trade practices or standard operating procedures — they must constantly search for better ways of doing business in a time-conscious society. According to George Stalk, Jr., and his colleagues at the Boston Consulting Group, many service or product providers demand compromises from their customers. Customer-focused companies can exploit these unneccessary concessions to find a competitive advantage. Figure 4.5 lists seven ways that Charles Schwab has revolutionized the discount brokerage industry and prospered by breaking industry compromises for nearly a quarter of a century.[6]

1. Shop the way customers shop. Schwab pioneered around-the-clock service, which included automated phone trading for securities as well as PC-based electronic trading.

2. Pay careful attention to how customers really use the product or service. By really listening to their customers, Schwab eliminated the need for follow-up confirmation calls.

3. Explore customers' latent dissatisfactions. Schwab's One-Source created a single point of purchase and account statement for hundreds of mutual funds.

4. Look for uncommon denominators. Schwab separates high-volume equity traders from ordinary investors with simpler financial management needs.

5. Pay careful attention to the anomalies. Schwab's concept of retail sales offices ran contrary to the prevailing mindset in the industry (i.e., discount brokers do not need costly overhead). Yet, the retail network generated substantial walk-in traffic and provided reassuring sites for current clients to transact business.

6. Look for diseconomies in the industry's value chain. Schwab became a financial intermediary in the mutual fund sector via One-Source rather than creating its own product line of funds.

7. Look for analogous solutions to the industry's compromises. Schwab demonstrated that firms could break the industry compromise between low price and reliable service (similar to Southwest Airlines).

**Figure 4.5. How Charles Schwab Redefined the Brokerage Market** (Adapted from Stalk, G. et al. (1996) Breaking compromises, breakaway growth, *Harvard Business Review*, 74(Sept./Oct.), pp. 131–139.)

## The Value Proposition: Strategic Implications

As markets change, so must firms' value propositions. Consider the approaches used by the office superstores — Staples, Office Depot, and Office Max. Staples uses its extensive database for target marketing, promotional activity, and product enhancements. This office supply store chain learned that, as many of their small business customers grew larger, they defected to competitors with delivery services. Staples recently introduced this value-added option to do a better job retaining customers.[7]

Because they sell essentially the same products and have similar service and pricing strategies, Office Depot and Office Max have opted for image-based differentiation. The former company signed on Dilbert, Scott Adams' cartoon character, as spokesperson: "Business is crazy; Office Depot makes sense." Office Max counter-attacked with its own animated creation called StickMax and removed all Dilbert products from its stores.

The competitive situation and potential niche opportunities should guide management's thinking about the appropriate value proposition to employ. The convergence and deregulation of the financial services industry means that everyone is entering each other's business. One industry expert noted that retail insurance services could evolve into one of a bank's top three businesses. To accomplish this, five new value propositions might be considered: instant insurance, deep discount insurance, transformational insurance (to deal with life changes), indexed insurance (automatically adjusts to income levels), and solutions-based insurance (for example, a single policy for a homebuyer's financial risk protection rather than mortgage insurance, title insurance, homeowner's insurance, disaster insurance, etc.). It is interesting to note that none of these products is being offered to bank customers at this time.[8]

After years of tremendous success, Toys 'R' Us has recently struggled due to complacency and lack of innovation, as well as competition from Wal-Mart, Target, and other discount giants and membership warehouse chains and new/creative competitors in the educational toy market. As part of the business renewal process, organizations should use cost/benefit analysis periodically to assess how their value proposition compares to competitive options.

As Figure 4.6 shows, companies may occupy one of five positions — best value, discount value, expensive value, fair value, or poor value — in the mind of the customer. Discount, fair, and expensive values have

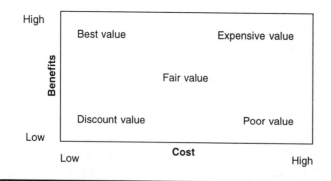

**Figure 4.6. Assessing a Company's Value Position** (Adapted and expanded from Reidenbach, R.E. (1996) Follow the value chain to superior performance, *The Bankers Magazine*, Nov./Dec., p. 51.)

---

### Customer Value Checklist 4.
### Ten Basics of Customer Value

1. Who is your customer?
2. How does your customer experience value?
3. What is unique about your value proposition?
4. Are you competing primarily on price or value?
5. Do you design products and services that deliver the desired value?
6. Do you design effective sales and service channels?
7. Do you recruit and equip employees to deliver and increase customer value?
8. What are you willing to do to deliver better value?
9. How have you added value to customers of late?
10. Do you refine and measure the value proposition to ensure customer loyalty and retention?

(Adapted from Tucker, R.B. (1997) *Customer Service for the New Millennium: Winning and Keeping Value-Driven Buyers,* Franklin Hills, NJ: Career Press; Larrew, T. (1998) The six steps of convergent marketing: putting customers at the center of business decisions, *Credit World,* Jan./Feb., pp. 18–19.)

---

benefits consistent with their costs. Best value (above the fair-value line) represents a strong competitive advantage, while poor value (below the fair-value line) is a prescription for failure for an organization. Bradley Gale, a leading thinker on customer value, explains that the fair-value line is the line of points at which competitors would neither gain nor lose market share with respect to price-quality tradeoffs.[9]

In the case of Toys 'R' Us, we can conclude that the company lost ground in the marketplace, moving from the "best value" to "fair value" position. Their Toy Registry initiative is a relatively new strategy aimed at winning back some of the lost market share. The Registry acts as a "wish list" to let family and friends know what toys children want for birthdays, holidays, or special occasions.

Finally, you are encouraged to review the ten questions in Customer Value Checklist 4 to explore the key customer value concepts discussed in this chapter.

## Summary

The value proposition establishes the basis for developing a unique position in the marketplace. Quality, service, and value-based pricing are the core elements of the VP (these issues are detailed in the next two chapters). Companies that are value winners also use image, innovation, and intangibles to strengthen their value statements. Rather than viewing the VP as separate elements, good managers try to create synergy among all of the components to achieve differentiation and secure competitive advantage. Furthermore, you should reshape the value proposition when changing market conditions call for the adoption of a revised business strategy.

## Customer Value Action Items

1. Define your company's value proposition.
2. What do your customers value?
3. What core aspect of the value proposition (VP) does your company emphasize — quality, service, or price?
4. How does your company augment its VP through the 3I's: image, innovation, and intangibles (e.g., time, specialized knowledge, etc.)?
5. What is unique about your VP?
6. How does your company work at being different and better than the competition?
7. Has your company broken any industry "rules" lately? If so, explain.
8. Does your firm offer a best value, discount value, expensive value, fair value, or poor value?
9. What can your organization do to deliver truly superior customer value?

## References

1. McDonald's Corporation (1998) *1997 Annual Report*, Oak Brook, IL: McDonald's Corporation.
2. Webster, Jr., F.E. (1994) Defining the new marketing concept (part 1), *Marketing Management*, 2(4), pp. 22–31.

3. Callan, C. and Mara, J. (1997) Living the value proposition, *Banking Strategies,* Nov./Dec., pp. 16–20.
4. Kim, W.C. and Mauborgne, R. (1997) Value innovation: the strategic logic of high growth, *Harvard Business Review,* Jan./Feb., pp. 102–112.
5. Grayson, Jr., C.J., and O'Dell, C.S. (1998) Mining your hidden resources, *Across the Board,* April, pp. 23–28.
6. Stalk, Jr., G., Pecaut, D.K., and Burnett, B. (1996), Breaking compromises, breakaway growth, *Harvard Business Review,* 74(Sept./Oct.), pp. 131–139.
7. Reichheld, F.F. (1994) Loyalty and the renaissance of marketing, *Marketing Management,* 2(4), pp. 10–21.
8. Kaytes, D.G. (1997) Jump starting insurance sales, *Banking Strategies,* 73(Nov./ Dec.), pp. 104–108.
9. Gale, B.T. (1994) *Managing Customer Value: Creating Quality and Service That Customers Can See,* New York: The Free Press.

**Defining and Managing Service Quality**

Quality is a journey, not a destination.

As we saw back in Chapter 1, quality is one of the core components of value. Along with price, product quality and service quality serve as the foundations of the value triad. Today, quality has become the most powerful competitive force facing U.S. companies. In a recent American Management Association survey of North American, Western European, and Japanese managers, 78% indicated that improving quality and service to customers is the key to competitive success.

The search for quality is arguably the most important business trend of the past two decades, as demanding customers have come to expect service that is fast, reliable, and friendly. Disney Chairman Michael Eisner established the "Disney Vision of Excellence — Quality, Service, and Smiles", a value proposition that inspires service personnel to deliver a memorable customer experience. This chapter explains what quality is (and what it is not), the essentials of service quality, why quality is important, and how to improve service quality. You will note that quality is examined here in a "generic" fashion, yet the emphasis in our discussion will clearly be on service quality.

## What Is Quality?

Today, many of the products and services we use have become standardized so that even private-label brands meet or exceed minimum standards. Modern communications permit and in some cases encourage customers to shift their patronage from one producer to another. Global competition has resulted in increased choice and has raised customer expectations of what constitutes acceptable quality. Marketing is a contest for consumer's attention, and the Internet is now competing for that attention, as nearly 90 million consumer worldwide now utilize the Web for making purchases or acquiring information.[1] The Internet will shift power away from businesses to consumers, who can quickly compare products and prices from a range of suppliers as never before. Now competition is "just a click away". All these developments point to the need for companies to offer customer-defined quality that differentiates them in the global and digital marketplace. But, what do we mean when we say quality?

Quality is one of those elusive concepts which are easy to visualize but difficult to define. Quality has many definitions ranging from specific to general and varies by functional area. For example, Philip Kotler, a leading marketing guru, defines quality as "the totality of features and characteristics of a product or service that bear on its ability to satisfy stated or implied needs."[2] To expand on this definition, we would add that quality must provide goods and services that completely satisfy the needs of both internal and external customers. Moreover, quality serves as the "bridge" between the producer of goods or services and its customers.

Quality gurus such as W. Edwards Deming viewed quality as reducing variation. Table 5.1 presents Deming's quality philosophy summarized in his 14 points aimed at changing both cultural and organizational systems of a company.

Juran, on the other hand, defined quality as "fitness for use" — products possess customer-desired product features and are free from deficiencies. The Juran philosophy of quality is centered around three basic quality processes: planning, improvement, and control. Juran believed that there must be a continual striving toward quality, consisting of a number of steps from research, development, design, specification, planning, process control, etc. and then back again to research.

Crosby, another leading quality guru, defines quality as "conformance to requirements, not as goodness." Crosby believes that quality is created by a system of prevention, not appraisal (doing it right the first time), where the performance standard is "zero defects — meeting specifications 100% of the time." Crosby also believes it is necessary to build a quality-driven corporate culture.

Garvin takes a more aggressive and strategic approach to defining quality. He views quality as a means of pleasing customers, not just preventing annoyances. He eschews the defensive quality posture practiced by many U.S. companies in favor of a more strategic approach based on a combination of eight quality dimensions, including a product's performance, features, reliability, conformity, durability, serviceability, aesthetics, and perceived quality. Implied in Garvin's eight quality dimensions are five overall categories of quality: [3]

1. Transcendent — some form of innate excellence
2. Product-based — measurable based on attributes of the product itself
3. Manufacturing-based — conformance to requirements
4. User-based — quality is in the eyes of the beholder
5. Value-based — defined in terms of price/cost tradeoffs

Sparks and Legault take Garvin's eight dimensions of quality and apply them to the firm's business cycle. Figure 5.1 illustrates the elements of the quality process as viewed by the customer, as well as those that the customer never sees but which help define quality from the producer's viewpoint.[4]

Integrating the voice of the customer ensures a practice known as quality function deployment (QFD). This process precedes new product or service introductions in order to ensure design quality. QFD enables companies to identify and prioritize customer needs and respond to them effectively. Toyota improved its rust-prevention record from being one of the worst to one of the best in the world by coordinating design and production decisions to focus on this key customer concern. Using the "house of quality" model (see Figure 5.2), designers were able to break down the concept of body durability into 53 items covering everything from climate to modes of operation.

The importance of each design dimension in Figure 5.1 also varies by product (or service). For example, aesthetics would be less important for Dell Computer, which sells direct via the phone or Internet. The goal of QFD is to determine not only what customers want, but which product or service attributes are most important to them.

## Table 5.1. Summary of Deming's 14 Points

| Principle | Explanation |
| --- | --- |
| 1. Maintain a constancy of purpose. | Continuation of business requires a core set of values and a purpose that is stable over time. |
| 2. Adopt the new philosophy. | Learn new responsibilities and take on leadership of change. |
| 3. Cease dependence on mass inspection. | Quality does not come from inspection, but rather from improvements in the process. |
| 4. End the practice of awarding business on the basis of price alone. | Price has no meaning apart from perceived quality; work on minimizing total costs. |
| 5. Improve constantly and forever the system of production and service. | Build quality into the product in the first place; systems should be redesigned continually for improved quality |
| 6. Institute training. | Equip managers and workers with the tools they need to evaluate and improve systems, including basic statistical methods. |
| 7. Institute leadership. | Leaders should know the work they supervise; the aim of leadership should be to help workers do their jobs better. |
| 8. Drive out fear. | Deming claimed that workers perform best when they feel secure; fear breeds hidden agendas and padded numbers and may cause workers to satisfy a rule or quota at the expense of the company. |
| 9. Break down barriers among staff. | Workers in various functional areas need to work together as a team. |
| 10. Eliminate slogans, exhortations, and targets. | Such exhortations only create adversarial relationships; the real cause of low quality is in the system. |
| 11. Eliminate work quotas. | An emphasis on extrinsic motivators, such as quotas or other numerical goals, works against quality and productivity improvements. |

**Table 5.1. Summary of Deming's 14 Points (cont.)**

| Principle | Explanation |
| --- | --- |
| 12. Remove barriers to pride of workmanship. | Remove any bureaucratic hindrances that rob workers' of pride of workmanship; listen and follow up on worker suggestions and requests. |
| 13. Institute a vigorous program of education and self-improvement. | Deming advocated life-long learning, both formal and informal. |
| 14. Put everyone to work on the transformation. | Everyone needs to be involved if business systems are to be improved. |

*Source:* Adapted from Deming, E. (1986) *Out of Crisis*, Cambridge, MA: MIT Center for Advanced Engineering.

## Service Quality Guidelines

Until recently, most managers associated quality with manufactured goods and production. However, during the 1980s, there emerged a broadened definition of quality that included services as well as goods. Defining quality for services is more difficult than for products, due to the intangible, variable nature of service characteristics. A recent study of U.S. consumers by the *Yankelovich Monitor* confirms this phenomenon; 72% of those surveyed said they needed a better way to evaluate the quality and value of what they buy. Furthermore, unlike product

| Design —— | Production —— | Sales Process —— | Delivery —— | After the Sale |
| --- | --- | --- | --- | --- |
| Performance<br>Features<br>Aesthetics<br>Reliability<br>Durability<br>Safety/Security | Conformance | Facilities<br>Communication<br>process<br>Transaction<br>system | Quantity<br>On-time<br>Place | Unanticipated service    Anticipated service |
| | | **Overall Impression** | | |
| | | **Perceived Quality** | | |

**Figure 5.1. Quality and the Business Cycle** (Adapted from Sparks, R. and Legault, R. (1993) A definition of quality for total customer satisfaction: the bridge between manufacturer and customer, *SAM Advanced Management Journal,* 58(1), Winter, p. 17.)

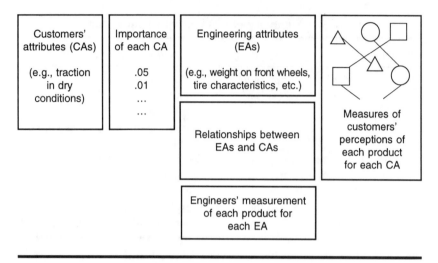

**Figure 5.2. House of Quality**

quality, consumers frequently lack the necessary information to evaluate service quality. For example, consumers of durable goods such as cars or major appliances often conduct research before making a purchase, allowing them to use *search* quality prior to the purchase. Moreover, consumers can also use *experience* quality, based on post-purchase evaluation of the product to determine whether their expectations were met.

With services, however, consumers are usually limited to using *credence* quality to evaluate the experience, relying solely on the overall credibility of the service provider. A consumer receiving legal services or medical treatments has little basis on which to judge the quality, other than the reputation of the law firm or medical facility. Here consumers are not always sure what to expect and may not know for some time, if ever, whether the outcome was performed satisfactorily. These factors make it more difficult for consumers to evaluate services in advance while at the same time creating greater risk. Managers can help reduce this risk by providing information that helps customers evaluate alternatives before the purchase as well as provide documentation of the firm's service reputation.

Another challenge presented in assessing service quality arises when viewing services along a continuum ranging from pre-sale to post-sale activities. Figure 5.3 shows the progression of these activities and where the potential for service failures may occur in the process. For example, a brokerage house might offer free seminars on estate planning as part

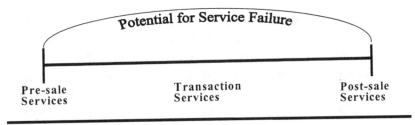

**Figure 5.3. Continuum of Services**

of pre-sale services, providing valuable information that participants can later use when choosing a particular investment plan. Lincoln Suites Hotel proactively manages pre-sale services by calling its guests several days before their scheduled arrival date to confirm their arrival and departure dates, the number of people in the party, and their smoking/nonsmoking preferences and to provide directions to the hotel. This attention to detail prior to check-in minimizes hassles later and eases travel anxiety by addressing last-minute concerns. By the same token, firms risk alienating prospects by poor handling of pre-sale services. Most of us have experienced the frustration of calling a firm's toll-free line only to be placed on seemingly endless hold or getting trapped in the voice-mail maze.

Customers also form perceptions of quality during the service transaction — how effectively and efficiently the service was delivered and the speed and convenience of completing the transaction. Anyone who has purchased a product over the phone has experienced the frustration when the "computers go down" and processing the order and payment grinds to a halt. Amazon.com, the online retailing pioneer, has revolutionized book buying and flawlessly handles customer purchase transactions. For starters, it builds customer profiles by preference with each visit, recommending titles within categories and sending e-mails to prompt browsing. Most importantly, it gives the customer a sense of power over the entire retail transaction, from initial entry to random search to final selection and ordering. There is no need to supply your name, address, and credit card number each time you shop, either, as Amazon.com creates a user profile on your initial visit.

Finally, customers evaluate support activities that occur after the transaction — that is, post-sale services. Joe Girard, who holds the Guinness record for most retail automobile sales, believes that when a customer returns with a complaint or needs service, he should drop everything and make sure the customer gets the best service available. He maintains that, "The sale begins after the sale." He is also known for sending out birthday cards to his customers every year. Sales follow-up in the form of phone calls, letters, or cards shows a genuine concern for the customer and leads to repeat business and business loyalty. Phil Breslin, a Domino's Pizza franchisee in Baltimore, requires his store managers to make customer calls at the end of each business day, even if that means letting close-outs wait until the next business day. Both these examples demonstrate a commitment to build repeat business through effective post-sale follow-up.

Generally, a user of services has a set of attributes or characteristics in mind when judging service quality. Using extensive, in-depth interviews with 12 consumer focus group interviews, Parasuraman, Zeithaml, and Berry found that customers assess service quality using the following ten dimensions:[5,6]

1. Reliability —dependable and accurate performance of promised service
2. Responsiveness — willingness/readiness to provide prompt service
3. Competence —knowledge and skill to perform the service
4. Access — approachability and ease of contact of service personnel
5. Courtesy — politeness, consideration, and friendliness of service personnel
6. Communication — keeping customers informed; listening to customers
7. Credibility — trustworthiness, believability, honesty
8. Security — freedom from danger, risk, or doubt
9. Understanding/knowing customer — knowing customer's needs
10. Tangibles — physical evidence of service

Note that later empirical verification reduced the above ten dimensions to five overall factors (tangibles, reliability, responsiveness, assurance, and empathy).

Parasuraman and his colleagues found that service quality is a measure between service perceptions as well as expectations. Service quality stems from a comparison of what a consumer feels a service firm *should* offer (desires or wants) vs. their perception of what the service firm actually does offer. Thus, ensuring good service quality involves meeting

## Table 5.2. Service Quality Gaps

| Service Quality Gap | Definition |
|---|---|
| Consumer expectation/management gap | Managers have difficulty in translating customer requirements into service quality specifications or precise performance standards. |
| Planning and design gap | Performance standards and specifications (as well as systems) do not always measure up to what customer expects. |
| Implementation gap | There is a discrepancy between service quality specifications and the delivery of service performance in accordance with those specifications. |
| External communications gap | There is a discrepancy between the level of service quality delivered and the communication of that delivery to the customer (i.e., over-promising and under-delivering). |

*Source*: Adapted from Parasuraman, A., Zeithaml, V., and Berry, L. (1985) A conceptual model of service quality and its implications for future research, *Journal of Marketing*, 49(Fall), pp. 41–50.

or exceeding consumers' expectations. Hotel patrons, when asked to indicate what they consider most essential, revealed five factors that indicate their likelihood of a return visit: cleanliness, providing breakfast, friendliness of the personnel, value, and check-in speed.

These researchers further determined that customer perceptions are influenced by a series of "gaps" which are presented in Table 5.2. The task of managers is to close the gaps using the following recommended strategies:

1. Gap 1: Learn what the customer values and values most, using such tools as benchmarking, quality function deployment, and competitive analysis.
2. Gap 2: Design a proper system using blueprinting and other quality tools such as fishbone diagrams.
3. Gap 3: Control the process using such quality tools as statistical process control and pareto charts.

4.  Gap 4: Provide accurate information by informing customers of the true level of service they can expect and holding to those pledges.

Parasuraman, Zeithaml, and Berry later operationalized these gaps in the form of SERVQUAL, a 22-item instrument that measures both expectations and customer perceptions of the service encounter. SERVQUAL can serve as an effective diagnostic tool for uncovering broad areas of a company's service quality shortfalls and strengths.[7] This scale serves as a suitable generic measure of service quality, transcending specific functions, companies, and industries. Service quality ratings are obtained from the scale when consumers compare their service expectations with actual service performance on distinct service dimensions — reliability, responsiveness, assurance, empathy, and tangibles. Poor service quality results when perceived performance ratings are lower than expectations, whereas the reverse indicates good service quality. There is also evidence from their research that these service dimensions vary in importance, with reliability being consistently most important, followed in order by responsiveness, assurance, empathy, and tangibles. Managers can use these insights to make appropriate decisions for improving service quality.

Service quality can also be defined according to both the "what" and "how" of a product or service and its delivery. Gronroos distinguishes between technical quality and functional quality.[8] Technical quality is concerned with the outcome of the delivered product or service, such as a restaurant meal that is well prepared or an acceptable haircut or styling. Customers use service quality attributes such as reliability, competence, performance, durability, etc. to evaluate technical quality. For example, when bringing a videocassette recorder (VCR) in for repair, the customer would expect the VCR to be properly serviced to eliminate the problem and prevent it from occurring again. Functional quality has more to do with how the technical quality is transferred to the consumer. Back to our VCR example, the customer would expect not only competency and accuracy in the repair but also helpful and courteous service personnel. Service quality attributes such as responsiveness and access would be important in helping the customer judge the functional quality of the service encounter.

Service quality can also be judged by considering the various "spheres" or thresholds of the service offering as presented in Figure 5.4. The core

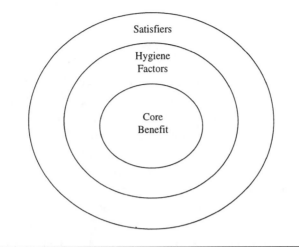

**Figure 5.4. Three Levels of Service**

benefit is the most fundamental level for which the service offering stands — that is, what the consumer is actually seeking. The core benefit represents basic reasons why people buy, such as hunger, safety, convenience, confidence, status, self-esteem, and so on. Gonroos uses the term "service concept" to indicate the core of a service offering, such as offering car rental as a solution to a short-term transportation need.[9]

The hygiene factors constitute the minimally acceptable level of service attributes that customers would expect to be present in the service offering. For example, a mid-priced hotel catering to business travelers would be expected to offer such services as express checkout, a fitness room, a fax and/or computer hookups, a restaurant, and a lounge. Failure to offer these services or to deliver them poorly will likely lead to dissatisfaction. In contrast, simply offering these services and performing them adequately will not delight the customer — the customer expects them as part of doing business.

Truly delighting customers requires service providers to carefully consider satisfiers. Satisfiers are those service attributes that differentiate the service firm from its competitors, while at the same time exceeding customer expectations in one or more areas of service by delivering above what is expected. According to Naumann, hygiene factors need to be delivered at an acceptable level before satisfiers become important.[10] Satisfiers have the potential to create high customer satisfaction levels once expectations regarding hygiene factors have been met. Firms that would offer satisfiers need to consider the value-added services that would both delight and surprise the customer.

Before a guest ever sets foot in Le Parker Meridian Hotel in New York they can use the hotel's QuickTime Virtual Reality (QTVR) tour, which enables potential guests to "walk" through the lobby and rooms. In addition to virtual reality tours, the site offers in-depth, timely information about room rates, events, and points of interest for the business and pleasure traveler. The hotel also welcomes repeat guests with amenity baskets accompanied by handwritten notes.

Ritz-Carlton works hard at learning its customers' preferences to serve them better in the future. From the moment guests book a room for the first time at a Ritz-Carlton hotel, their guest-history profile begins. Every preference they have is recorded, and all 30 Ritz-Carlton hotels and resorts have access to the information. Ritz -Carlton employees take every opportunity to note guest preferences; in fact, employees carry guest-preference pads to note comments, which are later recorded in the guest-history files. For example, if a guest likes an iron in the room, or prefers not to have turn-down service, or requests a Cadillac instead of a Lincoln when needing car service to the airport, the information will be recorded and will follow the guest to every subsequent stay.

Finally, it should be emphasized that quality is more than simply meeting specifications and that the customer's point of view on quality is key. That is, *quality is what the customer says it is.* Remember, it is the customer not the company that sets the quality and value agenda. A recently conducted study found that consumers define quality as including reliability, durability, easy maintenance, easy use, a trusted brand name, and low price with a high value. The losers in the quality battle will be those who attempt to do things right, while the winners will be the organizations that learn to do the right things.[11] The next section discusses the importance of quality and the payoffs that a quality-oriented culture produces.

## Why Quality Matters

Xerox once enjoyed a near strangle hold on the copier market until the late 1970s, when it saw its nearly 100% market share devoured almost entirely by more cost-efficient Japanese producers. In the late 1970s, Fuji Xerox, its Japanese subsidiary at the time, launched a total quality

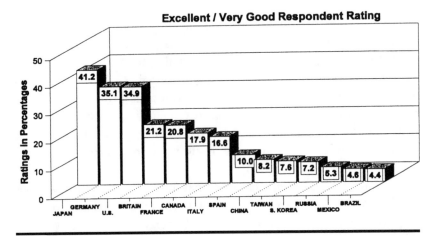

**Excellent / Very Good Respondent Rating**

**Figure 5.5. Overall Quality Leaders** (From 1996 Bozell-Gallup Worldwide Quality Poll.)

process under the name "New Xerox Movement" with the goal of better satisfying customer requirements and bringing costs under control. Quality circles were introduced, and quality tools became the norm. The turnaround was nothing short of spectacular. The prestigious Deming Quality Award was bestowed on Fuji Xerox, while revenues and profits soared. Xerox learned firsthand that quality works.

The global market as we know it is becoming more competitive every day, as companies continually search for new ways to gain an edge over their competitors around the globe. Global competition and deregulation in a number of industries are forcing companies to turn to quality in order to survive. General Electric's CEO, Jack Welch, recently commented, "Quality is our best assurance of customer allegiance, our strongest defense against foreign competition, and the only path to sustained growth and earnings." The Council on Competitiveness conducted a study examining the competitiveness of the U.S. economy since 1985 and found that the factors accounting for the largest gains in U.S. competitiveness included: (1) product, process, and management of innovation; and (2) focus on quality and customer needs. While U.S. companies have made great strides in improving quality during that time, their products still lag behind those of Japan and Germany according to a Bozell-Gallup Worldwide Quality Poll.[12] The study found that consumers around the world rated Japanese products "excellent" or "very good" 41.2% of the time and American goods "excellent" or "very good" 34.9% of the time (see Figure 5.5).

Perhaps the most important reason for pursuing quality is that quality pays. Deming stressed the favorable economic outcomes that result from a strategy of offering high quality. In Walton's book, *The Deming Management Method*, Deming is quoted as saying, "I want to make it clear that as you improve quality, your costs go down. Continual reduction in mistakes, continual improvement in quality mean lower costs ... less waste of materials, machine time, human effort. ... As costs go down, through less rework, the result is fewer mistakes, less waste, while productivity goes up."[13]

Research has also been conducted that shows a relationship between quality, market share, and return on investment. The exhaustive database from the Profit Impact of Market Strategy (PIMS) clearly documents these relationships. Higher quality yields a higher return on investment (ROI) for any given market share. For example, among businesses with less than 12% of the market, those with inferior quality averaged an ROI of 4.5%; those with average product quality, an ROI of 10.4%; and those with superior product quality, an ROI of 17.4 %.[14]

Quality also pays in the form of customer retention. Considering that the average business today loses 10 to 30% of its customers each year, customer defections represent a significant cost to companies. In a study by Michaelson and Associates, 69% of customers indicated "poor service" as the reason for leaving the company. Frederick Reichheld of Bain & Co. found that reducing customer defections by 5% can double profits.[15] Moreover, according to Forum Corporation, a Boston consulting firm, it is five times more expensive to get a new customer than to keep an existing one.[16]

Finally, adopting quality principles strongly correlates to corporate stock and earnings appreciation. A study conducted over a 5-year period assessed the performances of some 600 publicly traded winners of 140 annual quality awards given by state or private agencies. The study found that the award winners did about 50% better in stock appreciation and two to three times as well in growth of operating income, sales, assets, and employment (see Figure 5.6).[17]

A Swedish quality index has also shown a strong relationship between quality practices and performance. Companies in their study capable of increasing their quality index by one point every year for 5 years improved their average return on assets during that period by almost 12%.[18]

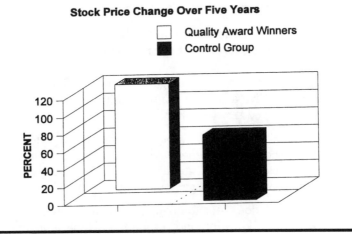

Figure 5.6. How Winners Win on Wall Street

# How To Improve Quality

Improving quality is a lot like taking vitamins, eating healthy foods, and exercising regularly. Although the results may not be immediate, long-term benefits are significant. Quality is neither a quick fix nor the program of the month, but rather a way of life for companies who are serious about improvement (see Customer Value Checklist 5 for help in diagnosing service quality problems).

Quality, as we have already seen, is fundamental to creating value, yet it is a moving target and must meet the customer's current definition of quality. Thus, we offer the following recommendations for improving service quality and ultimately delivering superior customer value:

- Design services in cooperation with customers. Learn what customers truly value by incorporating the voice of the customer earlier in the service development process. Also, it is important to determine not only the customer's preferred service attributes but their relative importance, as well.
- Focus your improvement programs outward, on market breakpoints. Only by defining these episodes, when the customer comes in contact with the organization, and by focusing on the ones most critical can you see things as the customer sees them. Also, visualize the complete sequence of the moments of truth a customer experiences in having some need met. Remember,

**Customer Value Checklist 5.
Probing for Service Quality Improvement**

1. Does your company do a good job of listening to its customers? Give a specific example of how listening resulted in improved service quality to your customers.

2. Reliability is the ability of the company to perform the promised services dependably and accurately. On a 10-point scale, where 1 is unreliable and 10 perfectly reliable, where would you place your company and why?

3. How well does your company perform the "service basics" — that is, knowing and responding to the fundamental service expectations in your industry (e.g., an automobile service department that fixes the car right the first time)?

4. How effectively does your company manage the service design elements or systems, people, and the physical environment? Provide an example of how a lack of planning in one of these areas resulted in a "fail point" during a customer encounter.

5. Service recovery refers to how effectively companies respond to service failures. Cite an example of when a service failure occurred in your company and how it was handled.

6. Teamwork is an important dynamic in sustaining service workers' motivation to serve and in minimizing service-performance shortfalls. Rate your company on its ability to foster teamwork on a scale of 1 to 10, where 1 indicates the absence of teamwork and 10 indicates maximum teamwork. How would you improve teamwork if you rated your company low on this attribute?

7. Internal service is crucial to service improvement, as customer satisfaction often mirrors employee satisfaction. To what extent does your company assess internal service quality (i.e., asking employees about the adequacy of systems to support the service, how the systems interact and serve one another, and where service failures are occurring)? Give examples of how internal service might be measured in your company.

the customer sees service in terms of a total experience, not an isolated set of activities. Mapping the service cycle helps companies see these activities as the customer sees them.

■ Create a tangible representation of service quality. Hotels and restaurants often advertise and display on their properties ratings by one of the major motor clubs, such as AAA or Mobil Oil. Hertz #1 Club Gold service communicates a premium, value-added bundle of services to business travelers seeking a hassle-free car rental experience.

■ Use teamwork to promote service excellence — service workers who support one another and achieve together can avoid service burnout. As the Preacher in *Ecclesiastes* (4:9–10) said, "Two are better than one, because they have a good reward for their labor. For if they fall, one will lift up his companion."

■ Create a service bias based on each of the following service quality determinants: professionalism, attitudes and behaviors, accessibility and flexibility, reliability and trustworthiness, service recovery, and reputation and credibility. These criteria can be used as guidelines for influencing positive service quality perceptions.

■ Develop proper measurements. Use metrics that are specific in nature, such as 95% on-time delivery, customer wait time, or order processing time. Benchmark the best practices for each service area being measured, such as wait time or order delivery.

■ Employee selection, job design, and training are absolutely crucial to building customer satisfaction and service quality. Structure the job of service workers to maximize their ability to respond quickly and competently to customer needs. Also, train service personnel in areas of service delivery and attitude. Role-play different service scenarios, showing various service recovery strategies. Provide service workers with some basic tools, such as those discussed in Chapter 3, to help control service quality variation and uncover service problems.

■ Reward total quality efforts in marketing. Look for opportunities to reinforce quality behaviors when they occur. Employees should be rewarded on the basis of these behaviors (commitment, effort) rather than strictly on outcomes, such as sales quotas. Rewarding a salesperson for meeting or exceeding quota with a bonus while giving a nominal award such as a pin or plaque to the person who fixes the product or process sends a clear message about the importance of quality.

- Think of service as a process, not a series of functions. Service quality occurs when the entire service experience is managed and the organization is aligned to respond accordingly.

## Summary

The modern quality revolution that began in Japan in the early 1950s and was exported to the U.S. during the 1980s has forever changed how corporations and institutions are managed. The sheer size of the service economy, competing demands on scarce resources, and more demanding customers force management to place greater emphasis on creating high-quality customer experiences. Competing in a global economy requires firms to understand what "world-class" quality really means. The challenge facing firms today is knowing their customer's definition of service quality and how to deliver that at a reasonable cost — in short, how to create superior customer value.

In this chapter, we have discussed various definitions of quality and the use of quality function deployment in determining service quality dimensions and their importance. We have also discussed the difficulty consumers have in assessing service quality. The gap model was presented along with some major service quality dimensions. The importance of service quality and its relationship to competitiveness, customer retention, and firm performance was explained. Finally, we offered some practical strategies for improving service quality by focusing on how services are designed, measured, and delivered.

## Customer Value Action Items

1. Why has quality become such a priority today?
2. What are some of the common denominators in the definition of quality?
3. How does quality function deployment bridge customer requirements with product/service features?
4. Determine the extent of *search quality*, *experience quality*, and *credence quality* for each of the following situations:

    a. Buying a personal computer

    b. Applying to graduate school

    c. Setting up a retirement program

    d. Dining at a local restaurant

    e. Visiting a theme park

5. Suppose you were interested in purchasing personal tax preparation software. Give examples of how service failures could occur during pre-sale, transaction, and post-sale phases of the buying process.

6. Suppose you were managing a mid-priced hotel catering to business travelers. Determine the key factors for assessing service quality; also, suppose you were a customer of that same hotel. What factors would you use to judge service quality? Rank your choices for each situation and then compare the two lists.

7. What evidence is there that quality and improving quality are important to the success of a business?

8. How can businesses improve service quality? Discuss.

# References

1. Hof, R., McWilliams, G., and Saveri, G. (1998) The click-here economy, *Business Week,* June, pp. 122–128.
2. Kotler, P. (1997) *Marketing Management,* 9th ed., Upper Saddle River, NJ: Prentice-Hall, p. 55.
3. Garvin, D. (1988) *Managing Quality,* New York: Free Press.
4. Sparks, R. and Legault, R. (1993) A definition of quality for total customer satisfaction: the bridge between manufacturer and customer, *SAM Journal,* 58, p. 17.
5. Parasuraman, A., Zeithaml, V., and Berry, L. (1985) A conceptual model of service quality and implications for future research, *Journal of Marketing,* 49(Fall), pp. 41–50.
6. Zeithaml, V., Parasuraman, A., and Berry, L. (1990) *Delivering Quality Service,* New York: The Free Press.
7. Parasuraman, A., Zeithaml, V., and Berry, L. (1988) SERVQUAL: a multiple-item scale for measuring consumer perceptions of service quality, *Journal of Retailing,* 64, pp. 12–40.
8. Gronroos, C. (1988) *Service Management and Marketing,* Lexington, MA: Lexington Books.
9. Gronroos, C. (1984) A service quality model and its marketing implications, *European Journal of Marketing,* 18, pp. 36–43.
10. Naumann, E. (1995) *Creating Customer Value.* Cincinnati, OH: Thomson Executive Press.

11. Johnson, W. and Chvala, R. (1995) *Total Quality in Marketing*, Boca Raton, FL: St. Lucie Press.
12. *Bozell-Gallup Third Annual Worldwide Quality Poll*, 1996.
13. Walton, M. (1990) *The Deming Management Method*, New York: Putnam, p. 26.
14. Buzell, R. and Gale, B. (1987) *The PIMS Principles*, New York: The Free Press.
15. Reichheld, F. and Sasser, E. (1990) Zero defections: quality comes to services, *Harvard Business Review*, Sept./Oct., pp. 301–307.
16. Sellers, P. (1989) Getting customers to love you, *Fortune*, March 13, p. 38.
17. Singhal, V. and Hendricks, K. (1998) The rewards of quality, *Business Week*, Sept. 21, p. 26.
18. Grant, L. (1998) Your customers are telling the truth, *Fortune*, Feb. 16, p. 166.

# 6 Communicating Value Through Price

"Price is what you pay. Value is what you get." (Warren Buffett, CEO, Berkshire Hathaway)

## Introduction

What does price mean? Price can vary greatly according to whose perspective is taken. For example, to marketers, price is used to signal value for their products or services, to differentiate their offer from those of the competitors, or to shift consumer demand. To consumers, price influences the perceived value, reflecting how much they have to give up in order to take possession of the product or service. From the competitor's standpoint, price is something to match, beat, or use as a competitive weapon to block a competing firm's market entry. Of course, competitors can also use price to penetrate an existing market, such as the approach AT&T took to enter the credit card market, initially offering their card at no annual fee for life.

Prices are often determined based on the type and location of the purchase. During a recent trip to Thailand, one of the authors shopped in a bazaar in the southern part of the country and found that the price of everything was negotiable. Even in more industrialized countries, prices for big-ticket items such as televisions, stereos, furniture, and automobiles are often subject to some price flexibility. Negotiated prices are even more common in business-to-business settings.

Today, managers set prices for goods and services before consumers and businesses ever meet. Managers often consider costs, demand, and competition — the hallmarks of value pricing — before arriving at a final price. This does not imply that pricing has become an exact science. Price is often set based on convention or rules of thumb, or even intuition about what the customer will (or should) pay. Regardless of whether setting a price is viewed as an art or science, the price set is only as good as the value delivered to the customer.

In today's competitive markets, companies cannot afford to neglect sound pricing policies. Often, setting the right price can make or break the bottom line, especially for new products and services. Although most companies view price decisions as important, prices are often set on purely tactical grounds or in response to a competitor's move. Instead of simply being a knee-jerk response to market conditions, pricing decisions should be made based on segmentation analysis, cost analysis, demand elasticities, and the firm's value proposition (see Chapter 4).

We have already discussed the quality components of the value triad. Product and service quality both influence the consumer's perception of value. Yet, price also serves as a major signal for quality. Innovative companies, however, recognize that value for their customers is more than simply low price. In this chapter, we will examine how price, the "give" component of the value equation, serves as an indicator of value. Next, we will look at how buyers evaluate price. We will also consider price in the context of a company's overall marketing strategy. The different approaches to pricing will then be discussed, as well as principles that lead to better pricing decisions. Finally, we will conclude the chapter with a brief overview of some future pricing issues.

## Relating Price to Value

Value today is often misunderstood to mean low price or bundled price. Yet, the real essence of value revolves around the tradeoff between the benefits consumers receive from a product or service and the price that they pay (see Figure 6.1). From a consumer's standpoint, price only has meaning when paired with the benefits delivered, both tangible and psychological. For a given price, value increases when product or service benefits increase. For example, Men's Wearhouse, a retailer of men's suits based in Fremont, CA, offers low prices on brand-name men's

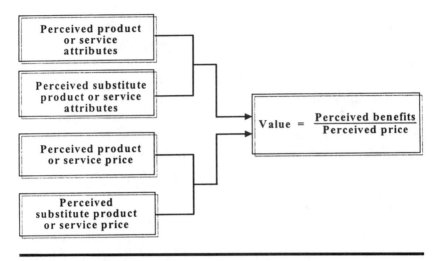

**Figure 6.1. Price, Benefits, and Value**

suits, but also offers free pressing for as long as the customer owns his suit, sportcoat, or trousers. Taco Bell, a value-pricing innovator, knows that for every dollar a Taco Bell customer spends, the company gets back 27¢ for food, 8¢ for advertising, 13¢ for overhead, and 12¢ for rent. They reasoned that rather than giving the customer 27¢ worth of food, give them 40¢ worth of food instead and find ways to reduce costs in the other areas.

By the same token, value decreases when perceived benefits go down relative to price. Many companies were initially attracted to managed health care because of their ability to control skyrocketing healthcare costs. Yet, despite the cost savings, employees of these companies were becoming frustrated by the loss of control over their medical destiny (i.e., reduced choice of physicians and reductions in certain types of care normally available under traditional fee-for-service coverage). Many of these managed-care companies were shortsighted by equating price to value.

Moreover, consumer value assessments are often comparative. Value judgments by consumers as to the worth and desirability of the product or service are made relative to competitive substitutes that satisfy the same need. Hewlett-Packard (H-P), the world's second largest high-tech company, is introducing a new line of PhotoSmart digital photography gear that will pit them against industry leader Kodak in the image processing market. H-P aims to turn its gear into the "home digital darkroom" of the future, offering consumers an alternative way to take and process pictures.

The prices of perceived product or service substitutes also go into consumers' evaluation of value. Kodak is slugging it out with their chief rival Fuji in the film market, where an all-out price war has erupted since mid-1997 at the low end of the film market. By bundling rolls of film in packs of 4 and 5, Fuji has forced the price per roll of film down to just over $1, recalibrating the value equation in this market. Thus, consumers determine the value of a product or service based on a company's perceived benefits and price, as well as those of a competitor's offer.

## How Buyers Evaluate Price

Buyers often use price as a perceptual cue to indicate product or service quality. That is, all things being equal, the higher the price, the higher the perceived quality. Historically, product quality has been treated as the mirror image of price. This is still particularly the case when the brand is relatively unfamiliar to the buyer, such as with medical-related products. The quality/price link also tends to be stronger for durable goods than for non-durable goods.[1]

Buyers also use frames of reference to evaluate prices. Consumers evaluate purchases in terms of gains or losses, relative to a referent point. The referent point is the consumer's state of well-being at the time of the purchase. According to the Prospect Theory, buyers are influenced by anticipated changes in well-being.[2] For example, suppose two companies sell long-distance calling plans. Company A advertises their plan for $25 per month, with a $12 rebate for continuing the contract for at least one year. Company B advertises their plan for $24 per month, with a $12 surcharge for dropping out of the program before a year is up. Which is the better deal after one year's worth of calls? The answer, of course, is that the economic costs are identical here, yet most consumers would be more psychologically influenced to buy the call plan from Company A. Consumers would prefer the offer from Company A because of the way it has framed the price, leading to a perceived "gain".

Not only does framing affect how consumers evaluate price, so do price benchmarks or reference prices. Reference prices are any prices against which other observed prices are evaluated.[3] Reference prices may be internal, stored in the consumer's memory, and may serve as a basis for judging or comparing actual prices. These internal benchmark prices are influenced by the product's perceived quality and by previously acquired information based either on prior purchasing situations or on advertising cues. Consumers approach purchase situations with a target price (usually a price range) in mind and react positively or negatively when price deviations fall within the region of acceptance. Thus, the challenge for marketing managers is to determine what that acceptable range is and to set prices accordingly. Sellers can enhance a buyer's value perceptions by comparing a lower selling price to a higher advertised reference price.

Reference prices may also be external, determined in the presence of some marketing stimuli such as point-of-purchase shelf tags that indicate suggested retail price or the price of another product against which the price is compared. For example, it is not uncommon for stores selling private-label brands to encourage shoppers to compare the house brand with the nationally advertised brand. Sellers can also create value for their customers by showing the suggested retail price beside the sale price. Buyers respond favorably to this approach, as long as the suggested retail price is not inflated. Furniture retailers have been attacked for misleading and deceptive advertising practices when they advertise furniture at bogus discount prices. Burdine's, a Miami-based department store, was recently investigated by the Attorney General's Office for advertising a dining room set at a sale price for eight consecutive months, effectively making it the regular price.

## Strategic Pricing

Today, intelligent pricing (or the lack thereof) is determining winners and losers in a host of competitive markets such as airlines, fast food, and telecommunications, just to name a few. Price is a critical element of a company's marketing mix and is the only one that directly generates revenue. Yet, price cannot be considered apart from the other marketing mix variables, given their interdependence, and thus must be viewed in the context of the overall marketing strategy. Too often pricing is treated as a tactical response in the marketplace instead of part of a well-integrated marketing strategy. Pricing messages, like all others, need to be strategically integrated with all other brand messages in order to send customers and potential customers a coherent, meaningful statement.[4] Moreover, the price established must be consistent with the company's overall value proposition.

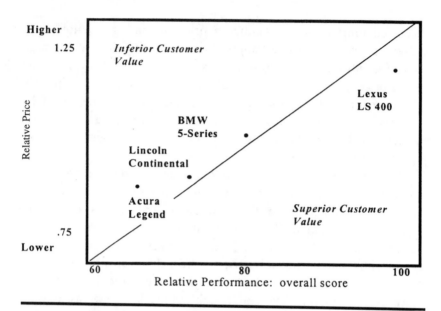

**Figure 6.2. Customer Value Map: Luxury Cars** (Data from April 1993 *Consumer Reports* ratings.)

Price also tends to be managed by functions within organizations, such as finance or sales, who frequently have their own agendas and conflicting views with marketing. Because of these competing agendas, companies end up with a pricing policy that bears little or no connection to marketing. Surprisingly, most companies do not manage pricing cross-functionally even though pricing can have a much greater bottom-line impact than other marketing initiatives.

We recommend that firms can become more strategic in their pricing decisions by considering the following:

- *Prepare a value map.* A value map shows the value position of each competitor in a market by comparing relative price to relative quality (see Figure 6.2).[5] A value map represents an exceptionally powerful tool for comparing value positions within an industry, suggesting strategic shifts in either price or quality depending on the company's location on the map.
- *Relate pricing to the target market's demand elasticity.* Any given industry, such as the airlines or hotels, is comprised of customer segments with varying degrees of price sensitivity. The challenge for management is to determine the price floor and the

price ceiling of the offering, along with the price-value segments in the middle. For example, airlines use very sophisticated "yield-management" systems not only to manage seat inventory but also to customize prices to match demand. Leisure travelers and business travelers may be buying tickets on the same flight, but they pay widely different fares. Leisure travelers are willing to book well in advance and are somewhat flexible in scheduling, but they are not willing to pay as much as business travelers, who book on short notice with little flexibility in scheduling and are less price sensitive.

■ *Make your pricing strategy reflect the perceived value of the service, not simply delivered value.* For example, Bugs Burger Bug Killers (BBBK), a pest control company, is able to charge ten times that of other firms serving the commercial property industry by focusing on a segment of the market that is not price sensitive (i.e., hotels and restaurants). BBBK meets a critical need of these establishments: pest elimination rather than simply pest control. This segment will assign such a high importance to the guarantee that price becomes almost irrelevant when they assess the value of the offering.

■ *Assign price-setting responsibility to a dedicated staff function.* Choose someone with a "blended" background in marketing/sales, finance, and economics to head up the department. Give this person the latitude to coordinate with other departments in aligning price with the overall business strategy. Industries such as airlines, telecommunications, services, and pharmaceuticals have already experimented with this approach.

## Pricing Methods

The purpose of this section is not to review all the possible pricing methods, but to discuss those that are truly customer oriented. Many traditional pricing methods are either cost or profit driven. Cost-driven methods seek to recover a reasonable return over the product's full cost. Profit-driven pricing attempts to maximize profitability by making trade-offs between price changes and changes in sales volume.

Value-driven companies may use any of the following five market-based pricing approaches:

- Price-driven costing
- Demand-based pricing
- Price customization
- Price differentiation
- Value-based pricing

Price-driven costing involves setting a price by starting with the estimated price customers are willing to pay and working backwards from this price specification. This requires the firm to figure out how to get the costs down in order to sell the product or service at the price indicated by customers, while allowing for a reasonable profit. Kodak followed this approach when pricing their instant camera in the mid-1970s. Before introducing the camera, Kodak conducted "concept tests" for the proposed product. Participants in the concept test were shown descriptions of different versions of the camera, each with different prices. Respondents were then asked to indicate their purchase intentions for each version, ranging from "definitely would buy" to "definitely would not buy". Kodak introduced an instant camera based on these data, arriving at an introductory price of $39.95.

Demand-based pricing requires that the price be set based on an estimate of volume that can be sold at different prices, based on market conditions, purchase situation, and price sensitivity. In certain situations, customers are sensitive to price increases, especially when their purchasing power has eroded. A local hotel in Jakarta, Indonesia, seized the opportunity when the Rupiah, the Indonesian currency, plunged in value against the dollar. The hotel set the price of their hotel rooms at a "fixed" exchange rate (see Figure 6.3). The prices for Super Bowl tickets or a pay-per-view heavyweight boxing match will often vary depending upon the teams and the fighters, respectively. Airfare prices "firmed up" considerably following the crash of ValueJet 592, as travelers gravitated back to the major carriers. Each of these examples demonstrates that price is often set based on what the market will bear.

Price customization, which may be a form of price discrimination, occurs when the company seeks to modify their price to accommodate differences in customers, locations, and the manner or time in which the product or service is used. Price customization — selling the same products to different buyers at different prices — is a legal practice as long as it does not have a negative effect on competition (price is set in "good faith" to meet the competition, or price reflects different uses of

Figure 6.3. Demand-Based Pricing Example

the product or distribution in different markets or sales at different points in time). Price customization is often based on the type of customer being served. For example, seniors or children frequently receive discounts at restaurants and entertainment activities. Prices may also be customized based on the channel of delivery. For example, staples such as soft drinks or milk are often priced higher in convenience stores than in supermarkets. Customers sometimes pay higher prices depending upon the urgency of the purchase, such as when placing a rush or custom order with a seller. Finally, a seller's price may be determined by time and place. For example, rates for hotel rooms, car rentals, or long-distance phone calls can vary depending upon the time the service is used. By customizing the price, marketers can recognize the convenience that customers incorporate into the value ratio.

Price differentiation is a pricing approach taken in response to competitive forces. Often the competitive strategy chosen to compete in a given market determines how prices will be established. For example, Wal-Mart has chosen a strategy of "beat their price" in competing in the mass-merchandising industry. Other companies, such as Circuit City, offer a low-price guarantee, boasting in their ads, "You can't get a lower price — we guarantee it!" and "We'll beat any legitimate price from a local store stocking the same new item in a factory-sealed box, and we'll refund 110% of the difference."

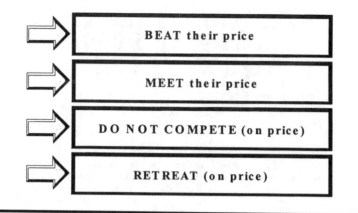

**Figure 6.4. Price Differentiation Strategies**

Companies may also resort to meeting the prices of their competitors. Airlines typically match a competitor's move to lower fares to selected destinations. For example, several years ago Southwest Airlines offered a round-trip fare from Baltimore, MD, to Los Angeles, CA, for $209; the same ticket on American Airlines was priced at $418. American quickly dropped their price to match Southwest's discounted fare.

Some companies choose not to compete, preferring to compete on non-price factors instead, such as service. Nordstrom and Tupperware are two well-known retailers who compete primarily based on their high levels of customer care. Customers appreciate and are willing to pay for the "extra" services they enjoy while patronizing these companies (see Figure 6.4). Sometimes it does not make sense to compete, because of a lack of resources or the scale economies; thus, firms in these cases should retreat on price. Xerox stopped competing in the financial services market when it was no longer profitable by cutting their losses and exiting the market.

Firms that pursue value pricing are committed to the belief that pricing should be set to reflect and capture customer value. Today, value pricing is often associated with low prices, such as McDonald's "extra-value" meals. Managers using value pricing need to educate the customer to redefine value from its current perception of being synonymous with "inexpensive". Value pricing involves adjusting the value equation either by lowering prices or raising quality, or both. Consider Hewlett-Packard color laser printers. While prices of Hewlett-Packard color printers have dropped almost 50% over the last two years, print quality (as measured by resolution, or dots per inch) has actually increased

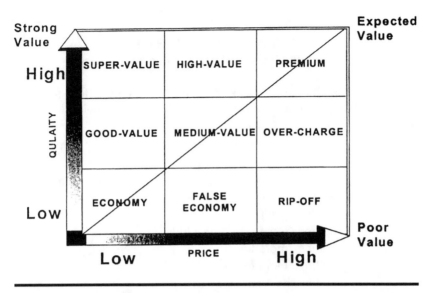

**Figure 6.5. Price/Quality Strategies** (Adapted from Kotler, P. (1997) *Marketing Management*, 9th ed., Englewood Cliffs, NJ: Prentice-Hall, p. 496.)

quite dramatically. Also, air time charges for digital wireless communications have dropped in half in the past year, while transmission quality has increased with the advent of digital networks and handsets.

Berry and Yadav recommend that companies pursuing value pricing consider using service guarantees to reinforce this approach. For example, Hampton Inn will refund a guest's money if, for any reason, they were unhappy with their hotel room.[9] They also recommend using relationship pricing, such as offering "price bundling" by selling two or more services together at a cost lower than if the individual services were purchased separately. Bundled offerings of some telecommunications firms can include long-distance telephone service, paging, video-conferencing, Internet access, and even cable television for a set price.

A useful tool for guiding value pricing is the price-value grid, which helps firms determine the efficacy of their value pricing. As shown in Figure 6.5, this grid is defined along the price and quality dimensions, the cornerstones of value creation. A firm offering a high-quality offering at low prices would possess a strong value proposition (e.g., Wal-Mart selling sell-known brands at everyday low prices or Southwest Airlines offering reliable and enjoyable air travel at extremely affordable prices). Firms whose offerings have low perceived quality at high prices would represent a poor or troubled value proposition. People in many local

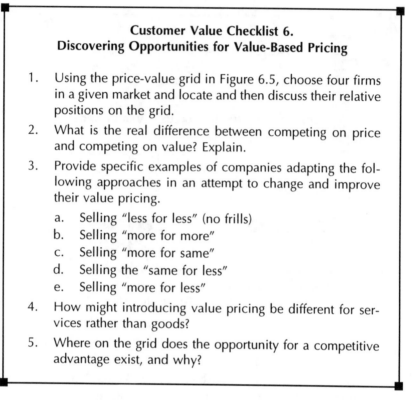

**Customer Value Checklist 6.**
**Discovering Opportunities for Value-Based Pricing**

1.  Using the price-value grid in Figure 6.5, choose four firms in a given market and locate and then discuss their relative positions on the grid.

2.  What is the real difference between competing on price and competing on value? Explain.

3.  Provide specific examples of companies adapting the following approaches in an attempt to change and improve their value pricing.
    a.  Selling "less for less" (no frills)
    b.  Selling "more for more"
    c.  Selling "more for same"
    d.  Selling the "same for less"
    e.  Selling "more for less"

4.  How might introducing value pricing be different for services rather than goods?

5.  Where on the grid does the opportunity for a competitive advantage exist, and why?

communities view cable service as a poor value due to regular price increases with limited measurable improvement in programming quality. This value proposition puts firms at a major competitive disadvantage if reasonable substitutes are available. The point here is that value pricing will be effective to the extent that both price and quality are considered in tandem. Customer Value Checklist 6 provides guidance to firms considering value pricing.

## How To Make Good Pricing Decisions

Pricing decisions draw on many areas of marketing expertise. The pricing decision requires a comprehensive understanding of the forces that shape the market, including competitive interactions, technology, and consumer psychology. Sometimes these forces interact; for instance, customers have learned to anticipate price reductions which often accompany technological innovation.

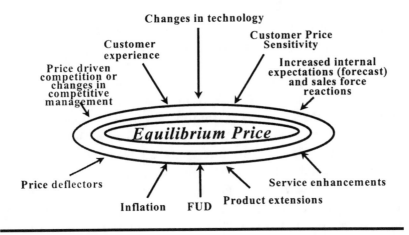

**Figure 6.6. Sources of Pricing Pressures** (Adapted from Mitchell, E. (1989) *Marketing News,* Nov. 20, p. 9.)

As Figure 6.6 shows, some of these factors are likely to put downward pressure on prices, such as substitutes, technological advances, price-driven competition, customer experience, and changes in internal focus, such as sales forecasts. Customer experience makes it difficult to raise prices, as repeat customers' ability to perceive incremental value of a company's product or service diminishes over time, especially as substitute or competitive products emerge. Increased internal expectations in the form of expected sales increases or new budgets can send prices on a downward spiral. Customer price sensitivity may also serve to keep prices in check, especially in the presence of available competitive substitutes or among a company's marginal customers.

Even in a deflationary economy, there are opportunities for keeping prices from dropping or even for raising prices. For example, product/ service enhancements or improvements often warrant maintaining, if not increasing, price due to higher customer perceived value. A case in point would be a hotel that offers a new business services center and may be able to maintain above-market rates. However, customers must perceive that these enhancements deliver a genuine, meaningful benefit, or they will continue to seek lower-cost alternatives.

Price deflectors, such as loyalty or frequency programs, may effectively insulate a company from destructive price competition. Many airline travelers, especially business travelers, will not select an airline based solely on price but rather on the mileage program in which they are members.

Finally, business customers who are motivated to reduce risk will not be overly concerned with prices as they evaluate value of a product or service. As we saw earlier, hotels feel that high-priced BBBK offers considerable value. The sightings of an undesirable pest can drive away many profitable guests. Risks may be internal as well as external. In the early days of the PC industry, Information Systems managers often reminded us, "No one ever got fired for buying an IBM," which suggests the importance of FUD (fear, uncertainty, doubt) in buying decisions.

Firms should be motivated to avoid price decreases that can erode margins and chip away at brand equity. In contrast, price increases can have a dramatic impact on the bottom line. Michael Marn of McKinsey and Company found that a 1% increase in price can boost a firm's profits by an average of 11.1%; a 1% increase in volume, on the other hand, produces only a 3.3% increase in operating profits.[10] It is quite easy to become seduced by the quick results produced by price discounting and fail to recognize the long-term consequences. Sometimes a firm will try to gain an advantage from being the lowest price competitor. This advantage disappears if competitors follow with price reductions of their own. Some marketers view this pattern as a form of the "prisoner's dilemma" game. In the classic prisoner's dilemma, if neither of two prisoner confesses, both go free; however, if only one confesses, he goes free but the other faces severe consequences. Therefore, each prisoner has to guess what the other will do.

Similarly, in a market with a small number of competitors, each firm must guess how others will respond to price reductions. If everybody drops their price, all will lose profits. Consider the example of Phillip Morris. Phillip Morris dropped the price on its leading Marlboro brand. In a sequence of events begun on "Marlboro Friday", other cigarette brands also dropped their prices, and soon some discount brands were introduced. As a result, Phillip Morris' net operating profits dropped by $2.3 billion, in spite of the increase in the brand's market share of 7 points.

Discounting as a regular practice is perilous for other reasons, as well. Brand loyalty usually suffers when firms engage in regular discounting. Price-seeking customers are rarely loyal, which pits one seller against another. They will maintain repeat patronage only until such time as the next deal is presented. The company unwittingly "prostitutes" the brand to the point where it eventually assumes a commodity status. Perpetual discounting also produces undesirable side effects in regard to the brand's image, often cheapening it. Izod Lacoste all but destroyed its brand's status in the late 1970s by repeatedly discounting the brand. Low prices ultimately made the "crocodile" become an endangered species. Finally, repeated discounting also conditions customers to seek price rather than looking at the value of the firm's offer. For example, owners of finicky cats have been conditioned to watch for sales of premium Fancy Feast cat food, when they stock up on the brand. Firms can avoid the pitfalls associated with price discounting by better understanding how their customers value different products or services and company attributes. The objective here is to find segments of customers who have problems for which unique and cost-effective solutions can be developed.

## Future Pricing Issues

This chapter may look different if we write another edition in 2002. The electronic marketplace is ushering in an era of sweeping changes that will leave no business untouched. Sales of goods and services online exceeded $5 billion in 1998, doubling the 1997 figure.[11] One of the major effects of the digital era will be fluid pricing as never seen before, as prospective buyers can now easily compare products and prices, putting them in a much better bargaining position. The more price information diffused across the Internet, the more skillful customers will become at haggling, and the less sellers can defend posted list prices. Today, online auctions let customers bid on everything from antiques to treadmills. The Internet allows such low costs of interactions that competitive bidding for everything is now possible.

So, what does this mean for marketers doing business in the 21st century? Clearly, the balance of market power has shifted from the marketer to the customer. Customers now have access to information that once was the exclusive purview of marketers. Customers using the Internet can now call up intelligent agents, or "bots", to search the Web, ruthlessly seeking the product or service at the best price according to specifications set by the user. Imagine the effect of these intelligent agents that work 24 hours a day, constantly searching for the lowest prices on branded products and services.

Companies are not powerless when competing in the digital arena, however. While the transparency of the Web will certainly expose price differentials, companies can and should respond by personalizing their products and services. Dell Computer is probably the best example of how to avoid "commodity selling" on the Web. Dell largely achieves its differentiation by maintaining direct contact with its accounts and allowing their salespeople to customize solutions to match clients' particular needs. "Dell's helping to define what customers are buying," says Jeff Gans of Eastern Consultants in Stamford, CN.[12] Dell also sets up customized intranet sites for its customers. Shell Oil, for example, has been using a customized intranet site, otherwise known as a premier page, to purchase computers from Dell. The site keeps purchasing managers up to date on product and pricing changes, while also tracking the order status of Dell computers purchased on the Web. When Shell employees need personal assistance, they can access the pager number of any marketing or technology employee that services their account.

## Summary

In this chapter, we discussed the importance of price as a key strategic element and value driver. Price does not communicate value by itself, but only in the presence of perceived product and/or service quality. That is, price only has meaning when it is paired with benefits delivered. We reviewed how buyers typically evaluate price. Buyers will use price as a cue, especially in the absence of other marketing cues, such as well-known brand names. Buyers will also evaluate products or services based on how marketers "frame" the price, as either a perceived gain or loss. Marketers need to understand price benchmarks or reference prices in each of their product or service categories. Consumers often use this reference point in determining an offer's value. We also stressed the importance of viewing pricing in the context of the firm's overall marketing strategy. Firms can become more strategic in their pricing by creating a price position in the company, using value maps, relating price to elasticity of demand, and ensuring that price reflects perceived, not simply delivered, value. A number of different market-based pricing methods were introduced, including price-driven costing, demand-based pricing, price customization, price differentiation, and value-based pricing. We concluded this chapter by discussing how to make good pricing decisions. We recommended considering the various industry forces such as competition, technology, substitutes, and buyer experience to make more informed pricing decisions. Finally, we caution against the overuse of discounting due to its "narcotic" effect on buyers and its adverse impact on brand loyalty.

## Customer Value Action Items

1. How well understood is the pricing function in your company? Discuss.
2. Discuss the relative importance of price in each of the following purchase situations:
   a. Automobile
   b. Life insurance
   c. Graduate education
   d. Hair cut or style
   e. Symphony tickets
   f. Health care
3. How much does price contribute to an offering's perceived value?
4. Select an industry and create a value map that shows individual brands and how they compare to one another on price and performance (follow the example given in Figure 6.2).
5. Price customization involves setting prices based on differences in customers and how they use the product or service and when and where the offering is used. Give several examples of how price could be customized in each of the following situations:
   a. Concert tickets
   b. Car rental
   c. Management consulting services
   d. Restaurant meal
   e. Airline travel
   f. Internet service provider (ISP)
6. Suppose a local used-car dealer is faced with the threat of an AutoNation opening up a few miles away. Which price differentiation strategy would you recommend, and why?
7. Determine your "reference" price for each of the following products or services:
   a. 2-liter bottle of soda
   b. Bestseller book
   c. Oil change for your car
   d. 1-hour massage

# References

1. Anon. (1996) Price still gets their attention, but ..., *Purchasing,* March 21, p. 24.
2. Berry, L. (1996) Retailers with a future, *Marketing Management,* 5(5), p. 42.
3. Peterson, R. and Wilson, W. (1985) The perceived risk and price-reliance schema and price-perceived-quality mediators, in *Perceived Quality,* Jacoby, J. and Olson, J., Eds., Lexington, MA: Lexington Books, pp. 247–268.
4. Smith, G. and Nagle, T. (1995) Frames of reference and buyer's perception of price and value, *California Management Review,* 38(1), pp. 98–116.
5. Biswas, A. and Blair, E. (1991) The effects of reference prices in retail advertisements, *Journal of Marketing,* 55(July), pp. 1–12.
6. Duncan, T. and Moriarty, S. (1997) *Driving Brand Value,* New York: McGraw-Hill.
7. Gayle, B. (1994) *Managing Customer Value,* New York: The Free Press.
8. Dolan, R. and Simon, H. (1996) *Power Pricing,* New York: The Free Press, p. 312.
9. Berry, L. and Yadav, M. (1996) Capture and communicate value in the pricing of services, *Sloan Management Review,* Summer, pp. 45–47.
10. Stern, A. (1997) The pricing quandary, *Across the Board,* May, pp. 17–18.
11. Hof, R., McWilliams, G., and Saveri, G. (1998) The click-here economy, *Business Week,* June 22, p. 122.
12. Marchett, M. (1997) Dell Computer, *Sales and Marketing Management,* 49(11), p. 51.

<br>
**7**

# Strategies for Adding and Promoting Value

"The whole value-added thing is in some ways like a new medium. It reminds me of the early days of cable: how do we know what we're getting?" (Stacey Lippman, Chiat/Day/Mojo)

A recent advertisement for SAS software proclaimed that you can delight your customers or your customers will be delighted to leave. The customer value approach espoused in this text stresses the need to go the "extra mile" as customer satisfaction and retention is today's key to business success. In addition to having a solid value proposition, firms can differentiate themselves from the competition by adding value to their goods and services and promoting the organization's uniqueness to their target markets. This chapter discusses the unique selling proposition (USP), positioning, and value-added marketing strategies.

## The Unique Selling Proposition and Differentiation

Advertising executives know that having a strong, unique selling proposition is critical to support the firm's value proposition. In fact, some marketing professionals have begun to call USP the unique *service* proposition. We prefer this latter term, as it demonstrates that companies must distinguish themselves with respect to the offerings as well as the message.

Over the years, Avis has done a fine job using marketing communications to differentiate itself from Hertz, the market leader in the car rental business. Promotional themes have regularly emphasized Avis' underdog position to win the hearts of its target markets. Here are some of the advertising concepts Avis has used: "We're number two; we try harder!" ... "Rent from us; our lines are shorter!" ... "Rent from the employee-owners of Avis!" As you can see, a strong attention-grabbing promotional sound bite is often simple, basic, and powerful. Can you clearly articulate your firm's message in ten words or less?

An USP creates and communicates value. Once it is finalized, all components in the company's value proposition (product quality, service, price, and image) must work in harmony to support the firm's promise to its customers. Whole Foods, Inc., sells natural groceries to nutritious-conscious Americans. Using a multi-pronged strategy of offering healthy foods, large selection, reasonable prices (possible due to national purchasing power), product tasting/sampling, and knowledgeable and caring employees, this retailer has carved a solid niche in the marketplace that has been noticed by traditional supermarket chains.

To maximize value, an organization must stand out from the pack and be different from its competitors. If the firm is essentially the same as everyone else, it will not be perceived as being better than its rivals (in fact, the market may view it as not even necessary). The firm that is different may not be better, but it has a good chance to be seen as innovative and superior. Amazon.com's Internet-based virtual bookstore redefined the industry (see Figure 7.1). Barnes and Noble and Border's were forced to compete online and play catch-up to maintain their market leadership positions.

Rory Sutherland, creative director of Ogilvy One, says that a USP should give way to a more personalized approach known as the individualized selling proposition (ISP). Because mass marketing has been replaced by customized marketing, firms must tailor their offerings and promotions to relationship-seeking customers. MCI's "Friends and Family" phone plan and co-branded credit card promotions fit this bill.[1]

Differentiation means having an advantage over the competition. This advantage can be real (a more durable product or lower price) or perceived (based on an image). Tropical Swimming Pool's market edge is found in its extensive product line of pool types, on-call service options, and its 35 years of experience serving the South Florida market. While companies can actively reposition themselves via changing the

**Overview**

Founded in a Seattle garage in July 1995 by Jeffrey P. Bezos, a former whiz-kid hedge-fund manager on Wall Street, Amazon.com (named after the world's largest river) claims it is the world's biggest bookstore. Bezos, a Princeton graduate, was 31 years old at the time and realized the tremendous potential of the Internet as a sales and distribution channel.

Amazon offers more than 2.5 million book titles for sale, ten times as many as bookstores in the physical world. It keeps less than 500 titles in stock, relying on a system of distribution centers to ship books quickly to customers. In June 1998, Amazon.com launched an online music store with more than 150,000 CD titles available and has its eyes set on video sales.

Net sales for the first quarter ended March 31, 1998, were $87 million, a 32% net sales increase over the fourth quarter ending December 31, 1997. In spite of this impressive sales gain, the company reported a $9 million loss (at the time of this writing, Amazon.com has yet to show a profit). The bulk of the company's capital goes to visibility enhancement with ads on popular websites as well as some traditional media such as the *New York Times Book Review*. Cumulative customer accounts grew more than 50% during this quarter to nearly 2.3 million. Amazon.com is now the third largest bookseller in the U.S. (after Barnes and Noble and Borders). The company ranks in the top 20 across all Internet sites, and is the leading online shopping site.

**Customer Value Strategy**

Amazon.com's value proposition stresses service, selection, and price. Other online bookstores operate in a similar way, but none is as successful as Amazon.com. The business model is simple: comprehensive selection (if it is in print, it is available) and discounted prices (10 to 40% off). Amazon.com knows that in today's chaotic lifestyles, time saving and great service are highly valued.

A 5-day guarantee for regular delivery is provided for in-stock books at the distribution centers (overnight service is offered). Amazon's ability to maintain records of customer preferences and then act on that information (e.g., an e-mail notification when a new book by a favorite author has arrived). Customized book selections create "bookworm" forum communities which provide interactivity between readers and authors.

Millions of dollars are invested in their website and brand-building strategy, which takes precedence over generating short-term profits. The site is rich and resourceful. It emphasizes information over graphics and includes separate pages for each book, featuring brief descriptions and author and customer reviews. The site is easy to use, fun, colorful, and browser-friendly and loads quickly. Visitors are prompted for ways to make the service even better. Online contests and announcements encourage customers to return to see what's new at Amazon.com.

Promotional deals have been signed with Alta Vista, America Online, Excite, Netscape, Prodigy, Search Network, Yahoo!, and other Internet search engines. More than 30,000 associates have links to Amazon.com which yield commissions of 3 to 8% per order.

**Figure 7.1. Company Profile of Amazon.com** (Prepared by Norapol Chinuntdej and Art Weinstein.)

product or service mix, image-based positioning is more often the approach through which unique market identities are created. Hence, as Ries and Trout note, positioning is often done in the minds of the customers.[2] In our over-communicated society, those companies that can best break through the "noise clutter" with clearly focused promotional campaigns will strike responsive chords with their target markets and succeed in the marketplace. Miller Lite and Molson Golden are two brewers that have excelled in this area.

## Three Levels of Positioning

Apple Computer is a good example of a firm that was a market leader in the 1980s, fell on very hard times in the 1990s, and is trying to find its way in the new millennium. Steve Jobs, architect of the firm's successes in the glory days, is making nice progress in getting Apple on track after being essentially banished from the company for many years. Because value creation is a dynamic process, repositioning must be ongoing.

There are three levels of product positioning: core, extended, and total products.[3] The core product is short-term positioning and typically works for a year or less. In this phase, companies focus on the tangibles — price, quality, and technical specifications. Packard Bell used its borrowed name recognition (from Hewlett-Packard and the Bell phone system) and price leadership philosophy to become a dominant force in the low end of the retail personal computer market. Acer's inspired idea of colored computers as decorative furniture quickly catapulted the firm into the top ten in the U.S. home user and small office/ home office (SOHO) market segments. While the core product variables are relatively easy to adjust, it is difficult to "own" such market positions. Competitors can quickly emulate a low price of comparable quality strategy.

A more effective approach is to build the extended product. In this phase, firms create the necessary infrastructure to develop strong marketing relationships with channel members, suppliers, and, of course, customers. This strategy tends to last, in the intermediate term, 1 to 5 years. Compaq's diverse product line can be found in computer stores, office supply superstores, department stores, and other retail outlets. Dell Computer's direct marketing machine enables it to serve *Fortune*

500 firms and other business users effectively. Extended product positioning takes time, money, and process innovations.

Companies that position themselves at the total product level have clearly identified who the company is and what they stand for. Firms that have garnered a long-term position (lasting more than 5 years) have clearly won the market's respect. Hewlett-Packard's reputation for high-quality products and IBM's computer know-how and excellent service have been established over the decades. These companies have well-earned reputations which stress positioning on the intangibles. A total product image gives these companies the benefit of the doubt if they occasionally stumble. Remember IBM's PC Jr. fiasco? The halo effect enabled them to quickly recover from this misguided marketing move. A less-respected firm may have found it difficult to recover from such a market blunder.

## How To Add Value to Products

As differentiation implies, companies must constantly search for new ways to add value to their goods and services to distance themselves from their rivals. Here are 13 ways to accomplish this vital strategic objective (note: a baker's dozen adds value).

1. *Additional features and benefits:* The telephone companies do a great job of adding special services for their residential and business customers. Call blocking, call forwarding, call retrieval, and three-way calling are some low-cost options that create satisfied customers. Hotels are responding to customer desires by adding business amenities, exercise centers, free breakfast buffets, and social hours.

2. *Affordability:* Price is closely related to value. Customers will pay more for a product that is highly valued. Nevertheless, the marketing challenge is to provide offerings that are affordable to the masses. Although PC sales in the U.S. leveled off in 1997, the industry was reinvigorated when computers broke the $1000 price point. Some attribute this new growth to more of a psychological barrier than an economic impasse.

3. *Branding:* The power of brand building is unquestioned. In the hypercompetitive environment of the 21st century, the brand

name and equity it generates create lasting value for organizations and their customers.[4] The brand creates an image and identity to distinguish it from competitive offerings. Brands such as Coca-Cola, Disney, Dole, IBM, Kodak, Mercedes, McDonald's, Nike, Sony, Sunkist, Virgin, and others have become ingrained into pop culture. Realize that commodities and business products as well as consumer goods and services can be successfully branded. AllEnergy, Amoco Ultimate Gold synthetic oil, EnergyOne, Ensoure, and PanEnergy are examples of some strong brand names in the energy market.[5]

4. *Customer involvement:* Successful companies know how to add value and establish strong bonds with their customers. Rock music stations attempt to get close to their radio listeners through concert and music request phone lines, community-based special events, contests, informative/interactive websites, sponsorship of concerts, and other promotional strategies. These marketing activities build customer loyalty and attract national as well as local advertisers.

5. *Customization and choice:* Twenty-first century companies are moving from segmented to one-on-one marketing. Levi's now offers Personal Pants which are custom-made to fit the individual measurements of women. The *Farm Journal* publishes more than 1000 different versions of each issue for readers whose interests vary widely by acreage, crops, and geography.

6. *Enhanced quality:* Motorola and General Electric are companies renowned for outstanding products and their pursuit of six sigma (and beyond) quality. Whether manufacturing digital pagers or locomotives, being the "best in the class" is not just a management goal; rather, it is an intrinsic part of the corporate business culture.

7. *Exceptional service:* The Ritz-Carlton hotel chain, a Malcolm Baldrige National Quality Award winner, is known for unparalleled customer service which is highly personalized, genuinely caring, and super-attentive to detail. Management empowers its employees to "move heaven and earth" to satisfy customer needs. Using a master database of customer profiles, employees track customer desires in amenities and room features and other facets of guests' stay patterns and preferences. Requests for hypo-allergenic pillows and peanut butter (rather

than chocolate chip) cookies will be noted in computerized files for repeat customers.

8. *Frequency marketing incentives:* In today's highly competitive environment, customers seek reasons to remain loyal to firms. Building on the frequent flyer concept developed by American Airlines, it seems as if everyone is jumping on the frequency marketing program bandwagon. Car rental firms, hotels, restaurants, and small businesses now offer frequency-based clubs to encourage continued patronage by their valued customers.

9. *Simplifying or bundling the offering:* Microsoft has greatly profited from this adaptable, yet practical business strategy. Case in point: their Word (word processing) application is available as a free-standing unit, upgradable product, or in a variety of integrated suite packages with multiple other software products such as Access, Excel, Outlook, PowerPoint, etc. Microsoft also offers flexible service packages for which customers can pay by the minute or incident, buy annual contracts, and/or select from other fee-based programs.

10. *Solving customer problems:* The old sales adage that customers do not buy drill bits but buy round holes is even more true today than ever before. Customers want answers to their questions, and they will do business with those companies that best know how to provide realistic solutions to important problems. Witness the explosive growth of Andersen Consulting as they spun off from their giant accounting firm parent. As Andersen continues to build its business reputation as a preeminent management advisor, look for a second spin-off of its fast-growing computer consulting operation.

11. *Technological leadership:* State-of-the-art technology can be a great source of differentiation (and competitive advantage) for businesses. Customer databases, electronic promotional techniques (brochures, catalogs, and websites), inventory control systems, sales automation equipment/procedures, and "the latest and greatest" technologies in your industry are approaches likely to be valued by your customers. For example, Click Camera and Video's investment in expensive digital technology and one-stop service for all photographic needs set them apart from drug store and supermarket competitors in the film processing and photo-finishing business.

12.   *Uniqueness:* Effective marketing creates interest for customers. Exciting restaurant concepts such as Outback Steakhouse, Rainforest Café, and Roadhouse Grill have prospered recently, largely because their value propositions are so different from mainstream dining establishments. Many credit unions now offer computer loan programs as part of a grander business strategy to provide home banking services to their membership bases.

13.   *Warranties:* Service marketers know that a sale does not end when the purchase is made. Post-sale servicing differentiates excellent companies from average enterprises. Case in point: Kensington stands behind its product line. If a computer/cable lock combination fails, they cheerfully and expeditiously replace this item, no questions asked. When customers have a need for another Kensington product, they will be confident that they are buying from a company that cares not just about its products, but also about its customers.

## Other Value-Added Approaches

Companies should not limit themselves to these 13 value-adding strategies. The use of ambiance and atmospherics (Saturn automobile dealerships), dominant merchandise assortments (Bass Pro Outdoor World), hassle-reduction (Take-Out Taxi), one-stop shopping (Pep Boys), segmented marketing (utilities providing specialized market knowledge and energy management information to their small commercial customers), speed (FedEx), supply-chain management (Motorola's relationships with their suppliers), or other sound and creative customer value strategies can provide a sharp competitive edge in the marketplace.

## Implementing a Value-Added Services Program

Karl Albrecht is a leading thinker in the area of services marketing. He notes that value is the result perceived by the customer. Furthermore, he adds that value is a four-level hierarchy. *Basic value* is the fundamental component of your value proposition required just to be in business. *Expected value* is what your customers consider the standard for your industry. *Desired value* includes added-value features that customers know about and would like but do not necessarily expect from you or your competitors. Finally, *unanticipated value* is the "surprise" features that can set your firm apart from the pack and yield long-term customer loyalty.[6] Hence, the marketing implication for management is to go beyond the basics and expectations (customer satisfaction) and strive to offer truly superior customer value by providing desired or unanticipated values.

Clean Rite Centers is a chain of progressive self-service laundromats in the New York City area. Superstores which are five times the size of typical mom-and-pop laundromats offer a multitude of value-added features. These include childrens' play areas, clean bathrooms, on-site parking, smart-card-operated machines, televisions playing the latest movies, security systems, and, most important of all, customer-friendly help (keep in mind that many customers visit weekly for 2-hour periods).[7]

A process for adding value in a retail context follows (note that this approach is readily adaptable to service firms). The six steps are (1) specifying business objectives (e.g., increasing traffic, increasing sales, targeting best customers, etc.); (2) designing a program to accomplish said objectives; (3) being sure that the value offered really includes an *added* value; (4) determining whether the program is sustainable both financially and in terms of consumer interest; (5) explaining and executing the program (sales associates must be involved and motivated); and (6) measuring and fine-tuning the program to maximize long-term results.[8] Customer Value Checklist 7 identifies seven issues that customer value managers must consider in developing a value-added program.

# Communicating Value Through an Integrated Marketing Communications Program

Mass-media advertising as we know it is on its deathbed.[9] Direct marketing, sales promotion, the Internet, and other "in-touch" new forms of interactive media have taken center stage. These communication sources break through the clutter and provide information value to customers and prospects. An intriguing approach to promoting value is integrated marketing communications (IMC). IMC is the concept of designing all promotional activities — advertising, personal selling,

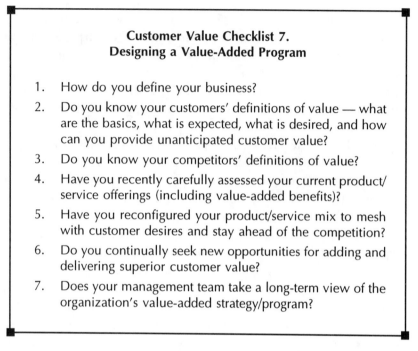

**Customer Value Checklist 7.**
**Designing a Value-Added Program**

1. How do you define your business?
2. Do you know your customers' definitions of value — what are the basics, what is expected, what is desired, and how can you provide unanticipated customer value?
3. Do you know your competitors' definitions of value?
4. Have you recently carefully assessed your current product/service offerings (including value-added benefits)?
5. Have you reconfigured your product/service mix to mesh with customer desires and stay ahead of the competition?
6. Do you continually seek new opportunities for adding and delivering superior customer value?
7. Does your management team take a long-term view of the organization's value-added strategy/program?

sales promotion, and public relations — to provide a synergistic, consistent message (one look, one voice) to targeted audiences. A sound, concise definition of integrated marketing communications is offered by Duncan and Everett. They state that IMC is "… the strategic coordination of all messages and media used by an organization to influence its perceived value."[10] Don E. Schultz, a professor at Northwestern University, has researched and written extensively about IMC over the past decade. Some of this guru's major thoughts on this emerging strategic marketing area are summarized in Table 7.1.

Overall, companies are doing a reasonably good job utilizing an IMC philosophy, in spite of the newness of this approach. Research has found that about 75% of firms now coordinate all or most of their promotional activities. As shown in Table 7.2, we can see that retailers do this best (85%), while service firms are least successful in their IMC endeavors (55%). Service firms tend to farm out a lot of promotional work to different vendors in the areas of direct response, public relations, and sales promotion, which partly accounts for this discrepancy from the norm.[11] Standardizing promotional campaigns becomes a much greater challenge to marketing managers in service businesses.

## Table 7.1. Forces Impacting Integrated
## Marketing Communications (IMC)

| IMC Drivers | IMC Restraints |
|---|---|
| Small organizations | Large organizations |
| Business marketers with a strong sales force; marketing communications is a support technique | Consumer marketers with a brand-management system |
| Single brand or line of products under one brand name | Multi-brand packaged goods companies |
| A database of customers/prospects and their purchase histories | Limited usage of databases |
| View marketing communications as an entity | View marketing communications as a segmented process |
| Acceptance of risk-taking | Unwilling to take a risk |
| Willing to re-think the system of promotional incentives | Locked into traditional rewards for promotional activities |
| Strong top-down management | Bottom-up management |
| Less formal marketing structures, limited marketing history | Formal marketing structures, sophisticated marketing organization |
| Realization that IMC is a major value creator for the organization | Promotional strategies just another part of the marketing mix |

*Source:* Adapted from ideas offered by Schultz, D.E. (1991) Integrated marketing communications, *Journal of Promotion Management*, 1(1), pp. 99–104.

The corporate database (marketing information system) is the key to success for IMC. Although the integrated marketing communications idea is being well received by organizations, implementation is a problem for business marketers. Only 15% of companies take database

## Table 7.2. Coordination of Marketing Communication Activities

| | All Firms | Business | Consumer | Retail | Service |
|---|---|---|---|---|---|
| Fully coordinated | 46% | 62% | 46% | 50% | 34% |
| Mostly coordinated | 29% | 19% | 33% | 35% | 21% |
| Partly/not coordinated | 26% | 19% | 21% | 15% | 45% |

*Source:* Adapted from McArthur, D.N. and Griffin, T. (1997) A marketing management view of integrated marketing communications, *Journal of Advertising Research*, Sept./Oct., pp. 19–26.

marketing to a higher level than mailing lists (which 70% of the firms maintain). The failure to implement an IMC program is due to lack of expertise, budget, and/or management approval.[12]

## Creating an Integrated Marketing Communications Program

Here is an eight-point plan for initiating an IMC program in your organization.

1. *Use zero-based budgets.* Most companies use incremental approaches in allocating promotional budgets. For example, if they spent $10 million last year, they may "tack on" another 5% to get this year's figure. Other companies base their decisions on competitive spending, industry averages, or a percentage of sales. A preferred approach is the objective and task approach. Start with a zero budget and force all promotional managers to justify their investment. This might result in a budget of $9 million or $12 million (or many other possibilities) for IMC activities.

2. *Focus primarily on current customers.* Many organizations direct 80% or more of their advertising and selling effort activities to trying to win new business (conquest marketing). An IMC program recognizes the importance of retention marketing (see Chapter 8) and inverts that ratio so that a majority of the promotional activity is earmarked for relationship building with existing customers. This reduces customer defection, upgrades business relationships, and creates advocates for the firm's services.

3. *Use highly targeted mass promotion.* Direct mail, specialized lists, trade publications, and the Internet can be used effectively to reach prospects rather than suspects. Business-to-business interactive direct marketing sales are projected to be about $20 billion by the year 2002. For every $1 direct marketers invest in Internet advertising, $7 in sales are generated.[13] A website has become an indispensable marketing technology for 21st century companies. It has evolved into a one-stop, online corporate information source, customer support tool, distribution channel, order taker, product catalog, price list, promotional vehicle,

research technique, segmentation source, and a strategic and tactical marketing differentiator.

4.  *Build marketing relationships.* Strategic partnering is a major part of a good IMC program. In addition to the Internet (discussed in item 3) and intranets (protected corporate information resource centers), progressive companies are creating extranets which link an enterprise's extended family of suppliers, distributors, retailers, and partners.[14] Hence, customer, channel, referral, and stakeholder relationships can all be nurtured through carefully conceived promotional efforts.

5.  *Note that everything an organization does sends a message.* Image and atmospherics are very important in communicating value to customers. The little things, such as stationery, signage, telephone greetings, and website design, etc., should all reflect professionalism and a consistent message to the marketplace.

6.  *Two-way dialogue is key.* In an over-communicated society, the marketing challenge is to establish a meaningful dialogue with customers as to how the firm's service mix can provide maximum benefits/value. Interactivity and involvement on the part of the customer is important for sharing information and creating firmer bonds. The Web is an ideal medium to accomplish this objective. Its selectivity and flexibility create a customized business experience for each user.

7.  *Use 21st century communication technologies.* In today's changing marketplace, companies must seek new and better ways to stay in touch with their target markets. Appropriate communication options include e-mail, electronic commerce, fax-on-demand, telemarketing, point-of-sale promotion, special events, multimedia, etc.

8.  *Measure promotional effectiveness.* Traditionally, advertising executives competed with sales managers for their "fair share" of the corporate promotional budget. Today, management requires accountability and demands to know and justify the return on investment of limited resources — they will no longer accept the nonmeasurable communications methods used by marketers in the past.[15] A marketing information system/database is the key tool for effectively monitoring and measuring the success of an IMC program. As part of this process, job descriptions and reward systems are likely to be redesigned. In

a strong IMC-centered environment, in-house competition is replaced with cooperation and teamwork. Joint rewards help the organization do what is best, rather than just protect individual turfs. Perhaps the sales manager will accept a 5% cut in new hires and the advertising manager will agree to a 10% reduction in advertising expenditures to redirect dollars to needed sales promotion or public relations activities if it is for the good of the organization. Under this scenario, if the overall net effect of the promotional strategy improves through implementing an IMC plan, all key players share in the rewards of their efforts.

## Summary

Service organizations must rethink the way that they compete from a strategic perspective. This requires a two-pronged attack: (1) add value to your offerings, and (2) use integrated marketing communications (IMC) to promote your value edge. First, this chapter reviewed the importance of creating a strong unique selling proposition (USP), competitive differentiation, and basic positioning techniques. Second, we explored 13+ strategies for adding value to your goods and services. Companies can use this foundation set as a marketing toolbox to enhance their current offerings. Third, we explained the IMC philosophy and presented an eight-step plan for implementing this approach. In our next chapter, we discuss how service companies can keep customers over time by using retention marketing strategies.

## Customer Value Action Items

1.  How does your firm differentiate itself from its rivals? Describe your *real* and *perceived* competitive advantages.
2.  Discuss your current unique selling proposition (USP). Can you develop an even stronger USP which simply but elegantly communicates maximum value to your target market(s)?
3.  Is your firm's positioning strategy based on the core, extended, or total product? What can be done to position your firm via a longer-term time horizon?

4.  Given the following value-added strategies, identify which techniques you are (1) currently using, (2) should be using, and (3) could use more effectively:

| | Using | Should Use | Can Use Better |
|---|---|---|---|
| Additional features/benefits | ____ | ____ | ____ |
| Affordability | ____ | ____ | ____ |
| Branding | ____ | ____ | ____ |
| Customer involvement | ____ | ____ | ____ |
| Customization/choice | ____ | ____ | ____ |
| Enhanced quality | ____ | ____ | ____ |
| Exceptional service | ____ | ____ | ____ |
| Frequency marketing incentives | ____ | ____ | ____ |
| Simplify or bundle the offering | ____ | ____ | ____ |
| Solve customer problems | ____ | ____ | ____ |
| Technological leadership | ____ | ____ | ____ |
| Uniqueness | ____ | ____ | ____ |
| Warranties | ____ | ____ | ____ |
| Other value-added (describe) | ____ | ____ | ____ |

5.  Explain how a retailer can use the six-step value-adding process to attract new business as well as do a better job satisfying and retaining existing customers.

6.  On a five-point scale, where 1 is "not very successfully" and 5 is "very successfully", how good a job does your company do with respect to practicing integrated marketing communications (IMC)? How can your firm improve its use of IMC as a foundation for communicating customer value and strategic promotional planning?

# References

1. Sutherland, R. (1998) The USP is past its sell-by date, *Marketing*, Feb. 5, p. 20.
2. Ries, A. and Trout, J. (1982) *Positioning: The Battle for Your Mind*, New York: Warner Books.
3. Nesbit, M. and Weinstein, A. (1989) Positioning the high-tech product, in *Handbook of Business Strategy 1989/1990 Yearbook*, Glass, H.E., Ed., Boston: Warren, Gorham & Lamont, pp. 30-1–30-8.
4. Schultz, D. (1998) What's in a name? Your brand could be your most valuable long-term asset, *Industry Week*, March 16, p. 20.

5. Ryan, K. (1996) Branded: what's really in a name?, *American Gas*, Aug., pp. 22–25, 37.

6. Albrecht, K. (1994) Customer value, *Executive Excellence*, Sept., pp. 14–15.

7. Anon. (1998) Service-centered innovation comes out of the wash, *Nation's Business*, Aug., p. 12.

8. Gill, P. (1991) Added value: relationship marketing is one way for retailers to build loyalty, *Stores*, Oct., pp. 39–40.

9. Rust, R.T. and Oliver, R.W. (1994) The death of advertising, *Journal of Advertising*, Dec., pp. 71–77.

10. Duncan, T.R. and Everett, S.E. (1993) Client perceptions of integrated marketing communications, *Journal of Advertising Research*, May/June, pp. 30–39.

11. McArthur, D.N. and Griffin, T. (1997) A marketing management view of integrated marketing communications, *Journal of Advertising Research*, Sept./Oct., pp. 19–26.

12. Cleland, K. (1995) Few wed marketing, communications, *Advertising Age*, Feb. 27, p. 10.

13. Berger, M. (1998) It's your move, *Sales and Marketing Management*, March, pp. 45–53.

14. McKenna, R. (1998) Marketing in real time, *Executive Excellence*, April, pp. 3–4.

15. Schultz, D.E. (1997) Integration is critical for success in 21st century, *Marketing News*, Sept. 15, p. 26.

# 8 Maximizing Value Through Retention Marketing

"Most companies are a lot better at prospecting for new customers than maintaining their customer list. ... I behaved as if every IBM customer were on the verge of leaving and that I'd do anything to keep them from bolting." (Buck Rodgers, former CEO of IBM)

Planet Hollywood, the celebrity-inspired and funded "eatertainment" chain has struggled greatly in the past year because diners are not coming back. After an initial dinner which often includes long waits, mediocre and overpriced food, and failure to see the stars (Arnold, Bruce, Demi, or Sly), relatively few customers are returning for a second visit. Clearly, this themed concept needs a stronger value proposition and a sound marketing strategy to keep customers; there are only so many tourists and one-timers to go around.

In this chapter, we explain how companies must develop customer retention (CR) strategies to maximize long-term customer and shareholder value. Specifically, we examine the importance of customer retention, an integrated customer retention model, how usage segmentation can assist in CR planning, a five-step process for designing a CR program, and customer retention approaches.

*Core service* (25%) — mistakes, billing errors, service catastrophes

*Service encounter failures* (19%) — uncaring, impolite, unresponsive, not knowledgeable

*Pricing* (17%) — high price, price increases, unfair pricing, deceptive pricing

*Inconvenience* (12%) — location, hours, waiting time

*Response to failed service* (10%) — negative response, no response, reluctant response

*Competition* (6%) —better service found elsewhere

*Other* (5%) — tangibles, crowding, problems with other customers, and seldom-mentioned incidents

*Ethical problems* (4%) — cheating, hard sell, unsafe conditions, conflict of interest

*Involuntary switching* (3%) — customer or service provider moved

**Figure 8.1. Switching Motives** (Adapted from Keaveney, S.M. (1995) Customer switching behavior in service industries: an exploratory study, *Journal of Marketing,* April, pp. 71–82.)

# Why Focus on Customer Retention?

Most companies spend a majority of their time, energy, and resources chasing new business. While it is important to find new customers to replace lost business, grow the enterprise, and expand into new markets, this goal should be secondary in importance to the main objective — keep your customers and enhance these customer relationships. As Figure 8.1 shows, customers leave service organizations primarily due to service reasons, but it is important to realize that these issues are controllable from the firm's perspective.

Frederick Reichheld, of Bain & Company, is a leading consultant on loyalty management. In his fine book, *The Loyalty Effect,* he builds a strong case for emphasizing employee retention and customer retention in business. Service companies must retain the best personnel to win and keep good customers (realize that the average company loses about half of its employees in 4 years). He notes that, "It's impossible to build a loyal bank of customers without a loyal employee base." Reichheld also shares these important statistics on the significance of customer retention:[1]

■ On average, U.S. corporations lose half of their customers in 5 years.

- A typical company has a customer defection rate of 10 to 30% per year.
- Raising the customer retention rate by 5% can increase the value of an average customer (lifetime profits) by 25 to 100%.
- Lexus has repurchase rates more than 20% higher than Infiniti. While Lexus only accounts for 3% of Toyota's sales, it contributes 30% toward their profits.
- State Farm determined that a 1% increase in customer retention will increase its capital surplus by more than $1 billion over time.

While a recent study by Marketing Metrics, a Princeton, NJ, firm, notes that corporations are now spending an all-time high of 53% of their budget on customer retention, there still is concern that most of the attention is spent wooing new customers or the great "one-night-stand". Douglas Pruden, a senior vice president at Marketing Metrics, urges us to look at this figure with skepticism. He notes that the definition of retention marketing is so broad that databases, satisfaction surveys, and couponing can qualify as retention activities (often such initiatives do not target existing high-value customers); compensation and promotions are generally based on demonstrating short-term profits (transaction business) at the expense of longer-term paybacks; and retention is viewed by many companies as the "fad of the week".[2]

We recommend investing at least 75% of your marketing budget on customer retention and relationship marketing activities. Research by the American Management Association has demonstrated that it costs five times more to get a new customer than keep an existing one.[3]

Philip Kotler, the internationally renowned professor at Northwestern University, states that "the key to customer retention is customer satisfaction." He notes that satisfied customers stay loyal longer, talk favorably about the organization, pay less attention to the competition, are less price sensitive, offer service ideas to the organization, and cost less to serve than new customers.[4]

## A Customer Value/Retention Model

Marketing managers know that it is critical to deliver superior value to their customers — this ensures business profitability. The customer

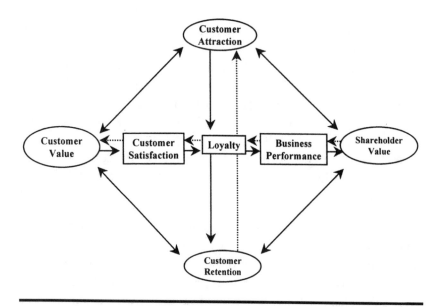

**Figure 8.2. The Customer Value/Retention Model**

value/retention model offers a good way of explaining the key relationships among the core elements that create value in an organization (see
Figure 8.2). As we have seen earlier in the book, customer value is built
through the proper mix of quality, service, and price (QSP) and image,
innovation, and intangibles (the 3I's), those elements that attract customers to the organization. Companies should segment markets via
demographic, psychographic, and usage approaches to locate new customers that find the firm's value proposition appealing.

Business firms typically use account size and industry as bases for
identifying and targeting markets. While these data are readily accessible, they often provide little insight into how specific goods and services are actually used by the customer; therefore, Anderson and Narus
recommend product application segmentation as a value-generating
tool. Consider the marine market as a case in point. A fabric manufacturer
may provide basic acrylic fabrics for powerboat and sailboat covers, as
well as higher value, custom-designed seat covers for inside the boat.[5]

A one-time buyer is really a tryer, rather than a customer. To move
beyond the transaction stage, organizational experiences must meet or
(preferably) exceed the buyer's expectations. Repeated incidents of high
satisfaction are sought through the effective utilization of relationship
marketing strategies, leading to higher customer loyalty. Loyalty (which

results from the quality of the customer-company relationship) in turn leads to improved business performance/shareholder value and increased customer retention rates. Furthermore, the ability to retain customers successfully results in increased market values.

Roy Ralston's "SURe" model states that as satisfaction (S) increases, the likelihood that customers will continue to use (U) a service increases, as does the likelihood of the customer recommending (Re) the service provider to another potential customer. Multi-industry research using regression techniques in the service sector found that a 5% increase in satisfaction produces a 3% increase in continued use (.6) and a 2.5% increase in recommending (.5); a 5% increase in use results in a 2% increase in recommending (.4).[6]

Feedback loops are also depicted in the customer value/retention model. Good value secures customers over the long term. Similarly, customers (both new and existing ones) want to maintain relationships with well-respected organizations that have high market values.

The customer value/marketing implications of the model are readily apparent. First, the key variables and their relationships to one another are clarified. This provides strategic guidance to management. Second, it stresses long-term relationships (retention) but still realizes that some customer defection and attrition will occur, so customer attraction must remain a priority. Third, the model is interfunctional and systematic — it ties marketing objectives to the big picture, the financial situation. Consider these two telling examples of the impact of CR on business performance:

1. A mere .1% of the U.S. automobile industry is worth $2.5 billion.[7]
2. A 2% increase in customer retention yields the same profit as a 10% reduction in overhead.[8]

## Usage Analysis and Customer Retention

Segmenting markets by consumption patterns can be quite insightful for understanding your customer mix. Differentiated marketing strategies are needed for the various user groups — first-time users, repeat customers, heavy users, and former users. By classifying customer accounts based on usage frequency and variety, companies can develop effective strategies to retain and upgrade customers. As Figure 8.3 shows,

Heavy, medium, light, former, and nonusers (A, B, C, D, X)

Heavy half segmentation (80/20 rule)

Users vs. nonusers

Competitive users

Loyal (degree) vs. nonloyal customers

Product/service applications by user group

Adopter categories (innovators, followers, laggards, lead users)

Geographic comparisons (customer penetration indices, growth)

**Figure 8.3. Usage Categories**

there are many highly informative, low-cost applications of usage analysis that should be considered by management.

For example, a hotel grades customers based on the number of rooms booked annually. The key accounts are A1 users — large organizations that reserve thousands of room nights and conference facilities. A2 customers also book a high volume of rooms without the conference arrangements. A third category of heavy users is the A3 account, which is a solid, loyal customer that generates hundreds of room nights annually. Four descending usage levels of B customers (B1 to B4) are considered medium users. Finally, five types of C accounts (C1 to C5) represent light users. The C5 guest may only visit the hotel once a year.

By classifying customers into usage categories, management can design appropriate strategies for each market segment. The objective is to move customers up the ladder, where possible. The implication of usage analysis is that all customers are not equal; some (the heavy users) are clearly more important than other categories.

For example, McDonald's actively targets "super-heavy" users. These customers are typically male and 18 to 34 years old and eat there three to five times a week, accounting for 77% of McDonald's sales.[9] In business and professional service markets, the best customers may be identified as key accounts based on customer ranking (e.g., our 100 most important customers), minimum sales volume level (e.g., $1 million in annual business), or market share (e.g., the annual account exceeds 1% of our total business).

The pareto principle, or 80/20 rule, is insightful in this context. In a typical business, approximately 80% of sales comes from about 20% of customers (also, note that generally about 80% of your sales comes from

20% of your goods or services). It is important to defend this core business, as heavy users (A accounts) are primary attraction targets to key competitors. These highly valued customers require frequent advertising, promotions, and sales calls and ongoing communication efforts.

Medium users (B customers) form the solid base of your business. Revenue-enhancement strategies such as cross-selling or value-added services can be used to keep these customers satisfied and to grow their business. Telephone calls, e-mail, and occasional sales calls are suggested to stay in touch with this group.

By knowing who our better customers are (the As and Bs) — through geographic, demographic, psychographic, and benefit research — we have a solid profile of "typical users". This information is very helpful in planning subsequent customer attraction/conquest marketing efforts. Realize that the marketing information system, the database, plays a key role in customer analysis and decision making.

For unprofitable customers (some C accounts), the company often needs to find new ways to serve them more effectively. Technology such as ATM machines can be used in this regard. Quarterly contact through a newsletters and direct mail or access options such as toll-free telephone numbers and websites maintain adequate communication with low-volume users. In some cases, it may even be desirable to sever the relationship with certain unprofitable customers.

A good understanding of our customers' purchasing patterns helps us keep our customers and gain a larger share of their business. Share of customer (customer retention focus) has supplanted market share (customer attraction focus) as a relevant business performance dimension in many markets. Share of customer is adapted by industry and goes by such names as share of care (health care), share of stomach (fast food), and share of wallet (financial services). If a company can increase a customer's share of business from 20 to 30%, this will have a dramatic impact on market share and profitability.

Recency, frequency, and monetary value (RFM) analysis is a helpful tool in evaluating customer usage and loyalty patterns. Recency refers to the last service encounter/transaction, frequency assesses how often these customer-company experiences occur, and monetary value probes the amount that is spent, invested, or committed by customers for the firm's products and services.

A couple of years ago, one of the authors purchased about $75 worth of brochure materials from a direct marketer for a one-time consulting project. This eager vendor immediately placed our writer into the preferred customer category and began sending him expensive catalogs about every three weeks without any follow-up orders. RFM analysis tells us that this is not sound marketing, as this company essentially treated all one-time tryers as "best" customers. Note that this transaction fared poorly on all critical RFM dimensions — recency (2+ years ago), frequency (a single purchase), and monetary value (relatively low).

A more effective strategy is to classify customers via usage analysis (as previously described) and design differentiated marketing approaches for each target market. In sum, usage analysis can greatly assist us in our customer-retention activities. Think about how to "hold" heavy users and key accounts, upgrade light and medium users, build customer loyalty, understand buying motives to meet or exceed expectations, use appropriate selling strategies for each targeted usage group, win back "lost" customers, and learn why nonusers are not responding to your value proposition.

## Designing a Customer Retention Program

To develop an effective customer retention (CR) program, organizations can follow this five-step process:

1.  *Determine your current CR rate.* It is surprising how few companies know the percentage of customers that leave (the defection rate) or the percentage of customers that they are able to retain annually (the retention rate). As shown in Figure 8.4, there are many ways to measure customer retention. Choosing an appropriate measure(s) provides a starting point for assessing a firm's success in keeping customers.
2.  *Analyze the defection problem.* This is a three-pronged attack. First, we must identify disloyal customers. Second, we need to understand why they left. According to Glenn DeSouza, there are six types of defectors. Customers go elsewhere because of lower price, superior products, better service, alternative technologies, market changes (they move or go bankrupt), and "political" considerations;[10] Figure 8.1 (switching motives) can also provide insight here. Third, strategies must be developed to

Annual and targeted customer retention rates

Weighted customer retention rates (accounts for usage differences)

Segmented retention indicators (sub-group analysis based on geographic,
  demographic, lifestyle, product preference, or other categories)

Share of customer

Lifetime value (LTV)

Recency, frequency, and monetary value (RFM)

**Figure 8.4. Customer Retention Measures**

overcome the non-loyal purchasing behavior (this will be discussed later in the chapter).

3. *Establish a new CR objective.* Let's assume that your company is currently retaining 75% of its customers. A realistic goal may be to improve client retention annually by at least 5%, to 80%, and to keep 90% of your clients within 5 years. Customer-retention objectives should be based on organizational capabilities (strengths, weaknesses, resources, etc.), customer and competitive analyses, and benchmarking with the industry or sector, comparable firms, and high-performing units in your company.

4. *Invest in a targeted CR plan to enhance customer loyalty.* The cost (potential lifetime value) of a single lost customer can be substantial. This is magnified exponentially when we realize the overall annual cost of lost business. Consider the impact of a 20% defect rate for a hospital. As Figure 8.5 demonstrates, a $6 million loss in revenues results in a $600,000 dive on the bottom

Number of patients annually = 15,000

Number of defections annually = 3000

Defection rate = 20%; retention rate = 80%

Average annual revenue per patient = $2000

Annual lost revenues = $6 million

Annual lost profits (10% profit margin) = $600,000

**Figure 8.5. The Cost of Lost Business for a Hospital**

line. The hospital that invests even $100,000 in patient retention training and CR program initiatives can dramatically improve its profitability. Targeted retention planning means that organizations should segment customers by relevant dimensions, such as geographic, demographic, and socioeconomic variables, and other criteria to best understand customer profiles and purchasing patterns. Cole Taylor is a Chicago-based bank holding company that ascribes to the "first dollar" principle. If the bank just has one dollar to spend on marketing (generally, not a problem for a $2 billion organization), they will invest it on existing customers rather than using it to attract new business.[11]

5.   *Evaluate the success of the CR program.* As an iterative process, the final phase in designing a solid customer retention plan is to ensure that it is working. Careful scrutiny is required to assess the program's impact on keeping existing customers (see Customer Value Checklist 8 for further guidance in this area). Upgrading current customer relationships may be a secondary business objective. At this point, we gather new information to learn to what extent our CR rate improved. We may need to revisit our benchmarks and further probe isolated causes of defection. CR strategies and tactics will be closely analyzed to determine which methods worked best and those that had little or no impact on keeping customers.

## Customer Retention Approaches

There are literally dozens of methods that can be used to keep customers. Customer retention tactics (for example, promotional incentives) are short term in nature, while CR strategies create lasting value for customers. Customer retention efforts should begin as soon as the firm acquires a customer. These efforts should include learning as much as possible about customer needs, responding promptly to any indications of disinterest, making customers feel truly cared for, resolving complaints quickly and efficiently, and being willing to negotiate with high-value customers who show signs of inactivity.[12]

As the customer value/retention model explained, companies must create loyalty from new customers in order to retain them. Some of the most common and effective approaches for enhancing retention include building a customer database/marketing information system,

---

**Customer Value Checklist 8.**
**Gathering Customer Retention Data**

1. What are your current and targeted CR rates?

2. Given your current defection rate, how often must you replenish your customer pool?

3. Has your CR rate increased during the past 3 years?

4. What is the lifetime value (LTV) of a customer?

5. What is the cost of a lost customer?

6. What percentage of your marketing budget is spent on customer-retention activities?

7. On average, how much do you spend on current customers annually?

8. What criteria does your company use for developing targeted retention programs by market segment?

9. Do you invest more on high-value (A) customers?

10. How does your firm use recency, frequency, and monetary value (RFM) analysis?

---

designing ongoing customer programs (continuity and loyalty-based initiatives such as frequent flyer miles), offering long-term services (membership/subscription programs), customizing promotion (using reminder advertising and press releases), focusing on key accounts and heavy users, using newsletters or informational materials to stay in touch with infrequent customers, attending trade shows, researching customers needs and wants, and welcoming suggestions and complaints.

Other innovative loyalty-building strategies include sending salespeople to work at the offices of your best customers, participating in customers' events, interviewing your customers' customers, holding a retreat with a major customer to share best practices, inviting customers to participate in training seminars, setting up a customer advisory council, developing a preferred-customer pricing strategy, rewarding customers for referring new business, developing 3- to 5-year business plans with customers, and partnering with key accounts on industry research projects.[13] Hospitals are turning to customer retention ideas to

*Image/promotion:* community service, direct mail, educational offerings, health fairs, integrated marketing communications, newsletters, regular contact with patients, useful informational materials, website

*Service quality:* continuous quality initiatives, convenience, customer service training, demonstrating that patients are highly valued, mystery shopping, patient representatives/ombudsman, service failure training, smiles, treating patients as family

*Research:* analyze defection rates/reasons, classify customers by usage/satisfaction/loyalty, develop targeted retention program, use "inside-out" (patient-focused) healthcare model

*Internal marketing:* loyalty task force, preparing "solutions" to recurring problems, sharing appropriate patient data with staff, rewarding and publicizing customer care patient of the month

*Patient-centered:* "dialogue" marketing, patient bill of rights, patient care councils, understanding patient expectations

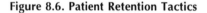

**Figure 8.6. Patient Retention Tactics**

keep patients in highly competitive environments. A list of patient retention ideas in five key areas is summarized in Figure 8.6.

As we can see, there is a multitude of potential customer retention ideas, tactics, and strategies that can be utilized successfully by value-creating managers. How do you know which approaches should be employed by your company? The following seven criteria provide a useful point of reference: (1) efficiency — low cost, (2) effectiveness — likelihood of success, (3) adaptability — strategic fit with your organizational culture, (4) consistency — works well with your current marketing plan, (5) competitive advantage offered, (6) ease of implementation, and (7) projected profitability.

## Summary

Companies that deliver superior value to customers on an ongoing basis are able to keep them over the long term. This chapter reviewed the essentials for establishing a customer retention focus. By maintaining consistently high levels of customer satisfaction and loyalty, customer defection becomes less likely. This results in enhanced business performance and increases shareholder value. Relationship marketing is the key strategy to obtain the desired results of retaining more customers, getting better customers, upgrading customer relationships, and using existing customers as advocates for acquiring new customers. This issue is discussed in the final chapter of the book.

## Customer Value Action Items

1. Identify five companies that do a good job in retaining customers and upgrading customer relationships.
2. What is the relationship among customer value, customer satisfaction, loyalty, customer retention, and business performance?
3. How can your organization use the customer value/retention model to do a better job getting and keeping customers?
4. Clarify the distinction between a company that focuses on products vs. one that focuses on customer needs.
5. In today's quickly changing and highly competitive market environment, customer retention is more important than customer attraction. Do you agree or disagree with this statement? Why or why not?
6. Should companies develop a separate marketing plan for keeping customers?
7. What are the top three reasons for customers leaving your company? How can these switching motives be overcome?
8. Does your firm segment its market through usage analysis? Describe your usage segments, and explain how you would implement a targeted customer value/marketing program for each key market segment.
9. Which of the CR measures listed in Figure 8.4 does your company currently use? Which measures should it use?
10. List some of the customer retention strategies and tactics that your organization uses. What are some additional CR approaches that they should think about using?

## References

1. Reichheld, F.F. (1996), *The Loyalty Effect: The Hidden Force Behind Growth, Profits, and Lasting Value*, Boston, MA: Harvard Business School Press.
2. Pruden, D. (1995) Retention marketing gains spotlight, but does reality match philosophy?, *Brandweek*, Feb., p. 15.

3. Zielinski, D. (1990) Focus on customer retention is a proven profit strategy, *The Service Edge,* June, p. 1.
4. Kotler, P. (1994) *Marketing Management: Analysis, Planning, Implementation, and Control,* 8th ed., Englewood Cliffs, NJ: Prentice-Hall.
5. Anderson, J.C. and Narus, J.A. (1991) Partnering as a focused marketing strategy, *California Management Review,* Spring, pp. 95–113.
6. Ralston, R.W. (1996) Model maps out a sure path to grow in the marketplace, *Marketing News,* May 20, p. 12.
7. Waldrop, J. (1994) How to succeed despite slow growth, *American Demographics,* April, pp. 52–56.
8. Marchetti, M. (1996) How the CEO of Unisys creates customer value, *Sales and Marketing Management,* Oct., p. 45.
9. Blattberg, R.C. and Deighton, J. (1996) Manage marketing by the customer equity test, *Harvard Business Review,* July/Aug., pp. 136–144.
10. DeSouza, G. (1992) Designing a customer retention plan, *Journal of Business Strategy,* March/Apr., pp. 24–28.
11. Taylor, B. (1996) The relationship builders: organizing around the customer, *Bank Management,* Jan./Feb., pp. 30–34.
12. Passavant, P. (1995) Retention marketing needs a new vision, *Journal of Direct Marketing,* Spring, pp. 2–4.
13. Brewer, G. (1998) The customer stops here, *Sales and Marketing Management,* March, pp. 31–36.

# 9 Creating Value Through Customer and Supplier Relationships

"If you're selling a service, you're selling a relationship." (Harry Beckwith, Founder of Beckwith Advertising and Marketing)

Think for a minute about the purpose of a business. Ask most business people, and they might reply "to make a profit" or "to grow shareholder value". As commendable as these goals are, should they be the primary focus of an enterprise? Harvard Business Professor Theodore Levitt once remarked, "The purpose of a business is to create and keep a customer."[1] The sale merely consummates the courtship, according to Levitt, at which point the relationship begins. Peter Drucker, a leading management theorist, puts it this way: "There will always, one can assume, be need for some selling. But the aim of marketing is to make selling superfluous. The aim of marketing is to know and understand the customer so well that the product or service fits him and sells itself."[2]

The traditional marketing paradigm consisting of the 4P's of marketing is beginning to lose some of its influence among marketers. This approach focuses on the transaction and the core product, taking a short-term perspective; customer attraction (conquest marketing) is the overriding goal. This perspective is no longer sufficient, as the powerful forces of industry globalization, the "value" movement, rapid advances in technology, and a shift in the balance of power toward customers have coalesced to change the rules for business success. Relationship marketing represents a fundamental transformation from traditional marketing, where relationships shift from adversarial to cooperative, and the goals shift from market share to share of customers. Phillip Kotler concurs saying, "Companies must move from a short-term transaction orientation to a long-term relationship-building goal."[3] The complicated nature of buyer/supplier interactions today makes repeated negotiations too much of a hassle and too costly, leaving success in marketing more dependent upon the relationship — creating and maintaining it.

You will recall that Chapter 8 examined retention marketing, looking at ways to create a loyal customer base. This chapter examines how to preserve the customer base following the principles of relationship marketing. We begin by defining relationship marketing as well as considering the rationale for following such an approach. We then contrast traditional vs. relationship marketing. The requirements for building healthy and lasting relationships are also explored. Finally, we present some of the keys for successfully practicing relationship marketing strategies.

## What Is Relationship Marketing?

The cornerstone of marketing is getting close to customers in order to better identify and satisfy their needs. Realize that marketing is responsible for more than "just the sale". We have witnessed a significant change in how business is conducted, with the focus shifting from the transaction to the relationship. This is particularly true for services marketing, where it is difficult to separate service operations and delivery from relationship building. Marketing in today's organization is now responsible for becoming an expert on the customer while keeping the rest of the company informed about customer activities. [4] Managing customer relationships continues to be paramount, yet so is the growing importance of managing relationships with suppliers and resellers.

Due to the strong interest in relationship marketing, several useful definitions have been offered. Len Berry, who is first credited with using the term "relationship marketing" in the services literature, says: "Relationship marketing is attracting, maintaining, and enhancing customer relationships."[5] An even more expansive definition is proposed by Parvatiyar and Sheth: "Relationship marketing refers to all marketing activities directed toward establishing, developing, and maintaining successful relational exchanges."[6]

While both of these definitions help us to better understand the nature and purpose of relationship marketing, we tend to endorse Gordon's view of relationship marketing: "Relationship marketing is the ongoing process of identifying and creating new value with individual customers and then sharing the benefits from this over a lifetime of association."[7]

Notice that relationship marketing is ongoing. A business relationship is like a marriage — success is achieved not just through good intentions but also through hard work and close attention to the other party's needs. Further, the goal is to identify and create new value with individual customers. Amazon.com does this via a "personalization" technology known as collaborative filtering. Once you have made a purchase from them, Amazon.com recommends a new book by comparing your tastes with those of fellow book buyers who have reported liking the kinds of books that you enjoy. Not only should new value be created, but the resulting benefits should be shared over the lifetime of the relationship. Compaq computers has reached an agreement with Internet service providers America Online and GTE Corp., along with online retailer Amazon.com, where each of the these companies agrees to share with Compaq a slice of the revenues generated using Compaq computers.

American Airlines created a program called "Airpass" for one of its large corporate customers, Perot Systems. When Perot employees book flights, they do not have to bother waiting for tickets; they just simply present a card at the ticket counter or gate. Miles are automatically credited to the employee's American frequent flyer account. Upgrades are readily available, and American allows Perot employees to use its Ambassadors Clubs for business and leisure travel.

## Traditional vs. Relationship Marketing

In the frenzied 1980s, companies focused most of their marketing efforts on acquiring new customers. Little attention was given to existing customers. With the cost of customer attraction continually going up, companies are giving much more serious attention to holding onto their existing customers. For example, for cellular phone companies, the cost of acquiring a new subscriber is now about $400, with an

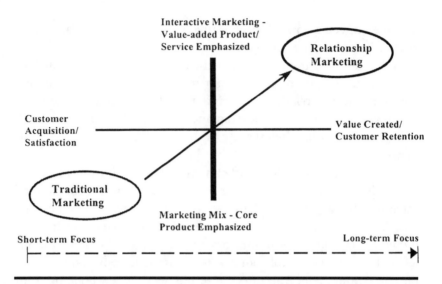

**Figure 9.1. Traditional vs. Relationship Marketing** (Adapted from Sheth, J. (1996) American Marketing Association Strategic Marketing Faculty Consortium: Evolution of Global Marketing and the Relationship Imperative, Arizona State University, p. 2.)

average pay-back period for the operator of 3 years.[8] Long-standing customers are less expensive to reach and less expensive to serve. Moreover, when taking into account the lifetime value of a customer, the financial toll of losing customers is staggering. Customer relationships are assets that should be evaluated and managed as rigorously as any financial or physical assets. Figure 9.1 presents an overview of how traditional marketing differs from relationship marketing.

As Figure 9.1 shows, relationship marketing not only focuses on customer retention but also takes a long-term perspective. Companies who exploit their customers for short-term advantage will win the battle but ultimately lose the war. In the mid-1980s, Ryder System, Inc., began a relationship with one of the large Bell operating companies via a short-term truck rental. Over time, Ryder has provided more value to the customer, including full-service equipment leases, drivers, a full outbound delivery network, and logistical solutions. In the last 3 years, Ryder also has assumed operation of all inbound transportation and distributor-center packaging, shipping, cross docking, and storeroom operations, all staffed and operated by Ryder personnel. From the humble beginning of a single truck rental, this account has grown into a totally integrated supply-chain system worth $30 million to Ryder, with a 1998 estimated account value of $50 million, including extended support into Latin America

Traditional marketing also differs from relationship marketing based on how the firm's marketing mix is treated. For example, packaged-good producers serving mostly consumer markets attempt to blend the marketing mix elements, although not always in an integrative sense. Further, the number of points of contacts with the customer are limited under traditional marketing. In relationship marketing, value is created in the relationships that companies have with their customers. The interactions that companies have with buyers (or prospective buyers) are not limited to nor always initiated by the marketing function or department. In fact, many of the contacts with the buyer are by "non-marketing" personnel, or what Gummesson refers to as part-time marketers.[9] Although their primary responsibility may be non-marketing (i.e., technical support, back-office, or front-line workers), they also perform crucial marketing tasks because of their vital customer contacts. Remember, customers evaluate value at every point of contact in the organization to determine if they received what was expected or promised.

The goals and outcomes of relationship marketing also differ from traditional marketing. Whereas the goal under traditional marketing is customer acquisition, under relationship marketing the focus shifts to creating value. Case in point: Nabisco created the ASSET (Account Specific Sales Expanding Techniques) program, a menu of tactics that can be executed at the store level for mass, club, and grocery chains in conjunction with Nabisco's national efforts. For example, around the national Cool School Bus promotion this year (which will give away buses full of Tiger Toys and Nabisco snacks to one winner per state), Nabisco has developed two major account-specific overlays: a store-by-store sweepstakes offering Thermos lunch totes filled with Tiger Toys and Nabisco snacks (a $100 value overall) and customized television spots. Kraft/General Foods has also been effective in creating value for its retail customers. Working with one retailer in upstate New York and using a merged database consisting of the retailer's frequent-shopper program members and Kraft's proprietary household database, Kraft prepared a customized mailing to households in the retailer's area.

If the goal is to create more value through interdependent, collaborative relationships with customers, the outcome is customer retention. As we emphasized earlier, relationship marketing is ongoing, constantly

## Table 9.1. The Relationship Marketing Mix

| Marketing Element | Rank |
|---|---|
| Customer sensitivity — employee attitude, customer treatment, and response to customers | 1 |
| Product — quality, features, and reliability | 2 |
| Customer convenience — availability to the customer, customer convenience, ease of doing business with | 3 |
| Service — post-sale and pre-sale service | 4 |
| Price — price charged, pricing terms, and pricing offers | 5 |
| Place — provider accessibility, provider facilities, and availability to customer | 6 |
| Promotion — advertising, publicity, selling | 7 |

*Source:* Adapted from Berry, D. (1990) *Marketing News,* Dec. 24, p.10.

looking for opportunities to generate new value. Thus, customer retention is not a given, especially when new value is not being created. BellSouth trains its service representatives to act as consultants for its small-business customers in order to work with them in addressing their communications as well as marketing needs. Many small-business clients have limited marketing budgets and appreciate the "bundled" solutions offered by BellSouth.

Retaining customers requires marketers to exhibit care and concern after they have made a purchase.[10] Dick Berry suggested modifying the original marketing mix, adding three new elements that focus more on "aftermarketing" elements. Based on a study with marketing managers, he recast the original marketing mix, adding an S and two C's to the standard 4P's. Table 9.1 describes the 4P's, as well as the three new items, along with a ranking of their importance to the managers he studied.[11] We believe the greatest opportunity for achieving high customer retention lies with these three new items: customer sensitivity, customer convenience, and service.

QVC's online shopping service is a good example here. Web shoppers can visit the iQVC site, then click on "My iQVC". Customers are then informed, "We'll ask you a few questions, you'll give us a few answers, and we'll deliver custom content right to your desktop." Shoppers who click on "My Mailing List" can choose from several categories, such as cookware, jewelry, toys, and collectibles. Once the customer has chosen, iQVC will e-mail the shopper with relevant news on the subject he or she has chosen. The site also offers "My Style Advisor", where customers complete an online questionnaire and receive a Style Advisor Profile, personalized for body line, face shape, and coloring. QVC then makes appropriate fashion and jewelry recommendations. QVC creates loyalty by being open 24 hours and offering efficient and helpful service before, during, and after the sale.

Having looked at how relationship marketing and traditional marketing differ, the next section will discuss the determinants of building strong customer relationships.

## Building Lasting Customer Relationships

Relationships, whether business or marriage, seem to be subject to the Second Law of Thermodynamics: unless maintained, they gradually deteriorate and wear down. Apart from sound management, the relationship erodes because the focus of both parties turns inward and moves toward insensitivity and inattentiveness.[12] Recall an American Airlines commercial a few years back where a senior-level manager is gathered with his subordinates, lamenting that, "We just got fired by our best customer." He reminded them that they used to conduct business with a visit and handshake — now it is by fax or voice mail. He proceeded to hand out airline tickets to each person present in the meeting, instructing them to pay a personal visit to each of their key customers. He, of course, was going to visit the customer who "fired" them. The message was never to take customer relationships for granted.

Sellers can resist this natural tendency toward decline and complacency by developing what we refer to as "relationship enablers". It is the seller's responsibility to nurture the relationship beyond its simple dollar value. Using the relationship enablers shown in Figure 9.2, sellers can minimize relationship decay and strengthen the bonds that lead to long-term, perhaps even lifetime associations.

First consider the effect of trust. Trust is an important factor in the development of marketing relationships and exists where there is confidence in an exchange partner's reliability and integrity. A seller can create confidence in the eyes of the buyer by being credible and following through on what they promise. FedEx dominates the market for overnight delivery because they promise to have the customer's package

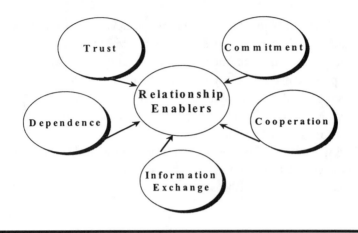

**Figure 9.2. Key Relationship Enablers**

there "absolutely, positively overnight". FedEx's customers rest easy at night knowing that this statement is not simply an advertising slogan, but a pledge to deliver on what they promise. The best tool you can use in establishing trust is communications. It is important to be open and honest, as well as clear and thorough. Establishing a good channel of communication can help you avoid countless potential disasters and loss of customer trust down the road. Remember, also, that trust is a "bank account" where deposits and withdrawals are made over time. The trust account accumulates interest only when the seller's messages and actions are clear, consistent, and reliable.

Another important relationship enabler is commitment. Whereas trust involves a reliance on the seller, commitment is an implicit or explicit pledge of maintaining and supporting the relationship. Although we make a distinction here between trust and commitment, a recent study we conducted found that trust actually leads to commitment.[13] A high level of commitment encourages both parties in a relationship to pursue their individual and joint goals. UPS and J.C. Penney recently formed a $1 billion partnership in which UPS becomes Penney's sole mail-order carrier, as well as their logistics carrier, bringing their equipment and expertise to the partnership. Such a commitment signals a willingness by each player to modify their existing systems to fit the other, inextricably binding these companies together.

We maintain that trust and commitment are the two most crucial relationship enablers. Finding a successful relationship without trust and commitment is rare. Moreover, trust and commitment seem to be strongly associated with complaint handling satisfaction. That is, successful customer complaint resolution leads to greater trust and commitment in marketing relationships.[14]

Cooperation, another relationship enabler, involves coordinated activities between buyer and seller and is aimed at producing desirable results for both firms. The gains experienced by cooperating can more than offset the loss of autonomy in a relationship. Furthermore, cooperation frequently involves a willingness to develop joint goals and even share resources. For instance, take Procter & Gamble (P&G). P&G actually manages Wal-Mart's inventory of P&G products, and it is P&G's responsibility to decide when Wal-Mart requires shipments. To do this, P&G has complete access to Wal-Mart's inventory. It manages everything and makes decisions on its own shipments. This arrangement is beneficial for both parties; Wal-Mart can charge less because it does not have the cost of tracking or storing inventory, while P&G has a much bigger share of business and it does not have to compete with other suppliers.

Even competitors can benefit from cooperation. For example, a recent alliance was formed between United Airlines and Delta Airlines to connect their frequent flyer programs and to sell seats on each other's domestic and, ultimately, international flights. This practice, known as code-sharing, would allow United to bolster its market reach through Delta's strong presence in the south and east, while Delta would gain an advantage from United's presence in the midwest and west, Latin America, and Asia.

Dependence serves as a further relationship enabler. Dependence is a willingness to invest time and dedicate resources for the purpose of establishing and strengthening a business relationship. In business-to-business marketing, resource-specific investments increase the dependence of retailers and vendors on each other.[15] Gillette's relationship with ADC, a promotional materials supplier, serves as a good example here. ADC's partner relationship with Gillette initially started when ADC was chosen to help develop a display program for Gillette's new men's toiletry line, The Gillette Series, consisting of shaving preparation products, deodorants, antiperspirants, and after-shave products. ADC's involvement began with the initial display concept, followed by prototyping, engineering, and assembling pre-packed displays which were shipped to Gillette's major distribution centers. ADC acted as an

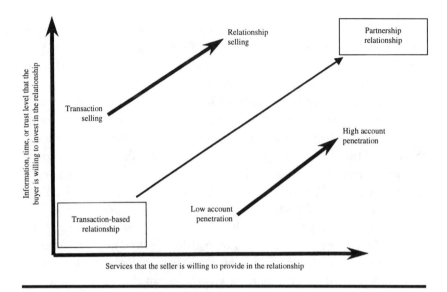

**Figure 9.3. Information Sustains a Relationship**

extension of Gillette's manufacturing and marketing by providing coordinated logistics, display development, pack-out, and distribution. ADC committed 54,000 square feet of manufacturing space and over 100 employees to this product launch.

Finally, information exchange is the lubricant that keeps the other relationship enablers from corroding. If price attracts a relationship, information sustains it. In fact, as Figure 9.3 shows, when buyers offer more information, sellers in turn are willing to provide more services, creating a win-win situation. McKesson Corporation, a major drug wholesaler representing thousands of independent pharmacies, helps the pharmacies set up accounting and inventory systems, as well as computer ordering systems (i.e., electronic data interchange, or EDI). The retailers gain value from improved stock planning, resulting in fewer stock-outs and more satisfied customers. McKesson benefits by creating "captive" retail accounts who grant McKesson unprecedented access to their sales and financial data.

Active information exchange between buyers and sellers can also result in product and process innovation. Von Hippel found that in some industries more than two thirds of the innovations he studied could be traced back to a customer's initial suggestions or ideas.[16] In the fragrance industry, suppliers are much more involved in new product planning than in the past. One case in point is Vanilla Fields, the blockbuster mass market scent from Coty. Coty presented Fragrance Resources, one of its suppliers, with a challenge to find "the musk of the Nineties". Fragrance Resources came up with vanilla but also gave Coty a lot of other marketing information, such as ways they could position a vanilla fragrance.

In many cases, knowledge exchange between buyers and sellers develops informally over time through interfirm interactions. The key is to use the information obtained to create value for the exchange partners. For example, Fuji and Xerox have attempted to codify this knowledge by creating a communications matrix, which identifies a set of relevant issues (e.g., products, technologies, markets, and so on) and then identifies the individuals (by function) within Fuji and Xerox who have relevant expertise on that particular issue. This matrix provides valuable information regarding where relevant expertise resides within the partnering firms.

In summary, each of the relationship enablers will be evident to some degree in most successful buyer/seller relationships. Clearly, some of these factors will become more important over the life of the business relationship. Trust and cooperation, for example, are critical during the initial stages of relationship building; commitment, dependence, and information exchange become more important later in the relationship. Using Customer Value Checklist 9, evaluate the your customer relationships based on the relationship enablers discussed above, and determine the extent to which your relationships lead to long-term business goals. Our discussion of relationship marketing up to this point has been limited to buyer/seller relationships. Just as the opportunity to work with customers in creating new value is important, so is working with supply-chain partners to accomplish the same purpose. Creating new value through improved supply-chain relationships is discussed next.

## Improving Supply-Chain Relationships

So far we have focused mainly on promoting and improving relationships between firms and their customers. Firms increasingly recognize that the value added through the supply chain contributes to overall end-customer value. For example, downstream intermediaries (distributors, wholesalers, retailers) add value to the offering that the producer

**Customer Value Checklist 9.**
**Diagnosing the Health of Buyer-Seller Relationships**

1. Using the Relationship Enablers in Figure 9.2, choose a key customer (or supplier) and rank the relative importance of each relationship enabler in building the business relationship. Provide a rationale for your rankings.

2. Using the same customer or supplier from the previous example, rate how it performs in regard to each relationship enabler:

|  | Excellent (4) | Good (3) | Needs Improvement (2) | Not Acceptable (1) |
|---|---|---|---|---|
| Trust | —— | —— | —— | —— |
| Commitment | —— | —— | —— | —— |
| Dependence | —— | —— | —— | —— |
| Cooperation | —— | —— | —— | —— |
| Information exchange | —— | —— | —— | —— |

3. The goal of relationship marketing is to achieve some long-term business goal leading to a sustainable competitive advantage. Using the same customer or supplier as before, what is the likelihood that improvements in the business relationship will produce positive business outcomes (i.e., a sustainable competitive advantage)? Using a 7-point scale, where 1 indicates "No Chance" and 7 indicates "Complete Certainty", assess how likely it is that improvements in your relationship with your buyer or supplier will lead to positive business outcomes.

|  | Probability |
|---|---|
|  | No Chance → Complete Certainty |
|  | 1  2  3  4  5  6  7 |
| a. What is the probability that improvements in this relationship will substantially reduce costs or lead to better asset utilization? | — — — — — — — |
| b. What is the probability that improvements in this relationship will improve customer service as indicated by the customer? | — — — — — — — |
| c. What is the probability that improvements in this relationship will result in higher profitability for both partners? | — — — — — — — |

cannot easily or economically do. Furthermore, an intermediary can be an enduring source for creating new value with end customers by maximizing speed and minimizing costs and investment.

As such, channel integration must be an integral part of the marketing mix, with channel decisions being carefully evaluated and managed. A marketing channel is the exchange pathway through which goods and services are moved, flowing from the production point to intermediaries and finally to the ultimate consumers. As products are distributed, value must be created by middlemen. Intel's successful "Intel inside" promotional campaign demonstrated that even a components supplier can be very important to discriminating customers.

We find that distribution strategies are often uncreative. Firms tend to employ obvious and safe paths (imitative approaches). The effective use of innovative, value-creating distribution options such as Amazon.com's virtual bookstore, Dell Computer's build-to-order direct strategy, the airlines' SkyMall program, and supply-chain management (SCM) practices can provide a strong competitive edge to firms. This latter issue is addressed further in this section.

Supply-chain management revamps channel strategy from an area relatively neglected to an actively managed marketing/logistics function. According to a recent study, about 50% of companies worldwide and 42% in North America have maintained key supplier relationships for 6 or more years. Yet, less than 25% of global organizations and only 20% of North American companies involve their suppliers in key business processes.[17] Hence, a major opportunity exists to further leverage ongoing business relationships.

Supply-chain management means that collaboration rather than competition becomes the *modus operandi* as disparate organizations now jointly focus on satisfying customers by aligning and integrating business processes. All participants in the "extended channel" work in harmony to find new ways to add value at varying points in the distribution cycle. Furthermore, costs may be cut, product or service quality enhanced, delivery time reduced, and overall business performance improved through an effective SCM system.

Suppliers play a key role in the relationship between seller and buyer. There are twelve criteria (in six areas) for being perceived as a world-class supplier. These are product (features and quality), service (features and quality), overall cost (level and stability), responsiveness (lead time and due-date performance), organizational capability (resources and stability), and corporate responsibilities (social and environmental).[18] It should be noted that each customer will value a different set of criteria; hence, each will have its own view of whether or not it is working with a world-class vendor.

Li & Fung is Hong Kong's largest export trading company and is a leader in SCM practices. On behalf of American and European customers, Li & Fung adds value through design, engineering, and production planning in raw material and component sourcing (front-end activities) and via quality control, testing, and logistics in managing production (back-end activities).[19]

According to Mary Lou Fox, senior vice president of Manugistics (Rockville, MD), a supply-chain management software and services firm, there are five evolutionary stages of SCM. In the first stage, the emphasis is on quality and cost control. Customer service is the focus of stage two. Coordinating supply-chain processes across the enterprise occurs in stage three. Looking for ways to provide profitable customized products via the extended supply chain is the objective of progressive stage-four companies. Finally, the formation of tightly knit supply-chain communities is the aim of stage-five organizations.[20]

## Keys to Practicing Relationship Marketing

Relationship marketing represents a shift in thinking about how companies do business. Because relationships are fragile, the attributes of trust, commitment, dependence, cooperation, and information exchange are crucial for enabling and maintaining strong relationships. In this section, we will review the major factors that contribute to success in practicing relationship marketing

First, and most important, relationships are strengthened when sellers create more value for their customers (see Figure 9.4). Customers are likely to offer their patronage to sellers who supply greater benefits or lower costs, or both. Companies should look for opportunities to offer new features or services, to customize their offering, to unbundle or bundle services, to enhance product or service quality, and to offer guarantees. Zane Cycles, an independent bicycle retailer in Branford, CN, understands this principle well. For example, owner Chris Zane offers free lifetime service for each bike purchased at his store. Zane also offers customers toll-free numbers — both voice and fax — as a way of

1.   Look for opportunities to add value
2.   Respond quickly to customer needs
3.   Apply "mass customization"
4.   Track each relationship

**Figure 9.4. Keys to Practicing Relationship Marketing**

adding value to the customer relationship. Furthermore, if a Zane customer wants to buy something that costs less than a dollar, Zane gives them the item at no charge and thanks them for their business. Adding value does not always require doing something for the customer in a big way; sometimes it is the tiny little touches that delight customers and intensify their loyalty, as shown by Zane Cycles (see Chapter 7 for more examples of value-added strategies).

Customer relationships are also improved by responding to customer needs. Recall that in Chapter 5 when we discussed the major determinants of service quality, responsiveness was one of the key predictors of service quality perceptions. Consider the case of Hartness International. Hartness is a producer of high-speed, case-packing machines that load bottles of soda, syrup, or ketchup into cartons before they get shipped. For Hartness' customers, time is money, as a down bottling line can cost the customer as much as $150 per minute. Hartness recognizes the importance of this potential problem and hires only service technicians who are licensed pilots. That way, whenever Hartness has to fix a machine, technicians are not held hostage to airlines schedules — they can fly one of the company's four planes. Today, Hartness has 5000 customers in 90 countries.

Companies who successfully practice relationship marketing have mastered mass customization. In many markets it is not only possible but imperative to mass customize for customers. Buyers often have individual problems that require unique solutions. Giving customers what they want and how they want it will develop their loyalties. Dell Computer has known this since Michael Dell began custom-building PCs in the mid-1980s. Dell is now planning to introduce a new customer service plan which uses the Internet to automate and customize service much the same way in which they have streamlined and customized PC production. By using communications over high-speed private net-works and the Internet, Dell plans to not only to provide personalized Web pages to non-corporate customers, but also to answer customers' technical questions with lightning speed. In fact, Dell's message to its employees is "Dell wants *you* to *own* your relationship with the cus-tomer."

New technology enables efficient customization of products and services, even when the customer base is quite large. Technology can also assist companies in differentiating customers as being most valu-able, offering maximum growth potential, and not valuable. Several times a year, US West sifts through its customer list looking for money losers who have the potential to be more profitable in the future. By looking at demographic profiles, plus the mix of local vs. long-distance calls or whether a customer has voice mail, they can estimate a customer's potential telecom spending. Next, US West can determine how much of the customer's likely telecom budget is already coming its way, thus helping it know where to set the cutoff point for how much to invest in marketing to this customer before profitably suffers.

A final key to practicing relationship marketing is to track each relationship. We discussed the concept of the lifetime value (LTV) of a customer in Chapter 8. LTV is simply a projection of what customers are worth over a lifetime of doing business with them. Calculating LTV is important because of the impact of retention levels on profitability. A hypothetical automobile example helps illustrate this concept. Suppose that, over a 50-year purchasing lifetime, a typical customer buys a new car every 4 years at a purchase price of $25,000 (in constant dollars). Based on this scenario, the lifetime value of this customer exceeds $300,000. Most customer service experts say that, on average, a satisfied customer will tell at least one other person about their experience. Thus, when a second loyal customer is created as a result of positive word of mouth who repeats the cycle, we are now looking at a customer worth over $600,000! Of course, you would have to factor in the cost of acquiring and servicing this customer when performing this calculation. Nevertheless, calculating these kinds of numbers can be sobering, espe-cially for companies experiencing high customer attrition. Executives at Taco Bell have estimated that a repeat customer is worth as much as $11,000. Data such as these need to be shared with employees in order to see the true "cost" of losing a customer.[21]

## Summary

A massive shift has taken place from marketing to an anonymous sea of customers to developing, nurturing, and managing business relationships with individual customers. Just as the marketing concept focused businesses on seeing customers as the center of the universe, relationship marketing takes a quantum leap forward by concentrating on satisfying and keeping each customer over time.

Which brings us to an important question. Based on what we have already learned, how will leading-edge service companies compete successfully in the future? Recall that value now represents the key strategic driver, regardless of the scope in which the firm competes. Superior value is most likely to occur in firms that practice a customer orientation. Because customer-oriented firms are more proactive in anticipating their customers' wants, they are better positioned to discover the emerging value drivers. Process improvement is also crucial to creating superior value. Processes add value when they allow customers control over how and when they buy, while eliminating errors and inconvenience. Moreover, competing on value requires effectively managing and communicating the value proposition. The value proposition involves the proper "blending" of price, product, service, innovation, and image as a means for establishing a unique position in the market. Finally, strong relationships — end customer and supply chain — are necessary for creating and sustaining value. Business relationships are a fundamental asset and require ongoing investments of time, trust, and commitment. Savvy companies understand that value is created in the relationship they have with their customers — how they connect with them personally and systematically. Companies successful at practicing relationship marketing look for opportunities to add value through their business relationships, offering new features, services, or customized offerings.

## Customer Value Action Items

1. Compare and contrast traditional and relationship marketing.
2. Why has interest in relationship marketing grown over the past decade?
3. Discuss how to create "win-win" relationships with customers.

4. Are there situations when relationship marketing is not advisable? Why?

5. Using the companies listed below, provide examples of how practicing supply-chain management would create more value for their end-user customers:
   a. Sears
   b. GM
   c. Motorola
   d. Disney

6. Discuss how supply-chain management enhances each of the following value elements:
   a. Price
   b. Service
   c. Quality
   d. Time

# References

1. Levitt, T. (1981) *The Purpose of an Enterprise,* Harvard Business School Case No. 9-481-146, Boston, MA: HBS Case Service.
2. Drucker, P. (1973) *Management, Tasks, Responsibilities, Practices,* New York: Harper & Row, pp. 64–65.
3. Kotler, P. (1991) Phil Kotler explores the new marketing paradigm, *Marketing Science Institute Review,* Spring, pp. 4–5
4. Webster, F. (1992) The changing role of marketing in the corporation, *Journal of Marketing,* 56(Oct.), p. 14.
5. Berry, L. (1983) Relationship marketing, in *Emerging Perspectives on Service Marketing,* Berry, L., Shostack, G.L., and Upah, G., Eds., Chicago, IL: American Marketing Association, pp. 25–28.
6. Parvatiyar, A. and Sheth, J. (1994) Paradigm shift in marketing theory and approach: the emergence of relationship marketing, in *Relationship Marketing: Theory, Methods and Applications,* Sheth, J. and Parvatiyar, A., Eds., Atlanta, GA: Center for Relationship Marketing, Emory University.
7. Gordon, I. (1998) *Relationship Marketing,* Toronto: John Wiley & Sons, p. 9.
8. Cane, A. (1997) Churn blightens the development of the telecommunications business, *Financial Times,* Nov. 11, p. 2.
9. Gummesson, E. (1990) *The Part-Time Marketer,* Karstad, Sweden: Center for Service Research.
10. Vavra, T. (1992) *Aftermarketing,* Burr Ridge, IL: Business One Irwin, p. 15.
11. Berry, D. (1990) Marketing mix for the '90s adds an S and 2C's to the 4P's, *Marketing News,* Dec. 24, p. 10.
12. Levitt, T. (1983) After the sale is over, *Harvard Business Review,* Sept./Oct., p. 90.

13. Feldman, L., Johnson, W.C., and Weinstein, A. (1998) Trust, commitment, and long-term manufacturer-supplier relationships, presented at the 1998 Research Conference on Relationship Marketing, Atlanta, June 1998.
14. DuPont, R. (1998) Relationship marketing: a strategy for consumer-owned utilities in a restructured industry, *Management Quarterly*, 38(4), p. 11(6).
15. Ganesan, S. (1994) Determinants of long-term orientation in buyer-seller relationships, *Journal of Marketing*, 58(April), p. 14.
16. Von Hippel, E. (1988) *The Sources of Innovation*, New York: Oxford University Press, p. 89.
17. Tait, D. (1998) Make strong supplier relationships a priority, *Canadian Manager*, Spring, pp. 21, 28.
18. Stevens, K. (1997) World class perceptions, *Supply Management*, Jan. 30, pp. 38–39.
19. Magretta, J. (1998) Fast, global, and entrepreneurial: supply-chain management, Hong Kong style, *Harvard Business Review*, Sept./Oct., pp. 103–114.
20. Anon. (1998) What customers value most, *Chief Executive*, pp. 8–16.
21. Kotler, P. (1997) *Marketing Management*, 9th ed., Upper Saddle River, NJ: Prentice Hall.

# Part 2. Customer Value Cases

# Analyzing Business Cases: The Customer Value Funnel Approach*

"As marketers, we should be committed to the proposition that the creation of customer value must be the reason for the firm's existence and certainly for its success." (Stanley F. Slater)

To compete successfully, organizations must evaluate all pertinent actors and factors in a market. Two value concepts are preeminent: (1) maximizing economic value, and (2) responding to the relevant values of constituencies. This briefing develops a managerial perspective featuring a four-stage value funnel framework. The customer funnel approach is a valuable tool for understanding and assessing business dynamics and situations. You are encouraged to utilize the questions at the end of this section when analyzing the case studies (which follow) in this book.

## A Values-Based Managerial Perspective

Management's objective should be to maximize value over time, realizing that customer values have a major impact on both business processes

---

*  This section builds on ideas in the article by Art Weinstein and Randolph A. Pohlman (1998) Customer value: a new paradigm for marketing management, *Advances in Business Studies*, 6(10), pp. 89–97.

and performance. There are six important assumptions upon which a long-term value creation commitment is based:[1]

1. Creating/adding value is a challenge and opportunity for marketers; an increase in value is good.
2. There are various value-based segments in a market; value is subjective.
3. Organizations must formulate their own unique value philosophies/statements; customers can vote for or veto value propositions.
4. Knowledge creation leads to value creation; markets provide valuable information that should be tapped and utilized.
5. What is valued by customers should drive action programs (e.g., product development, communications programs, and related strategic decisions).
6. Value trade-offs frequently exist in the marketplace; as customer values can compete or be complementary, they must be assessed and responded to on a regular basis.

Hence, the enhanced customer value approach offers management an alternative view of how to compete effectively in dynamic and volatile markets. This value maximization premise means that corporate success should be evaluated in a new light. We propose that business performance should be built on a dual foundation of paramount value concepts: (1) anticipating and responding to the relevant values of all constituencies (e.g., customers; stakeholders; employees; collaborators, competitors, suppliers, and regulators; and society), and (2) value maximization — how economic value and knowledge are created and applied throughout an organization to best serve its target customers.

While the former element is largely qualitative in nature, the latter is mostly a quantitative dimension. This approach provides an insightful basis for designing a value-based model for managers to assess business situations as we enter the 21st century. The conceptualization of the value-driven model is developed in the subsequent section.

## The Customer Value Funnel

The customer value funnel captures and summarizes the salient attributes of the two sets of value concepts in action (see figure). As the

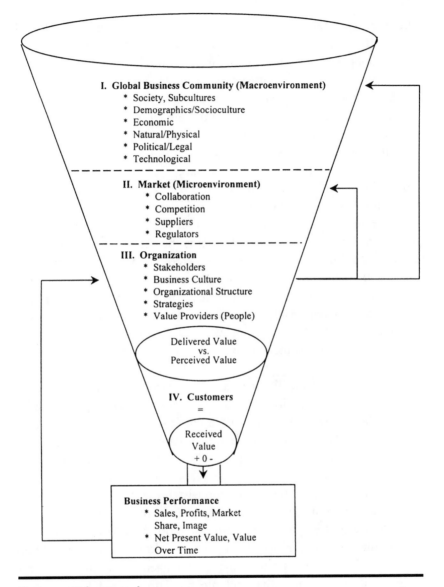

I. **Global Business Community (Macroenvironment)**
* Society, Subcultures
* Demographics/Socioculture
* Economic
* Natural/Physical
* Political/Legal
* Technological

II. **Market (Microenvironment)**
* Collaboration
* Competition
* Suppliers
* Regulators

III. **Organization**
* Stakeholders
* Business Culture
* Organizational Structure
* Strategies
* Value Providers (People)

Delivered Value
vs.
Perceived Value

IV. **Customers**
=

Received
Value
+ 0 -

**Business Performance**
* Sales, Profits, Market Share, Image
* Net Present Value, Value Over Time

**Customer Value Funnel**

framework illustrates, organizations must deal with a set of macro issues as well as customer-specific concerns to excel in business. Viewing the four levels of the model — global business community, market, organization, and customers — through a broad to narrow lens ultimately impacts the performance of a business unit.

The interdependency of the four levels is readily apparent. The dotted lines in the figure (between levels) indicate that each successive level is part of the preceding one. For example, as Drucker notes, there would be no companies without customers; similarly, organizations are part of markets, which, in turn, are part of the global business community.[2] The values of the major "players" in the model must be carefully scrutinized as to value identification and congruency and value delivery options (these are the relevant values). From the top down, the value drivers are what: (1) society values (level I); (2) suppliers, partners, competitors, and regulators value (level II); (3) owners and employees value (level III); and (4) customers value (level IV).[1]

A realistic assessment of value-creation opportunities (value maximization) throughout the funnel is the next step. Organizations consist of value providers. If the delivered value of these employees exceeds the expectations of customers (perceived value), positive net transaction experiences result. This leads to ongoing satisfaction and increased customer loyalty. In these cases, organizations are faring well in their moments of truth (points where value transfer occurs); hence, isolated favorable transactions evolve into continued, long-term relationships.

The value over time (lifetime value) of a customer is measurable and, in many cases, substantial. For example, leading supermarkets typically generate about $50,000 from households ($100 per week for 50 weeks for 10 years); Ford Motor Company estimates the lifetime value of an average customer at more than $200,000; and Ryder System expects about $9 million from customers (3 years at $3 million per year).

For the most part, the funnel model represents a downward flow, with each successive level being a component of the level above (e.g., markets are part of the global business community, organizations are part of markets, etc.). However, the feedback loops evidenced in levels I, II, and III demonstrate that market intelligence and knowledge are ongoing, iterative, interactive, and integrated processes. If business performance does not meet corporate objectives, strategic or tactical changes are mandated. The organization (level III) can adjust internally via rethinking its overall direction, implementing training and development initiatives, revising business plans, etc. Often, however, external adaptations are required due to changes taking place in the macro/global or micro/market environments.

# The Customer Value Funnel: Concluding Remarks

In sum, the customer value funnel offers executives and "students of the market" a tool to help achieve a competitive business edge. The long-term value of the organization is maximized by being in harmony with the relevant values in the marketplace, and the energy of value providers is harnessed to deliver excellence in all endeavors. Realize that the value paradigm is still in the formative stage. A strength of the customer value approach is that it is pragmatic and consistent with the managerial need for integrating business functional areas. The information presented in this book can provide a springboard for the creation and refinement of marketing/customer value management strategies.

# Customer Value Cases: A Primer and Questions for Analysis

The case studies that follow provide in-depth examples of customer value concepts and applications in diverse service-related industries. By reviewing these cases, you can learn more about the types of planning and research that go into customer value thinking, the market factors with which these organizations must contend, marketing and management decisions and strategies, and how market performance may be enhanced through sound business practices.

Think about how the focal organization uses competitive differentiation to take maximum advantage of market opportunities. As a framework for analysis, the five guiding customer value funnel questions below will help you assess the relevant customer value issues in each case study. To gain further insights into the business situation, you are also encouraged to review the questions at the end of each customer value case.

# Customer Value Funnel Questions

1. Identify the relevant macroenvironmental factors (level I) in the case study. What impact do these issues have on the focal organization?

2.  Discuss the market factors (level II) in the case study. How do collaboration, competition, supplier, and regulators affect the performance of the focal organization?
3.  Explain how the focal organization (level III) creates value for its customers. What strategic changes are required to deliver outstanding value to its customers?
4.  Do customers (level IV) perceive value as unsatisfactory, satisfactory, or superior? Why? Which attributes do customers value that are not receiving adequate attention by the organization?
5.  Critique the organization's business performance based on traditional (e.g., sales, profits, market share, and image) and value-based (e.g., net present value, value over time) performance criteria. What can the organization do to improve its performance?

# References

1.  Pohlman, R.A. (1997) *VTM: The Value Theory of Management,* Working Paper Series #97-01, Fort Lauderdale, FL: Nova Southeastern University.
2.  Drucker, P.F. (1974) *Management: Tasks, Responsibilities, and Practices,* New York: Harper & Row.

# Case 1. AAA Motor Club – Responding to Change*

## Background

T he Automobile Association of America (AAA) was established in 1902 as the Chicago Motor Club with 1000 members. Over the years, additional AAA clubs evolved to various membership sizes, and some states had several clubs. As AAA progressed into the 1980s, there were more than 135 clubs throughout the U.S. and Canada (including affiliates such as franchises and divisions owned directly by AAA National).

As the economies of business were building, smaller affiliates were being bought and absorbed into the larger affiliate clubs that offered greater financial and operating strengths. During the 1990s, when the total number of clubs began to decline, AAA National made a strategic decision to divest itself of the divisions it owned and become a corporate support entity to the clubs. In 1997, AAA divested itself of the last of 11 divisions owned by AAA National and relinquished Florida to Auto Club South (ACS). ACS's geographic market coverage is shown in Figure C1.1.

Today, AAA represents the largest motoring and travel club, with over 40 million members in the U.S. and Canada. AAA National is now

---

* This case was prepared by Miles J. Volin, Regional Sales Manager, AAA Auto Club South Florida.

**Figure C1.1. AAA Auto Club South Territory Map**

headquartered in Heathrow (Orlando), FL, to support the over 90 AAA clubs in the system, each independently owned and operated but complying with the bylaws of AAA National. During the past 5 years, membership growth for East Florida and AAA National has been 2.6%, annually (see Table C1.1). This growth is expected to continue at a 3 to 4% annual rate for the next several years. ACS is now the third largest club, with over 3 million members and encompassing Florida, Georgia, and Tennessee operations, but it is still behind the two largest clubs, southern California and Michigan, respectively (see Table C1.2).

## Internal Business Environment and Culture

A radical shift in thinking began in the mid 1980s that caused U.S. companies to expand product lines as well as turn their emphasis to

**Table C1.1. AAA Membership**

| Year | AAA National | East Florida |
|------|--------------|--------------|
| 1997 | 40,380,309 | 1,368,796 |
| 1996 | 39,371,068 | 1,333,064 |
| 1995 | 38,117,346 | 1,302,823 |
| 1994 | 36,752,727 | 1,227,712 |
| 1993 | 35,291,651 | 1,151,655 |

*Source:* Data from AAA National Headquarters, Heathrow, FL.

multi-national operations. A major change was already occurring at AAA, moving it from being a motor club to a comprehensive travel services company.

Product and service diversification at AAA clubs has been increasing in order to provide the benefits demanded by the marketplace. Competitors in this highly competitive market were making strong overtures to look like AAA, targeting the most attractive AAA product areas and making direct product comparisons. AAA countered by offering an increased menu of travel products available at any given AAA office. AAA stepped up its market awareness by promoting its store-front locations with a variety of services no other travel organizations offered. This approach far exceeded those of its competitors, who simply partnered with AAA to sell their traveler's checks at every AAA location.

In 1996, AAA East Florida, acknowledging the quality movement in selling travel-related services, pursued the coveted Florida Sterling Award program. This program is similar to the Malcolm Baldrige Award and is given to organizations representing the highest quality operations among the elite companies in Florida. AAA East Florida was a finalist among the candidates for 1996 and, although they did not win, planned a strong entry for 1997, prior to their merger into Auto Club South. The continued pursuit of the Sterling Award has and will continue to change the way ACS views its customers and internal processes.

The improvement of customer-driven processes at ACS has affected service in the following areas: financial services, insurance coverage, travel packaging, lodgings and special packages, luggage, attractions/discounts, automated travel planning, and others. For example, after studying customer flow in the travel offices, initial customer contact in

### Table C1.2. Auto Club South
### Membership Growth/Acquisitions

| Year | Acquisition | Membership |
|---|---|---|
| 1998 | Acquired East Florida | 3,139,973 |
| 1997 | | 1,645,697 |
| 1996 | | 1,587,164 |
| 1995 | | 1,499,706 |
| 1994 | | 1,435,981 |
| 1993 | | 1,355,967 |
| 1992 | | 1,285,218 |
| 1991 | | 1,256,600 |
| 1990 | Acquired Mid-South Auto Club | 1,250,503 |
| 1989 | | 1,134,504 |
| 1988 | Acquired Georgia Motor Club | 1,129,861 |
| 1987 | | 867,760 |
| 1986 | Acquired St. Pete Motor Club | 830,000 |
| 1985 | | 551,917 |
| 1984 | | 518,302 |
| 1983 | | 491,178 |
| 1982 | | 453,881 |
| 1981 | | 429,000 |
| 1980 | | 390,000 |
| 1979 | | 370,000 |
| 1978 | | 350,000 |
| 1977 | | 300,000 |
| 1975 | | 250,000 |
| 1972 | | 200,000 |
| 1968 | | 100,000 |
| 1959 | | 50,000 |
| 1947 | | 10,000 |
| 1940 | | 1000 |
| 1938 | | 97 |

*Source:* Data from *Employee Handbook: Working Together,* Auto Club South, 1998.

the offices shifted to the receptionist, queuing members via computers to the desired departments for services. This eliminated a great deal of customer confusion about which service representative to see, as well as preventing out-of-sequence servicing conditions, leading to fewer dissatisfying customer encounters.

AAA initiated Express Desks for members needing only maps, tour books, or pre-marked travel planning packages to speed up service for members and to minimize waiting time. AAA also implemented cell phone rental vending machines (similar to soft-drink vending machines). Members can rent a cell phone for up to 15 days at a nominal fee and use a credit card for the transaction. These innovations set AAA apart from other travel services operations, resulting in faster service and one-stop shopping for each trip.

## Competitive Differentiation

Competitors often attempt to undermine AAA products and services, portraying themselves in their advertising as superior to AAA for a particular product or service. AAA is responding by constantly repositioning itself, all the while trying to secure special negotiated vendor contracts (e.g., cruise lines, tour operators, attractions, etc.) in order to gain a market edge. AAA strives to create service superiority by promoting the famed Trip-Tik© travel guide, a copyrighted service that no other travel company can access or duplicate, although many have tried to imitate it with very cumbersome computer printouts.

AAA offers one-stop shopping and bundled services to members, resulting in greater customer value as well as incremental income gains. While emergency road service (ERS) continues to be the core service of AAA, oil companies and automobile producers continue to offer their own roadside services. These competitive inroads into such a key market have led AAA to improve and enhance their ERS call centers, dispatching, and on-the-road servicing.

## Current Situation

The January 1, 1998, merger placed tremendous pressure on systems, procedures, computers, and functional departments. Both clubs experienced computer hardware/software operating problems, and work hours extended well beyond the norm. Computers in the East Florida office were used for tracking members entering the AAA office. Logical waiting/queuing service and sequencing, identification of services requested at check-in (no more guessing games and missed sales opportunities), and better servicing would follow.

After computerizing hotel reservations were added, bookings tripled daily, and commissions increased threefold. Sales and revenues increased nearly three times from 1997 for the East Florida operation due to specific contracts (i.e., hotel chains and specific hotels). This improved operation also attracted additional members and new customers for services.

Marketing exploded on the AAA East Florida coast with new products, increased service level demands, an expanded list of vendors, internal market and travel packaging with significant discounts, discount tickets for attractions (previously limited to the greater Orlando area), and in-office on-display/pickup purchasing at the customer's fingertips.

Internally, this created increasing pressures on the staff to be more travel-product knowledgeable, to produce faster output, and to diversify their skills, such as gaining computer software literacy. Today's AAA employee must be able to juggle travel routes and destinations (maps and Trip-Tiks), make hotel reservations, and sell attraction tickets, traveler's checks, luggage, and other services to create a one-stop travel and entertainment shopping experience. Training, education, workshops, and seminars all provide means for equipping office personnel with the skills necessary to deal with market dynamics and customer demands while achieving the corporate goals of sales, profits, and productivity.

The job criteria required to build and enhance value include expanded skills and the ability to perform multiple tasks. AAA service workers are also being held more accountable for their ability to add value, as illustrated by some of the examples below:

- Offer a variety of products and services (e.g., hotel reservations — one reservation for every two Trip-Tiks, traveler's checks, attraction tickets, luggage)
- Increase speed of service (minimal wait time)
- Acknowledge customer within 60 seconds

## The ACS Vision and Mission

Auto Club South's vision continues to focus on creating greater value for its members through membership development/retention and developing its employees. ACS has a threefold vision that includes the following:

1.  We believe that highly knowledgeable, motivated, and enthusiastic employees are the foundation of our success.
2.  We are committed to continuous improvement in employee satisfaction, job skills, and advancement.
3.  We must avoid increasing our members' dues while enhancing their perception of value.

ACS's mission is grounded in a number of strategic priorities. These priorities are built on its vision by emphasizing the following:

- Determine and focus on the most appropriate array of services for its members; currently only 7% of ACS members are ACS insured and only 20% are travel clients.
- Implement methods to improve member and customer access to services by extending hours via a telephone center, providing "fun" activities in branches so that wait times seem shorter, and designing the ACS website specifically for customers and members.
- Work toward dues stabilization for members.
- Implement the "people plan": create a more enjoyable and rewarding work experience, provide opportunities for improving job skills and career advancement, enhance employee communications via bulletin boards, a FICS-IT box for suggestions, and the *ACS Connections* (official employee publication).

## Customer Service

Although once known strictly as a motor club, AAA has diversified over the years into other travel-related businesses. For example, AAA now features an insurance agency representing a menu of carriers throughout the U.S. to provide insurance for auto, home, flood, life, and long-term care, as well as annuities and other coverage for its members (revenues are for internal operations use). This move and others were designed to position AAA as a comprehensive travel services company that offers a full-service travel agency, traveler's checks, tickets to Florida's popular attractions, co-branded VISA cards, vehicle financing and warranties, and even luggage.

AAA's bi-monthly magazine, *Going Places,* created additional opportunities to sell more products and services. Promoting these expanded services to its members though *Going Places* in addition to customer mailings helped stimulate demand for traditional travel services as well as some of their tertiary products.

Customer service is now being closely watched to monitor such conditions as lobby queuing and service order fulfillment. Regular follow-up with members booking hotels, cruises, etc. with AAA is also conducted. Customer satisfaction levels are continually reviewed. A customer satisfaction goal of 97% has been achieved in spite of exponential changes in staffing and systems. Much of the improvement in customer satisfaction came from listening to the customer. The customer was telling ACS that the following service attributes were important:

- *Quality:* products and services offering reliability and accuracy; good reputation
- *Functionality:* availability of services and products at any office; ease of use of services; access to online service; interactive, exchangeable, and refundable services and products with personal service
- *Deployment (delivery systems):* self-serve, vending capabilities, user friendly, computer ease of use, simplicity, card-swipe technology, voice-activated verification

This direct feedback from the customer resulted in rapid changes in systems and procedures. Process improvement occurred by closing the "gaps" between AAA's customers' perceived service quality requirements and the ability of their systems to satisfy those requirements.

## Performance

While the business economics improve through mergers, the actual number of independent clubs has steadily declined, resulting in much larger club memberships. The ACS merger effectively created the 19th largest travel agency among all travel agencies and the largest inside the AAA family of clubs (see Table C1.3). As of 1997, ACS revenues were about $218 million, and East Florida revenues were approximately $38 million. For 1998, the combined projections were in excess of $270 million revenues, and by the year 2000 revenues are expected to exceed $300 million.

**Table C1.3. Ranking of AAA Clubs
Among *Travel Weekly's*
Top 50 Travel Agencies**

| Rank | AAA Club |
|------|----------|
| 19 | AAA Auto Club South (ACS) |
| 29 | AAA Michigan/Wisconsin |
| 31 | AAA Cincinnati |
| 35 | AAA Carolinas |
| 37 | California State Auto Association |
| 47 | AAA Minnesota/Iowa |

Source: *ACS Connections*, August, 1998;
*Travel Weekly*, 1998.

## Future Strategy

AAA is a sleeping giant that is awakening. Strategic planning is now in place at National AAA, where the future marketplace outlook is being reassessed and new products and services are being sought which will allow AAA to be a key player in the growing travel services market. Over 1000 local offices will grow and expand in size and staff to combat competition, providing local service levels with toll-free calling capabilities. Satellite travel technology, on-board in-car CRT computers will provide state-of-the-art travel /directional assistance and emergency communications. Consortium programs with the U.S. government, General Motors test projects, and other high-tech capabilities will rapidly appear on the daily car travel and operational scene.

ASC recently launched a new initiative called "Beyond 2000 — A Galaxy of Opportunities", a plan to guide the club into the next millennium. As part of this initiative, new product and service introductions along with new locations are being highlighted. These changes will require greater staff expertise to fill the ever-changing AAA service positions.

## Questions

1. What technological breakthroughs will AAA need to align with future customer travel needs and requirements?

2. Strategy is the process of aligning the organization with changes in its environment. What were the major changes in the travel and financial services environment, and how did AAA respond to these?
3. Evaluate AAA's ability to create value for its members.
4. Visualize what AAA strategies of today will look like by the year 2005.

# Case 2. Ethyl Corporation — Becoming Customer-Oriented*

## Background

E thyl Corporation is a $1.4 billion petroleum additives company based in Richmond, VA. Ethyl develops, manufactures, and markets such products as lubricant packages for crankcase oils, automatic transmission fluids, and industrial gear lubricants, as well as a complete line of gasoline, diesel, and jet fuel and related fuel performance additives. Ethyl Corporation commands a 22% share of the global petroleum additives market, against such worldwide competitors as Lubrizol, Paramins, Shell, and Chevron's Oronite division, as well as several regional firms throughout the world. Ethyl's customer base spans the globe and includes such notable firms as Exxon, Mobil, Chevron, BP, Texaco, Shell, and other national oil firms in virtually every country.

The history of Ethyl Corporation came about through the development of a lead-based additive to reduce engine knock in gasoline engines in the 1920s and 1930s. The phrase, "Fill it up with Ethyl," resounded throughout the decades well into the 1980s, when fuel systems needed to change from lead-dependent fuels to the lead-free, catalytic converter systems used today.

* This case was prepared by Richard J. Chvala, Global Market Manager, Ethyl Corporation.

Ethyl Corporation grew from that first fuel-additive beginning into a conglomerate *Fortune* 200 company in the late 1980s. Ethyl Corporation has since spun off NYSE companies James River Corporation, a paper company now known as Fort James; Tredegar Industries, a plastics, packaging, and software firm; First Colony Life Insurance, which has since been sold to GE Capital; Whitby Pharmaceuticals, which was acquired by American Home Products; and Albemarle Corporation, a $1.3 billion specialty chemical company.

## Improvement Efforts

The success of Ethyl's spun-off sibling companies developed from a common link developed in the mid-1980s. Ethyl's board of directors charged the company executive committee with the task of developing the marketing ability of the myriad of mid-level managers positioned in each of the conglomerate's divisions. That directive gave way to the Marketing Forum, a once-per-quarter assemblage of the 50 to 60 top executives from each of these groups. The Forum would meet for 2 to 3 days at a time to review trends in such areas as competitive advantage, customer satisfaction, creating value-added service, and marketing strategy.

The Marketing Forum would enlist guest speakers for each of the sessions. Over the 3-year engagement of the Forum, such notables as Philip Kotler of Northwestern University, Michael Porter of Harvard, Marion Moore and Dan Laughun of Duke, and Tom Peters provided direction to the Ethyl Marketing Forum.

## New Service-Added Direction

Ethyl's management team used the Forum's study to redirect the strategic intent from a product orientation toward services valued by the customer. One such strategy session focused on how to assist customers beyond the product-need level ... actually talking with customer executives to determine what assistance Ethyl Corporation might provide in solving a customer's strategic problems. The impact of such a strategy would ultimately produce the following benefits:

- Helped determine and qualify Ethyl's core competencies.

- Established a team system to reveal customer needs (their value equation), to determine Ethyl's potential participation in solving that need, and to communicate that assistance value to the customer.
- Helped identify those support services that do not impact the customer and therefore may be reduced.
- Established lines of communication between executives of Ethyl and customers.
- Honed problem-solving skills beyond product venues.
- Platformed non-product synergies with alliance customers.

This program was first tested with two major customers who had recently undergone either a joint venture or merger with a previous competitor in the petroleum industry. Ethyl Corporation brought to customers the expertise of previous acquisition experience (Ethyl acquired Amoco Additives in 1992 and Texaco additives in 1995, successfully blending those organizations into the Ethyl framework). Ethyl leadership met with the customers' executives to map out the best approaches to integrating their new ventures. In the case of the customer acquiring a competitor, that customer enlisted Ethyl's help in establishing information resources (computer) integration, Human Resources policies, and facilitation of executive team communications and strategy synergy.

The joint venture customer took a different approach. In that case, Ethyl's expertise in SAP (the computer global logistics integration) and SMI (Supplier-Managed Inventory) systems were offered to the customer at a request from that customer's management team. The efforts by several Ethyl team members in coordination with the customer's teams provided a "speed up" in installing and utilizing the SAP system, as well as substantial savings in logistics and inventory control by way of the SMI program. In 1997, the customer named Ethyl Corporation as their "Supplier of the Year" for both products and the value-added service involved in their joint venture.

## Future

This type of service approach is completely new in the petroleum industry, and, with the exception of the computer industry, somewhat unheard of anywhere else. The goal of this style of value-added service is

*Perspective:* See entire business flow from our customers' point of view.

*Focus:* Concentrate on key products and services.

*Leverage:* Use our counselor salesperson skills to leverage and cross-sell.

*Alignment:* Organize ourselves to mirror customers' businesses and products.

*Quality:* Deliver highest quality products and services — best practices

*Speed:* Shorten time cycle of product and market research, design, development.

Superior product and service leadership are critical to our customer alliances and maintaining the preferred supplier position — and it is vital as we secure long-term positions and increased share of a customer's business over the years.

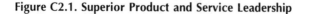

**Figure C2.1. Superior Product and Service Leadership**

to go beyond the call for quality products and to communicate beyond the ranks of sales and purchasing to gain insight of the customer's strategic problems. What Ethyl Corporation has been able to perform is a service for customers' top management teams — providing not products but peace of mind, as companies undergo the challenges of the competitive 1990s.

Ethyl Corporation further integrated this customer value approach into an actual system to explore customers' needs via a sales force trained to identify such needs and then transform that needs analysis into a team-based response unit. The tactical strategy, designated as the Ethyl Customer Service Approach, is illustrated in Figure C2.1. The approach established the following requirements for it to work effectively:

- Creating a framework to identify and match core competencies of Ethyl to the customer's problems and needs
- Training of sales people to identify customer issues and communicate solution responses upward in the customer's organization
- Development of customer-specific teams to support the salesperson in designing and delivering added-value solutions to the customer's organization
- Providing resources at support levels to guarantee quality in delivery of value added benefits to customers
- Developing a process to establish the customer's viewpoint regarding the value provided to underscore profit initiatives

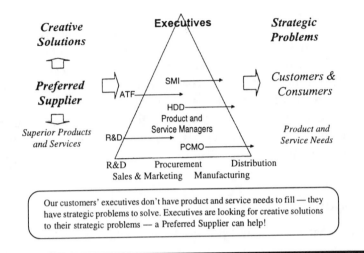

**Figure C2.2. Ethyl's Customer Service Approach**

The customer's benefits of such a program include, but are not limited, to:

- The program provides insights and ideas on strategic issues from a different perspective — a consulting approach rather than vending approach.
- The program serves as a solid foundation and trusted sounding board for customers in these times of significant change and continued consolidation — a long-term view.
- The program shares core competencies, world-class experiences, and global perspectives — acquisitions, supply chain, R&D, SMI, channel marketing, SAP, etc.
- The program changes priorities and promotes cost management (i.e., stop doing things that are not needed by the customer).
- The program strengthens customers' perceptions of the company in the value chain as a consistent, long-term supplier of superior products, service, and value.
- The program improves a customer's ability to improve and sustain a competitive advantage.

In Figure C2.2, the model for managing the service level for customers is detailed for each operational group. One might elect to develop the level of service within a customer's logistics department at a higher level, if the company sees that a core competency is logistics. If purchasing is a weakness for the supplier, then service efforts in that area may be reduced until the supplier's purchasing competencies are increased.

This process of adding value outside the parameters of product delivery encourages a new round of competition. The company that best understands its core competencies and delivers these benefits to the customer will possess the competitive advantage into the next decade.

## Questions

1. What benefits and drawbacks exist when a product-oriented company elects to offer expanded services to capture market share?
2. What might be Ethyl Corporation's competitors' strategy and tactics to defend against this new strategy?
3. Evaluate Ethyl's bid to become customer oriented. Did they succeed? Why or why not?

# Case 3. Glaxo Wellcome, Inc. — Internal Marketing Leads to Customer Responsiveness[*]

## Background

**L**ondon-based Glaxo Wellcome, plc, is an industry leader in discovering, developing, and producing innovative medicines that prevent and treat disease. The company operations are divided into five regions worldwide, with approximately 54,000 employees, 76 operating companies, over 50 manufacturing sites, and over 150 markets supplied. The company has seven products ranked in the world top 50 (IMS data, December 1997). Glaxo Wellcome concentrates in the following therapeutic areas: respiratory (Serevent®, Flovent®, Flonase®), viral infections (Valtrex®), gastrointestinal (Zantac®, Tritec®), central nervous system (Imitrex®, Amerge®, Wellbutrin SR®, Lamictal®), bacterial infections (Ceftin®, Raxar®), hospital and critical care (Nimbex®, Ultiva®), oncology (Zofran®), dermatology (Aclovate®, Temovate®), and cardiovascular (Trandate®).

---

[*] This case was prepared by Brett A. Gordon, MBA, and Pam A. Gordon, MBA, from the Pedagogus Group Consulting Firm.

The U.S. represents the largest market driving much of the company's outstanding growth for more than a decade. Glaxo Wellcome, Inc., the U.S. subsidiary, is located in Research Triangle Park, NC, and is actively involved in research and development, biotechnology, clinical development, and product supply.

Glaxo Wellcome is the product of a successful merger that took place in March of 1995. Both individual companies (Glaxo and Burroughs Wellcome) provided impressive pedigrees; each had roots established well over 100 years ago. Through the years, both companies enjoyed recognition as pioneers in many areas of science and medicine, leading up to their joining forces for the future and becoming one of the most successful research-based companies of this century.

While research, development, and marketing of innovative pharmaceuticals still provide the cornerstone of the business, Glaxo Wellcome, Inc., realized that service quality was an additional, important component in the success equation. For Glaxo Wellcome, Inc., creating customer value transcends all business areas; it is their new paradigm for the late 1990s.

## Customer Response Center

Glaxo Wellcome's commitment to understanding and meeting the needs of internal and external customers was formally written into their 1997 corporate goals and objectives plan. Part of the plan was to implement a Customer Response Center (CRC), which would be capable of handling product and general company information calls. In addition, they hoped to increase customer satisfaction and loyalty by 50% above previous levels. The overall mission of the Customer Response Center would be to increase Glaxo Wellcome's competitive advantage by maximizing the value of each customer contact.

During the analysis phase of the project, the CRC team interviewed 75 internal departments and 39 members of the sales force to gain a better understanding of why customers contact Glaxo Wellcome. From this inquiry, it was learned that there are approximately 1.5 million calls placed to Glaxo Wellcome, Inc., every month and that there are 1100 different types of contacts from customers to the company. The CRC team took those contact types and grouped them into 29 categories (general corporate information, product/therapeutic questions from healthcare professionals and non-healthcare professionals, etc.). They were then rated and ranked relative to costs and benefits — to Glaxo Wellcome as well as to the customer. Subsets were then identified for the purpose of initiating three phases of implementation: those functions that were to be implemented in phase I, ending in October 1997; phase II, which was the period 6 to 12 months out from October; and phase III, which covered the implementation taking place more than one year from October.

On October 1, 1997, the Customer Response Center was launched. During the first month of operation, the CRC responded to over 3500 customer inquiries; 68% of these calls were resolved at the first point of contact. This marked a significant improvement from earlier statistics that indicated that the average call was transferred six times. In addition, the service level, which is measured by the number of calls answered within 20 seconds, exceeded 90%.

Glaxo Wellcome recognized that employees were its most valuable asset; therefore, just as the CRC was designed to respond efficiently and thoroughly to customers' questions, the Employee Response Center (ERC) was developed to provide the same level of response to the employees. As of January 12, 1998, trained ERC representatives were able to provide timely, accurate answers and referrals to employees who inquired about:

- General payroll issues
- Direct deposit, tax changes, employment verification, and personal data changes
- General management policy
- Human resources procedures (e.g., hiring, transfers)
- Company programs (e.g., matching gifts, tuition reimbursement)

The Employee Response Center hours of operation are 8:00 a.m. to 8:00 p.m., Monday through Friday, and the center can be accessed internally, locally or by long distance.

During March, in order to support the increase in call volume, the CRC installed an on-line reporting capability, which measured the center's performance every 30 seconds and provided key information to representatives in seconds. Through proper project planning and execution, the additional call volume had a minimal impact on operations and resulted in the CRC continuing to provide a high service level of 88% of the calls being answered within 20 seconds.

The CRC took responsibility for 43,000 customer calls in the month of May, with continued growth expected in the months ahead. Customer satisfaction surveys from employees utilizing the center provided valuable input on ways in which the CRC could improve service in the future. The company reviewed potential alternatives for the CRC's voice messaging menus to provide more accurate selections and reduce the time to reach a Customer Response representative skilled to answer the customer's inquiry. The CRC also revised the call-monitoring process in an effort to improve quality of service and provide valuable input to the response representative as to ways they could improve service delivery to their customers.

During the month of June 1998, the CRC handled 45,000 inbound phone contacts and answered 87% of the calls within 20 seconds. Also, a variety of projects were finalized or implemented, further reinforcing the goal of providing value to customers. Included in these projects, was the launch of a computer software package that enhanced the CRC representatives' ability to service customer inquiries. Web-based communication from customers began migrating into the CRC.

## Future

The center is beginning two pilot programs for the end of 1998. The first is a video conferencing pilot with 250 physicians promoting some of the many pharmaceutical products Glaxo Wellcome manufactures. This pilot officially began June 1, 1998, and represents both inbound and outbound contacts with physicians. The project, utilizing the latest in communications technologies, has the potential to increase reach and frequency to important physicians when utilized in conjunction with field sales efforts.

The second pilot assists physicians who contact the CRC to locate a Glaxo Wellcome representative. This pilot also includes follow-up to physicians not seen by field representatives. Both pilots have been established to increase customer satisfaction and grow revenue. In addition, future projects include: e-mail correspondence, telesales, fulfillment automation, and enhanced functionality to improve telephone and data transmission with medical information.

The Customer Response Center remains committed to improving itself continually by carefully reviewing employee and customer survey information. Thus far, the company is pleased to report that the satisfaction level continues to increase dramatically since they began measuring results.

## Questions

1. Herb Kelleher, Southwest Airlines' CEO, once remarked, "Our employees come first, the customer second." Discuss the rationale for his philosophy and how it applies to Glaxo's introduction of the Customer Response Center.
2. Based on Glaxo's experience, how would you say internal marketing affects external customer expectations?
3. What are some other approaches that Glaxo could take to create greater employee satisfaction?

# Case 4. The Grateful Dead — Customer Loyalty and Service Quality[*]

What does it take to retain customers and create loyalty in them? This critical question faces all organizations today as customers have a multitude of choices for satisfying their needs and wants. Perhaps we can learn some valuable lessons not from a *Fortune* 500 company nor a company with considerable public data. Perhaps, instead, we can learn something valuable from an unlikely organization in an unlikely industry — the legendary rock band, the Grateful Dead. This choice is made because of the volatility of the music industry, an industry where bands come and go on a daily basis, an industry where response to rapid change is a requirement and has been for many years. The Grateful Dead was also chosen because the author has been actively observing this band for more than 25 years and is well acquainted with its unique history and customer service.

Throughout their career, starting in 1965, the Grateful Dead grew in popularity until 1995, when they disbanded after the death of lead guitarist, Jerry Garcia. They started out playing in a pizza parlor in Palo Alto, CA, for $50 a night, and by 1973 they played to the largest crowd

---

[*] This case was prepared by F. Barry Barnes, Ph.D., Assistant Professor of Management in the School of Business and Entrepreneurship at Nova Southeastern University, Fort Lauderdale, FL.

in U.S. history (estimated at 600,000) at Watkins Glen, NY. This is nearly twice as large as the crowd at Woodstock 4 years earlier. In 1991, total attendance at their concerts was 1.8 million, with an over 99% occupancy rate. Demand for tickets was always strong, and sales reached $52.5 million in 1994, the band's last full year of touring.

While these numbers are impressive, they do not capture the remarkable fan loyalty that lies behind them. The bond between the Grateful Dead and the Deadheads (as their fans came to be known) was often a lifetime relationship. Some Deadheads even changed their lifestyles to better match the Sixties values of music, peace, and harmony. Many Deadheads moved to the San Francisco Bay area, where more concerts were played each year than anywhere else. Others planned vacations to match the band's touring schedule. As many as 2000 Deadheads ordered tickets for *every* concert during the summer tours of 20 to 25 shows. Over the years, a virtual community of friends developed among the Deadheads as they moved from concert to concert year after year and became a "professional" audience. Many fans saw hundreds of Dead concerts over the years. Bill Walton, former basketball great and sportscaster, saw 600!

What could lead to this level of customer loyalty? What were the expectations of the Deadheads? How did the Dead match or exceed those expectations with the concert experience? Deadheads, like all consumers, have a set of expectations that determine their level of satisfaction with any product or service and the process of obtaining it. This set includes such things as the reliability or consistency of the product/service, its availability and accessibility, standards regarding tangible aspects of the product/service, concerns about the empathy and understanding shown regarding the process of obtaining the product/service, and responsiveness to customer needs and wants. How this set of expectations is met initially determines whether a customer is satisfied and retained, and over time it determines how loyal the customer will be for the long haul. If we examine each of these expectations held by Deadheads for the Grateful Dead, perhaps we can begin to understand the remarkable bond that developed between them.

## Reliability

Deadheads were looking for more than a canned performance that sounded just like the record. They wanted live, improvisational music, music that required their attention in the here and now, music that was adventurous. The Dead were happy to oblige. Their music was an amalgam of folk, bluegrass, blues, reggae, country, jazz, and rock that had been born in the heart of the Sixties' hippie revolution, yet continued to develop and grow through the years. No two concerts were ever the same, and the songs they played never followed a predictable sequence. Their active musical repertoire was 150 songs at any one time. Each song performance was different from every other performance due to the improvisational nature of their playing. In 1991, this author attended six concerts in 7 nights and saw more than 100 different songs performed with only two songs being repeated. Thus, the live Grateful Dead concert experience could always be relied on to offer a unique product, one which continued to keep demand high and fans coming back for more.

Reliability for Deadheads was also concerned with the quality and consistency of the performances. When things went just right at a Dead concert, there was a remarkable synergy between the band members as they played and between the audience, as well, that created a feeling of joy and ecstasy that is difficult to describe. This was often referred to as the X-factor. The band was always seeking this special synergy or X-factor, and although they did not always find it, Deadheads wanted to be there when they did. As concert promoter Bill Graham said, "The Grateful Dead aren't the best at what they do, they're the *only* ones who do what they do."

Reliability of performances was also demonstrated by the attitude of the band members who were dedicated to playing as well as they possibly could at every performance. During an interview in 1988, band members said, "We're just now starting to get good at this. We're just now where we wanted to be musically 20 years ago. Even an off night isn't too bad these days, but in the past we could be really bad." And rhythm guitarist and vocalist Bob Weir said, "We chase the music just as hard and as fast as we can." Fans knew this was true and respected the continual effort by the band to excel in every concert.

Finally, reliability was demonstrated by the constancy of the musicians in the band. When the band was formed in 1965, the founding members were Jerry Garcia, lead guitar and vocals; Bob Weir, rhythm guitar and vocals; Ron "Pigpen" McKernan, keyboards and vocals; Phil Lesh, bass and vocals; and Billy Kreutzman, drums. A second drummer, Mickey Hart, was added in 1968. During their 30-year career, the personnel of the band stayed remarkably constant. Only on keyboards did they have any turnover in personnel. In 1995, during their last concert tour, five of the musicians had been playing together for 27 years, a remarkable achievement for any organization, and a further guarantee of consistency and reliability of performance.

## Availability

Because their music was so varied and each performance unique, many Deadheads were not content to simply see the Dead perform once every few years and then fill in the time between listening to their records. They wanted the live experience and the possibility of the X-factor, and they wanted lots of it! The Grateful Dead again obliged them. For 30 years the Dead played an average of 77 concerts a year, more than 2300 in all. This is completely unlike other successful rock bands that tour only every few years to support a new album. Moreover, concerts were typically 2-1/2 to 3 hours long, but could even run 4 hours. On a few occasions, they played all night long and breakfast was served to the audience at dawn! Recognizing their fans were spread across the country and around the world, the Dead concert schedule typically included three tours across North America every year. They also toured Europe several times and even played at the Great Pyramid in Egypt. With this kind of availability, it is easy to see why fans could see so many shows.

## Tangibles

In order to continue to satisfy customers, tangible aspects of any product or service must improve over time. This is another aspect of customer satisfaction at which the Dead excelled. Their aim was to create the best possible sound at every concert, to reproduce their music as faithfully as possible, and to minimize listener fatigue produced by noise and distortion in concert sound systems. As a result, the Dead always had the most technologically advanced sound system in the world. In 1968, they helped establish a research and development group, Alembic, which constantly pushed the sonic envelope and created many innovations now used in all concert sound systems. In the early 1970s, the Dead pioneered the first stereo concert sound system, the Wall of Sound, which used no stage monitors. The Wall of Sound weighed 38 tons, took as many as 40 employees to maintain, and required four tractor-trailers to transport it. It was so cumbersome and expensive to maintain

($100,000 per month) that the band took their only extended break and did not tour in 1975. In 1991, the Dead pioneered the first fully digital concert sound system. The result of their efforts was the best concert sound in the world and the establishment of new industry standards. Deadheads quickly came to expect this high level of sound quality from all concerts but were often disappointed at concerts of other bands.

Another tangible aspect to the Grateful Dead concert experience was the lighting. The Dead were never concerned with creating a show or spectacle in their performances. There were no costumes, smoke, explosions, or giant props that might distract from the music. But, with their roots in the psychedelic Sixties, light shows were always a part of their concerts. The lighting effects were always subtle and sensitive to the music.

Another unique characteristic of the tangibles associated with the Dead was their tickets. When they began selling tickets via mail order (see Responsiveness section), the Dead began to add artwork to the tickets. Each concert bore a different Grateful Dead symbol, ranging from roses to dancing bears to skeletons. Each ticket thus became a piece of memorabilia for the fans. New Year's Eve concerts with the Grateful Dead became an annual party in San Francisco for Deadheads, hosted by concert promoter Bill Graham. The tickets for the New Year's Eve shows evolved over the years into spectacular pieces of art (see Figure C4.1).

## Empathy

A unique situation with their fans arose very early in the career of the Grateful Dead. Due to the improvisational nature of their music and the quest for the X-factor, fans began to record their performances clandestinely and then share them with friends. Although the band recorded their songs on record albums, the studio always failed to capture the dynamics of their live performances. The band recognized this, and for many years turned a blind eye to the covert taping. Finally, in 1984, the Dead officially recognized the "taping community" and set aside a "taping section" at each concert with the stipulation that, "Audio taping is for non-commercial home use only." As lead guitarist Jerry Garcia said, "When we're finished with the music, they can have it."

The sanctioned (and unsanctioned) recording of their performances has led to tapes being available for nearly every one of their concerts and has made them the most recorded band in history. It is not uncommon for fans to have tape collections of hundreds of their concerts. A huge

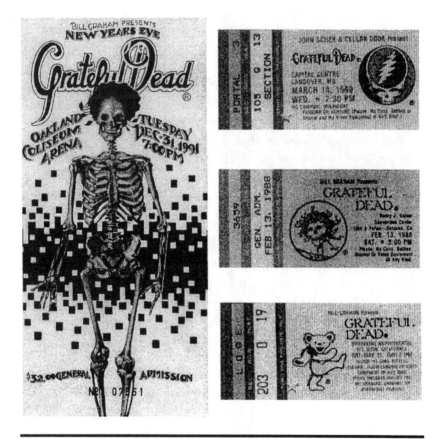

**Figure C4.1. Grateful Dead Concert Tickets** (Reprinted courtesy of GDP, Inc.)

community of tape traders has arisen through the years which trades the tapes with no money involved. This embodies the values of the Grateful Dead and the San Francisco psychedelic scene of the Sixties, as they gave away their music despite a recording career that included only one top-ten hit single. Their customer-friendly taping policy is a clear indication of their empathy toward Deadheads and has been adopted by a growing number of bands in the 1990s.

The Dead also established a Trouble line, which gave Deadheads a real person to talk to about problems with tickets, venue security, or any problem related to the band. This understanding by the Grateful Dead organization of the trials of getting tickets and traveling to see the band showed a remarkable degree of empathy and was another element that strengthened the bond between Deadheads and the Dead.

One decision by the band which was intended to be empathetic to Deadheads led to extremely challenging situations for the Dead as the following of fans grew. When there were fewer fans, before 1985, the band allowed Deadheads to sell food and T-shirts in the parking lots before and after shows. Fans freely used Grateful Dead logos and icons without paying royalties. An unintended consequence was growing numbers of people who would come to the concerts with no intention of seeing the show but just to hang out in the parking lot vending area. This created logistical nightmares for the band and local officials who had to manage and police the crowds. A second unintended consequence was the loss of tens of thousands of dollars in merchandise sales and licensing fees to the band. Members of the Dead organization worked closely with local officials to minimize problems with the crowds and urged fans not to come to concerts without tickets. And, in 1992, they began to protect their trademarks and logos more carefully and undertook an ambitious licensing program, often enlisting vendors from the parking lot scene.

## Responsiveness

As the Dead's popularity increased over the years, it became more and more of a challenge for Deadheads to obtain tickets. This was especially true if you wanted to see a concert in a city other than your own. In response to the concern expressed by many traveling Deadheads regarding purchasing tickets, the Dead set up a telephone hotline and established Grateful Dead Ticket Sales (GDTS) in 1983. The hotline was a recording of information about upcoming concert tours, special events, and band member information. This allowed Deadheads to easily determine when and where the Dead would be playing next and how to obtain tickets. GDTS quickly became responsible for selling up to 50% of the tickets for each venue directly to Deadheads via mail order, usually a month or more before they went on sale at the local venue. The combination of the hotline and GDTS allowed Deadheads to find out when the band was playing and then easily order tickets in advance, a very responsive move by the band.

The Dead was responsive to fans in many other ways, too. Many Deadheads believe that the music itself and even the X-factor were elements of responsiveness to the fans at concerts. Sometimes the music itself was clearly changed in response to Deadhead requests. One particular song, "Keep Your Day Job", just was not well liked by fans, and after 4 years it was dropped from the repertoire in 1986 at the request of Deadheads!

The Grateful Dead continue to be responsive to their fans even today, 3 years after they disbanded. They continue to release recordings at the unprecedented rate of three or four albums every year. The band's live performances from their 30-year career continue to be in great demand, and one ongoing series of recordings is Dick's Picks. For this series, Grateful Dead tape archivist, Dick Latvala, seeks considerable input from Deadheads, then chooses three or four concerts from the tape vaults to release each year. The Dick's Picks series is sold only through mail order from Grateful Dead Merchandising. Sales estimates for these albums range from 50,000 to 100,000 copies each, demonstrating an ongoing desire by the fans to continue listening to the music.

## Summary

Today, more than ever before, retaining customers and gaining their loyalty are the keys to business survival and profitability as we begin the new millennium. We often look to large organizations such as Microsoft, Ford, or Southwest Airlines when we seek models for loyal, satisfied customers. But, one organization that at its peak employed less than 100 full-time employees had a level of retention and loyalty in its customers that is only dreamed of by most organizations. Deadheads, like all customers, weighed their experiences and compared them to their expectations. What they found for 30 years was a continually surprising level of reliability, availability, tangibles, empathy, and responsiveness in their dealings with the Grateful Dead. Jerry Garcia once said, "I'd like to see what can be created from joy." Having attended 193 Dead concerts over 20 years, this author believes that the Grateful Dead consistently created superior customer value and experiences for their fans.

## Questions

1.  How would you rank the importance of the five service quality characteristics exhibited by the Grateful Dead? Why?
2.  How can these characteristics be used effectively by other organizations?
3.  Now that the band has stopped touring, can the remaining Grateful Dead organization continue to retain the Deadheads and earn their loyalty? What steps will they have to take?

# Case 5. Harrah's Entertainment — Brand Building*

Gambling is very big business in the U.S.; in 1996, industry revenues exceeded $500 billion, up from $17 billion in 1976. A major competitor is Harrah's Entertainment with 16 casino locations. Over the last 60 years, the Harrah's name has become synonymous with customer-focused, high-quality casino entertainment in more locations than any other competitor in its industry.

Harrah's is both differentiating itself from its competitors and generating loyalty in customer gambling behavior. Rather than competing on the traditional casino attributes of location and facilities alone, it focuses on providing assurance to gambling customers that they will enjoy an experience they have come to know, trust, and appreciate. With this brand identity, Harrah's believes that it is positioned to provide consistent value and a reliable, predictable experience for its customers.

Harrah's expects that competitors will have difficulty duplicating its strategy because its many locations give it more opportunities to build

---

* This case was prepared by Dr. William J. McDonald, general manager of New Thinking (http://www.newthinking.com) and author of two books: *Direct Marketing: An Integrated Approach* and *Cases in Strategic Marketing Management*. He has also published numerous articles in academic journals and industry magazines and created software packages for marketing planning, direct marketing, and international business. He holds Ph.D. and Master's degrees from the University of Chicago and a Master's of Management from Northwestern University.

relationships with customers. Many markets in which Harrah's has casinos have a limited number of licenses, most of which have been allocated, including the major regional markets of Lake Tahoe, Atlantic City, and Las Vegas. Today, one third of the U.S. population lives within a 3-hour drive of a Harrah's casino.

Beyond its strategy based on geographic distribution, Harrah's has the technological tools, knowledge, relationships, and experience with customers to offer a fundamentally different value proposition than its competitors can, all of which give customers a unique reason to choose Harrah's, not just in one market, but across its entire network of casinos.

As never before, casinos are seeking to know who their customers are, building vast databases, and using direct-mail marketing techniques to target specific people. Harrah's is the best example of this approach to casino hotel marketing. In this very competitive industry, casinos need a good database, basically to steal customers from the competition.

The competitive situation for casinos also includes a move toward joining gambling and other entertainment activities. Like Harrah's, most of the higher quality gaming companies position themselves as entertainment companies. Even in Las Vegas, the largest gambling location in the world, the money left there by visitors is channeled into other forms of spending because gambling is now part of a larger industry focus, which also includes hotels, restaurants, and shows. As a result, casinos are being transformed into vacation destinations, drawing millions of visitors who are not going to spend all their time putting coins in slots and betting at blackjack tables.

Although the majority of casinos are not marketed as family attractions, they are increasingly positioned as places for adults to bring their families. Several major Las Vegas casinos are promoting themselves as a vacation spot for families by adding theme parks and attractions geared more toward children than adults. As a result, many parents who previously would not have considered Las Vegas as an option for a family vacation are now spending time and money there.

All casinos want those who are 21 and older because that is where they make their money, but parents can bring the kids to family-oriented casino hotels because places such as the MGM Grand have theme parks and arcades. Rather than market to high rollers, casino hotel chain Circus Circus, which includes the Excalibur and Luxor hotel casinos, focuses on family-oriented attractions. With its dolphin tank, white tigers, and video game area, Las Vegas' Mirage Hotel is also family friendly.

# Harrah's Targets Its Best Customers

With a multi-market customer strategy that focuses on those who visit more than one market annually, Harrah's targets the 70% of gamblers who play in more than one market per year. These multi-market players have higher budgets than single-market players, and they make more trips to casinos. To implement the segmentation, Harrah's invested significant time and resources in learning who the best gaming customers are and what it can do to give them a highly satisfying gaming experience.

What if a high roller at a Harrah's casino in Las Vegas walks into a Harrah's casino in Lake Tahoe and expects to be recognized as a good customer? Harrah's solved this problem with its huge database that links all of its casinos. With the database, Harrah's identifies customers who gamble regularly and lose a lot of money, because a casino's success depends on how much money the average guest leaves behind. By tracking these data and developing very targeted offers, Harrah's can, for example, send direct mailings to those customers who visited one of its casinos in the last 30 days. Harrah's then invites them back with special offers. The database can also sort players by earning potential, which is about how much they spend and lose, which helps Harrah's create a marketing campaign to lure these players back. The database can also identify someone who has visited Harrah's casino in the past year and lost a lot of money each time. Harrah's focus on positioning and effectively targeting customers with direct marketing campaigns is classic database marketing.

The Total Gold customer program has increased traffic and retention for Harrah's (a 1% increase in retention is worth $2 million in net profit annually). These customers are given cards and earn points by gambling at any Harrah's casino. The points are redeemable for cash, merchandise, food, lodging, shows, or gaming chips. Harrah's places touch-screen kiosks at each of its casinos, where customers can check on their points or print vouchers redeemable for cash or other goods.

Harrah's also introduced its own VISA card, which funnels points earned as a percent of purchases directly into a member's Total Gold account. By using the card, the customer provides Harrah's with a detailed record of gambling and purchasing preferences, enabling it to solicit that person in more sophisticated ways with its databases.

Regular gamblers, such as those targeted by Harrah's, seldom participate in activities outside of the casino during their trips. This is one of the most dynamic differences between casino vacationers and other types of vacationers. Targeting the former means attracting vacationers to the casino floor, where they spend 3 to 6 hours a day gambling. Also, regular casino hotel guests, in comparison with other pleasure travel hotel guests, spend less time in their hotel rooms and much less time participating in activities available in the casino resort or in the local area — only the activities of walking, swimming in a pool, and sunbathing exceed a 10% participation rate by these people.

## Targeting Families

For family customers, casinos are now one part of a total entertainment experience. In Las Vegas, many casino hotel operators direct their marketing efforts toward families by enlisting architects and designers to create fantasy environments, including Disneyland-style theme properties that have broad appeal and an upscale, "good, clean fun" appearance. Casinos must satisfy the demands their guests have for choice and convenience. That means providing coffee and doughnuts in the morning near the blackjack pit or locating a pizza parlor across from the slot machines, as well as offering convenience and clothing stores, much like a retail shopping mall.

The concept of offering family appeal began in 1969 when Circus Circus opened in Las Vegas. Rather than market to high rollers, it wanted to attract other Americans. Since 1969, Circus Circus Enterprises has also built the Excalibur and Luxor hotel casinos, both with family-oriented attractions. The Luxor is shaped like an Egyptian pyramid with a 10-story replica of the Sphinx at its entrance. Similarly, the Treasure Island casino is a major attraction for family visitors because it has a moat featuring gun battles between full-sized pirate ships. The MGM Grand, the largest hotel in the world, features Las Vegas' first theme park, the MGM Grand Adventures, which has 35 acres of rides and shows, along with a youth activity center where kids can be checked in for supervised activities. The hotel also has a 35,000-square foot midway arcade with video and carnival-style games.

As a result, Las Vegas has managed to increase its number of visitors in tough competitive times by promoting itself as a family vacation spot. In that sense, Las Vegas is not just for gamblers anymore. Nevertheless, for most casino marketers, Las Vegas is still first and foremost considered an adult destination site. The vast majority of casinos do not attempt to market themselves as a family attraction; however, they are increasingly being marketed as places for adults to bring their families.

## Personalized Marketing

Even the more family-oriented hotel casinos use databases to collect information about customer gambling and buying habits and apply that data toward personalized marketing efforts. This helps to ensure that their hotel rooms are occupied by the highest-spending guests possible. For example, Caesar's Palace, with its landmark hotel and casino, is a sophisticated marketing organization. Visitors to Caesar's can marvel at its swank stores shimmering under a ceiling painted like a faux Roman sky, while Caesars' collects enough information for its computers to distill a precise customer profile. Conduits to Caesar's database are everywhere in its huge complex, from slot machines and gambling tables to survey cards in its restaurants and more than 1500 hotel rooms.

Caesar's calculates what a player is likely to spend, examines the incentives competitors offer, and creates special events for the best players. To focus on big spenders, Caesar's uses special interest codes which can show, for example, players who like boxing matches. It looks at when customers last visited, their gambling level, and traffic at its restaurants and shows and segments by sending marketing packages to get them to come back.

Even small-time gamblers who join the Emperor's Club for free get promotions. Caesar's sends them cards that offer a limited-time discount on hotel room rates. For more valued customers, an offer might center on the person's birthday or wedding anniversary and include dinner at one of its nicer restaurants such as the Bacchanal, which has a Roman theme.

At the MGM Grand, databases allow managers to personalize their relationships with customers. Even weekend gamblers enjoy being treated like high rollers, and casino management can confer status on the slot-machine plays and baccarat players alike. At the MGM Grand, returning players are called by name, handed their favorite beverage, and seated in a restaurant they enjoyed before. Similarly, the Golden Nugget casino provides hotel clerks instantaneous access to a customer's gambling history for determining what sort of room or premiums to offer.

## Mixed Results For Casinos

The diverse natures of gaming and entertainment do not automatically guarantee successful combining because each serves different customer needs and each requires different management strategies. Based on the Las Vegas experience, some types of entertainment constitute a better complement to gambling. For example, location-based entertainment such as revues and circuses are good combinations, as is shopping; however, interactive video and feature films are poor complements because they provide experiences similar to the games themselves.

Games, including casino gambling, have recreational value only when people actively engage in them. Playing a game involves behaving according to rules of the game. In contrast, entertainment is not usually defined by formal rules and is not normally interactive. Entertainment is presented to customers in a finished, ready-to-be-enjoyed form. However, because games and entertainment are leisure pastimes, some casino operators assume that gaming is just another form of entertainment. The distinction between games and entertainment is particularly unclear in Las Vegas because games have been packaged as fantasy and presented in conjunction with spectacular floor shows, inexpensive or free food and alcoholic beverages, and outdoor recreation such as golf courses, swimming pools, and tennis courts. Nevertheless, because the core business of casino hotels is gambling, the purpose of entertainment at those locations is to attract people to the games, and any entertainment that detracts from that purpose is a bad fit.

## Questions

1. What do you think about a high roller vs. family focus for casino marketing?
2. What are the advantages and disadvantages of pursuing the gambling vs. family vacation markets?
3. What strategies would you advise Harrah's to use in pursuing the gambling and family attraction markets?
4. What specific price, distribution, promotion, and service elements would you propose, and why?
5. What customer programs would you institute for each of the casino gambling and family entertainment markets, and why?

# Case 6. International Food Ingredients Supplier — Customer Value Analysis*

C ustomer value analysis is more than just a pricing technique or a market research method. It is a strategic marketing tool that audits the customer's needs, helps to position the company in relation to its competitors, and measures perception gaps in the buyer's and vendor's organizations. The example in this case has been drawn from a major chemical manufacturer in international markets and discusses how the customer value audit can be linked to development and implementation of a marketing strategy.

## Supplier Background

This study focuses on the Food Ingredients Division of a major multinational chemical manufacturer. This division markets four product groups in several key countries, as shown in Table C6.1. The complexity of the supplier's operations, brought about by the number of marketed products and the different countries served, can best be described by

---

* This case was prepared by Wolfgang Ulaga, Professor of Marketing at EDHEC Graduate School of Management, Lille, France, and Samir Chacour, a partner with ISOGROUP, an international management consulting firm based in Montreal and Paris.

**Table C6.1. The Supplier's Key
Product Groups and Markets**

| Product Groups | Key Countries |
|---|---|
| Hydrocolloids | U.S. |
| Cultures and dairy ingredients | U.K. |
| Brewery ingredients | Germany |
| Phosphates | France |

referring to Table C6.2, which shows four different levels of businesses in this company's industry. The overall objective of the supplier was to determine its competitive position and define its marketing strategy as a global supplier of food ingredients (D), including specific strategies by product category (B) and by country (C).

A first group of food ingredient manufacturers focuses on a single product category, selling the products only in the home country (e.g., the A in Table C6.2 representing hydrocolloids sold in Germany). A second group of manufacturers sticks to a specific product category which they sell in different countries (e.g., the B in the first row of Table C6.2 representing the sale of cultures and dairy ingredients in all four countries). A third group of suppliers sells different product categories in their home market only (e.g., the C in the first column in Table C6.2 representing all four product categories in the U.S.). Finally, a fourth group of companies can be identified as multi-product, multi-country suppliers, which is the case of the supplier that mandated the study (D in Table C6.2).

# The Example of the Hydrocolloid Business in Germany

Each of the businesses shown in Table C6.2 has its own context, which can be defined in terms of customer types, market characteristics, and specific competitors. For example, if we look at Table C6.2 at hydrocolloids in Germany, customer types include three segments: convenience food manufacturers, ice cream producers, and dairy product manufacturers. To reduce the complexity, our present case study focuses on one customer segment: the demand for hydrocolloids by convenience food manufacturers in Germany.

**Table C6.2. The Supplier's Levels of Business**

| Food Ingredient Group | U.S. | U.K. | Germany | France | All Countries |
|---|---|---|---|---|---|
| Cultures and dairy ingredients | A | A | A | A | B |
| Hydrocolloids | A | A | A | A | B |
| Brewery ingredients | A | A | A | A | B |
| Phosphates | A | A | A | A | B |
| All groups | C | C | C | C | D |

*Note:* A = specific-product, specific-country strategy; B = specific-product, multi-country strategy; C = multi-product, specific-country strategy; and D = multi-product, multi-country strategy.

Hydrocolloids are used as stabilizing agents in food products. They may be used for many purposes, such as extending a product's life cycle or changing its texture. Food manufacturers typically develop close long-term relationships with a limited set of suppliers providing them with valuable insight in their production processes. Customer needs vary considerably from single ingredients or premixed compounds to complex tailor-made ingredients combined into hydrocolloid systems, and for each single food product customers select the supplier most adapted to their specific need.

# Phase 1: Project Start-Up

The customer value audit (CVA) for hydrocolloids in Germany followed a three-step process. In the first phase, an internal CVA was undertaken with sales personnel from the vendor's organization. In a group session, participants were asked to estimate how customers perceive their products. The evaluation was conducted separately for each market segment. Table C6.3 shows the results of the CVA for hydrocolloids in the German convenience food segment.

The supplier's personnel were first asked to estimate how customers view the relative importance of price vs. overall product quality. Both categories were ranked by the participants as equally important in the customer's purchasing decision (50% for quality and 50% for price). They were then asked to assess the relative importance of the different

**Table C6.3. Hydrocolloids in Germany (Convenience Food):**
**Weighted Quality Attributes Resulting from Internal CVA**

| Type of Quality | Feature | Percentage of Total Quality Attributes (%) |
|---|---|---|
| Product-related quality (51%) | Product characteristics | 20 |
| | Range of products (breadth) | 14 |
| | Consistency of products | 6 |
| | Natural | 5 |
| | Ease of use | 5 |
| | Other | 1 |
| Service-related quality (34%) | Technical support/application | 13 |
| | Quick service/response | 10 |
| | Reliability and speed of supply | 8 |
| | Other | 3 |
| Promotion-related quality (15%) | Image, corporate identity | 6 |
| | Personal relations | 4 |
| | Reliability of company | 3 |
| | Other | 2 |
| Total | | 100 |

quality categories. Product-related aspects were perceived as most important (51%), followed by service-related criteria (34%) and promotion-related quality aspects (15%). For each of the sub-groups, items were then generated. The group members were asked to weigh the criteria relative to each other. The product's technical characteristics (20%), breadth of product range (14%), technical support (13%), quick service and response (10%), and reliability and speed of supply (8%) were considered by the participants as predominant in the customers decision-making process.

## Phase 2: Customer Survey

Key customers were identified in the three major market segments and, together with the supplier's sales management, were asked to participate in a customer value assessment project. In this step of the CVA process, in-depth interviews were conducted with 36 representatives of 12 companies in the convenience food segment. These representatives came from the purchasing, research and development/quality control, and production departments of each company.

Table C6.4 shows the results of the assessment of product value perceived by German clients of hydrocolloids in the convenience food business. The first column represents the relative importance of product quality attributes as perceived by the customers independently of any specific supplier. They were then asked to evaluate the chemicals supplier and its main competitors against these purchasing criteria (column 2 to column 6). A 10-point scale from Very Low Performance (1) to High Performance (10) with no verbal statements for points 2 to 9 was used. Column 7 computes an average competitor's position (average of column 2 to column 6). Finally, the client-company's position relative to this average is calculated (difference between column 2 and column 7).

The comparison of the actual customer results with the internal CVA results (i.e., Table C6.4 vs. Table C6.3) indicates the perceptual gaps between customer reality and internal perceptions of the supplier. For example, the supplier believed that price was as important as quality in the customer's purchasing decision. However, customers were significantly less price sensitive and weighted quality much higher than price (63.3% for quality vs. 36.7% for price).

Similarly, at the single-attribute level, customers considered product consistency as key (35% of product-related attributes, or 19.8% of total quality attributes), while the client-company weighted it as only 6% of total quality attributes. In addition, new issues were generated by customer interviews of which the supplier was unaware (e.g., the role of ISO certification).

The identification of these gaps was considered of great importance by the client company, as it helped in reallocating resources for customer priorities. Based on the survey results, value maps were then prepared which included the price/quality line which represented fair value positions as perceived by customers.

The supplier and its competitors were then positioned on the map according to how customers rated them on the price/quality scale. Figure C6.1 presents the value map corresponding to the results shown in Table C6.4. The dark line in the CVA map represents the price/quality slope. Companies positioned below the line were perceived as offering value lower than expected by the customers, while those above the line were perceived as offering a higher value. The reasons for the overall

**Table C6.4. Evaluation of Hydrocolloid Suppliers by German Convenience Food Manufacturers**

| | Importance (%) | Client Company | Competitor A | Competitor B | Competitor C | Other Competitors | Average Position | Relative Position |
|---|---|---|---|---|---|---|---|---|
| **Product-related attributes** | | | | | | | | |
| Consistency of product | 35.5 | 8.1 | 9.0 | 6.3 | 8.7 | 6.6 | 7.6 | 0.5 |
| Product characteristics | 32.9 | 8.1 | 9.0 | 6.3 | 8.7 | 6.6 | 7.6 | 0.5 |
| Natural | 14.2 | 8.0 | 8.3 | 6.3 | 8.0 | 7.5 | 7.5 | 0.5 |
| Ease of use | 8.8 | 8.8 | 8.1 | 8.3 | 7.0 | 8.3 | 7.9 | 0.2 |
| Range of products | 5.4 | 8.1 | 8.8 | 7.4 | 6.3 | 7.4 | 7.5 | 0.6 |
| Non-dusting | 3.2 | 8.2 | 8.3 | 8.5 | 9.0 | 8.3 | 8.5 | -0.3 |
| Subtotal | 100.0 | 8.1 | 8.8 | 6.5 | 8.4 | 7.0 | 7.7 | 0.5 |
| **Service-related attributes** | | | | | | | | |
| Reliability and speed of supply | 26.7 | 9.0 | 9.8 | 7.3 | 7.7 | 8.3 | 8.3 | 0.7 |
| Technical support/application | 23.3 | 5.7 | 8.8 | 5.8 | 5.7 | 5.1 | 6.3 | -0.7 |
| Quick service/response | 22.1 | 3.9 | 10.0 | 5.7 | 7.5 | 5.6 | 7.2 | -3.3 |
| Product innovation | 12.5 | 7.7 | 8.5 | 4.3 | 7.3 | 6.9 | 6.8 | 0.9 |
| Technical information/literature | 7.9 | 6.0 | 7.0 | 5.3 | 5.7 | 4.4 | 5.6 | 0.4 |
| Training/seminars | 4.2 | 4.8 | 5.7 | 6.3 | 8.0 | 2.9 | 5.7 | -0.9 |
| Global source of supply | 0.8 | 7.8 | 8.0 | 8.7 | 8.5 | 6.5 | 7.9 | -0.2 |
| Others | 2.5 | 1.0 | 1.0 | — | — | 10.0 | 5.5 | -4.5 |
| Subtotal | 100.0 | 6.3 | 8.8 | 6.0 | 7.0 | 6.3 | 7.0 | -0.7 |

**Promotion-related attributes**

| | | | | | | | | |
|---|---|---|---|---|---|---|---|---|
| Image/corporate identity | 5.8 | 7.4 | 9.6 | 5.5 | 8.3 | 5.7 | 7.3 | 0.1 |
| Personal relations | 27.5 | 4.8 | 9.4 | 6.8 | 5.7 | 5.4 | 6.8 | -2.0 |
| Reliability of company | 45.8 | 6.6 | 9.8 | 5.7 | 8.0 | 5.3 | 7.2 | -0.6 |
| Public relations | 0.8 | 2.6 | 2.5 | 1.5 | 8.0 | 2.8 | 3.7 | -1.1 |
| Upstream integration | 0.8 | 3.3 | 1.0 | — | — | 3.3 | 2.2 | 1.2 |
| ISO 9001 certification | 19.2 | 2.0 | 9.5 | 1.8 | 3.3 | 2.9 | 4.4 | -2.4 |
| Subtotal | 100.0 | 5.2 | 9.5 | 5.2 | 6.5 | 4.9 | 6.5 | -1.3 |
| **Total quality position** | — | 7.2 | 8.9 | 6.1 | 7.7 | 6.5 | 7.3 | -0.1 |
| Price position | — | 100.0 | 105.0 | 87.5 | 97.5 | 91.7 | 95.4 | 4.6 |
| Quality | 63.3 | | | | | | | |
| + price | 36.7 | | | | | | | |

*Note:* Product-related attributes = 55.8; service-related attributes = 29.2; promotion-related attributes = 15.0; average quality position (Qo) = 7.3; average price position (Po) = 96.3.

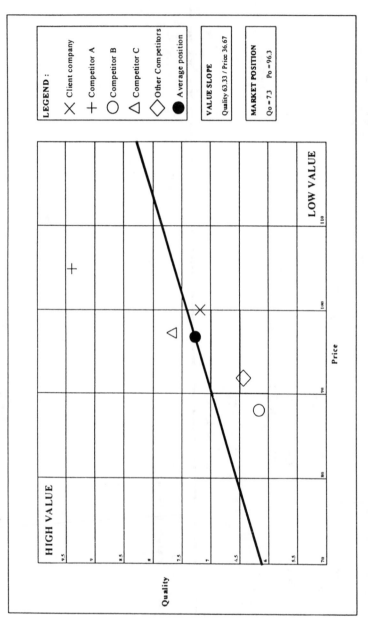

**Figure C6.1. CVA Map for Hydrocolloid Suppliers in Germany**

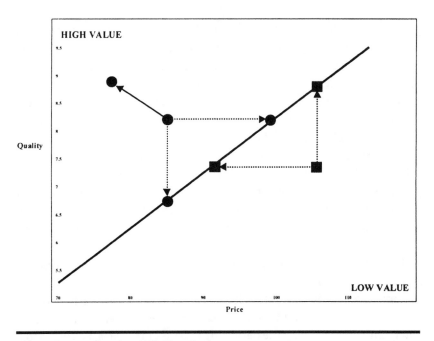

**Figure C6.2. Strategic Marketing Options**

positive or negative position of a company could be easily explained by analyzing the corresponding results. For example, the negative position of the client-company (X on the value map) can be partly explained by its perceived significant disadvantage (−3.3), relative to its competitors, on the "quick service/response" attribute, which was rated at 6.5% of total quality. This was due to the absence of a technical service office in Germany.

## Marketing Strategy Formulation

The importance of the value tables and maps resides in their ability to identify the key customer-perceived attributes which position a company against its competitors. Strategies can then be developed to improve the competitive position. The objective of a company positioned in the "low value" portion of the map is to reach the price/quality slope through a combination of price reduction and improved quality.

Companies perceived as offering "high value" have essentially three choices. First, they can improve their high-value position, thereby expecting to gain market share over time. Second, they can increase their price, while still remaining in the "high value" portion of the map, as they are currently perceived by their customers to be a bargain. Finally, they can reduce the level of quality which they are currently offering to decrease their costs and improve their margins. This strategy is considered the most risky because creating a perceived positive value takes time and represents a key asset to a company. These strategic options are represented graphically in Figure C6.2.

For example, the supplier in our study can improve its perceived value by selecting important attributes for which it believes it can improve its rating, such as improving the consistency of its products. This attribute was not highly rated in the internal CVA but ranked positive for the company against its competitors on average. Additionally, the company can address the attributes for which it compares negatively with its competitors, such as "quick service/response" or "personal relations of the commercial representative". It also can direct its interest to items given limited attention in the past (e.g., ISO 9001 certification).

Strategic options can be simulated on a CVA map and compared to determine those offering the best value increase for the least cost. Action plans by product and country can then be developed to implement the desired changes and achieve the required value rating improvements.

## Questions

1. What is the difference between customer value and customer satisfaction?
2. What are the differences between measuring value perceptions in consumer markets vs. industrial markets?
3. What are the steps for conducting a customer value audit (CVA)?
4. How can customer value analysis be linked to marketing strategy development ?
5. What course of action should the company take, based on its position on the CVA map (Figure C6.2)?

# Case 7. Larry Bird's Home Court — Brand Repositioning[*]

I n May 1997, the Indiana Pacers announced that former Indiana State University All-American and Boston Celtic great Larry Bird would return to Indiana as their new coach. With many of the same players from the previous year, Indiana enjoyed their most successful season in 1997/98 since entering the National Basketball Association (NBA). They won a franchise regular season record 58 games and took the defending champion Chicago Bulls and Michael Jordan to the final seconds of the seventh game before losing in the Eastern Division finals. As a result of the Pacers' success and his contribution to it, Larry Bird was selected the 1998 NBA Coach of the Year.

Bird was an All-State basketball player in the early 1970s at Springs Valley High School in French Lick, IN (population 2087). He committed to play for Coach Bob Knight and entered Indiana University but left school after 3 weeks, saying that the school was too large. In the fall of 1975, he enrolled at Indiana State University (ISU) in Terre Haute. By the time Bird graduated in 1979, he had become a legend. In his final

* This case was prepared by Robert D. Green, Assistant Professor of Marketing at Indiana State University. The author would like to acknowledge Max and Greg Gibson, Mark Bird, Michael Bonewitz, and The Greater Terre Haute Chamber of Commerce for their helpful information relating to this case. Mark Shaw's book *Larry Legend* (Chicago: NTC/Contemporary Publishing Group, 1998) provided insight and information about Larry Bird and his career.

year, he led the National Collegiate Athletic Association in scoring (33.3 points per game), as well as leading ISU to a 33-1 record, with the only loss occurring in the NCAA final game to Michigan State University and Magic Johnson.

The National Basketball Association Boston Celtics drafted and signed Larry Bird in 1979. In 13 seasons he was named an All-Star 12 times and NBA Most Valuable Player (MVP) three times, and the Celtics won three NBA championships. After being a member of the "Dream Team" at the 1992 Olympics in Barcelona, Spain, he retired as a player because of a recurring back injury. In the summer of 1998, Bird was elected to the Naismith Memorial Hall of Fame.

Upon his retirement as a player, Bird became an executive for the Boston Celtics. After 5 years in that position, he became bored, missing the game competition. The resignation in May 1997 of Larry Brown as the Pacers coach allowed Hoosier native Bird the opportunity to return to basketball and to Indiana. Those who knew Bird were not surprised he would be back in Indiana; however, some sports media critics quickly began pointing out that Larry Bird had not ever coached any team before being named to the Pacers position and questioned his ability to coach. He proved them wrong. What these critics failed to recognize was that Bird, as a player, was a "coach" on the floor.

Terre Haute and ISU are proudly identified with Larry Bird and his legendary basketball career. The respect and pride are mutual. Bird has business interests in and is a frequent visitor to Terre Haute. By moving from the Boston Celtics' front office to the Indiana Pacers' sideline, Larry has brought new excitement to the ISU campus, Terre Haute, and the entire state of Indiana with his second basketball career — as Coach Bird.

## Background

The Terre Haute Sheraton Hotel was opened by Michael Bonewitz in 1974 at 555 South Third Street (U.S. 41). He knew hotel franchising and the local hospitality market, having opened a TraveLodge in 1964 and later investing in several TraveLodges throughout the midwest. After a feasibility study and relying upon his prior experience in the Terre Haute market, Bonewitz built a 102-room, full-service Sheraton facility across the street from the TraveLodge. This was his first experience with Sheraton.

The hotel provided many services for guests. In addition to the 102 rooms, there was a dining room and an adjacent lounge. A removable wall allowed expanded seating for after-dinner live lounge entertainment. A banquet room with a 250-seat capacity was available for meetings, conferences, and conventions. An outdoor swimming pool was another amenity for guests. Bonewitz was able to "cross-sell" the Sheraton guest services — for example dining, lounge, and meeting facilities — to his TraveLodge guests. The Sheraton investment proved successful for Bonewitz.

Bonewitz decided in 1986 to sell the Sheraton to a group led by local businessman Max Gibson and Larry Bird. The timing was very good for both parties. Bonewitz had owned the property for 12 years, and Bird was at the height of his professional playing career in the NBA with the Boston Celtics. The residents of Terre Haute had already become Celtic fans. If they were not able to attend games in Indianapolis, Chicago, or even Boston, they could listen to live broadcasts by Johnny Most, "the voice of the Celtics", on WTHI-FM in Terre Haute, or they could watch the games via satellite television. Celtics baseball caps, T-shirts, sweatshirts, and bumper stickers were commonly seen in Terre Haute. The timing appeared right for the purchase of the Sheraton by Gibson and Bird.

Other motivations to purchase the Sheraton properties were apparent. Bird appreciated the fans in Terre Haute, even long after leaving the city for a playing and management career in Boston. Mark Bird, Larry's older brother, stated a defining reason for the consideration to acquire the hotel: "Larry always wanted to do something for Terre Haute. He wanted to have some place for people to see and enjoy trophies and other items he had received." The hotel provided such a venue.

Max Gibson, a successful Terre Haute businessman and owner of a large, diversified company, had been a confidant, advisor, and close friend of Larry Bird for many years. He had been very active in community projects and knew the market area well, thus the Bird-Gibson partnership was very logical. With Bird, Gibson could diversify his business interests further and bring a high-profile product back to Terre Haute. With Gibson, Bird could accomplish what he wanted — to make his fans in Indiana happy and continue his playing career in Boston.

After the Terre Haute Sheraton was purchased in 1986 by the Gibson-Bird group, the new owners quickly planned and implemented changes. The theme and motif were associated with Larry Bird and the Boston

Celtics, and the Sheraton franchise was canceled. The property became independent (not franchised) and was named Larry Bird's Boston Connection. Certainly the area market could relate to the new name, as they had had a Boston connection ever since the 1979/80 basketball season. Bird's ISU and Celtics basketball jersey number (#33) was even a part of the changes; the telephone number of the hotel was changed to 812-235-3333 and the toll-free number to 800-262-0033. Some speculated that the city would have been willing to change the address on South Third Street to 33 Larry Bird Avenue, if a street had not already been dedicated on the ISU campus adjacent to Hulman Center where Larry played his collegiate career.

Renovation and other modifications included changes in most areas of the hotel. Pictures, articles, awards (including Bird's NBA MVP trophy), and memorabilia appeared throughout the public areas of the hotel. Inside the main entrance into the lobby, guests were greeted by a life-size silhouette of Bird in a Celtic uniform (#33) shooting a jump shot, and the lobby area had parquet flooring similar to the Boston Garden. The lounge, named the MVP Room, offered gourmet dining for lunch and dinner and was available to overnight hotel guests without additional charge or to club members for an annual fee ($133).

Just off the lobby area was the restaurant, The Boston Garden. This area offered more than enjoyment of a good meal — dining there was an event! A basketball goal and a small hardwood court were constructed for those who would like to play on Larry Bird's "home court". A net was erected, apparently to protect restaurant guests dining from those who did not shoot with the accuracy of their host. The new owners changed the banquet rooms to a popular sports bar, The Bird Nest Lounge, which had numerous televisions for watching Bird in action (first as a player, and later as a coach) and offered drinks and a limited food menu.

The Sheraton had 102 hotel rooms, but with the renovation some rooms were changed to alternate uses. A gift shop, The Boston Connection, was opened in what had been a hotel room just off the lobby area and was an authorized NBA merchandise outlet. Three hotel rooms were enlarged and became suites. Small meeting rooms and a travel agency (Travel Connection) were added, which also accounted for reducing the number of hotel rooms available.

Because the former banquet rooms were converted to The Bird Nest Lounge, the Boston Connection was without such a facility until 1992.

Adjacent to, and owned by, the hotel was a single-story office building leased to an insurance agency. In 1992, the lease was not renewed. The hotel renovated and expanded the building and re-opened it as the Boston Connection Conference Center, available for meetings, conferences, banquets, and conventions. The facility had three rooms, varying in size, and could be opened to one large room accommodating 320 people. A full-service kitchen was added during the renovation.

The new owners made a quick and successful transition from the Sheraton to the Boston Connection. Gibson and his son, Greg, were active in the management of the property. During the NBA off-season, there were "Bird sightings" at the hotel and around Terre Haute. Larry was not able to be around the hotel as much as he would have liked, but there was an alternative. His older brother and corporate vice president, Mark Bird, was there regularly. The Terre Haute area was very responsive to the changes to the hotel, which made the venture a success for the community and for the investors.

## The Market Area

Terre Haute is in Vigo County, located 70 miles west of Indianapolis and 175 miles east of St. Louis on I-70. Chicago is 180 miles to the north. The population of Vigo County is 107,141; Terre Haute, 60,200. Total county employment is 64,963. Terre Haute has a large concentration of employment in the service sector (64%), followed by the goods sector (21%) and the public sector (14%). Of the area's 12 largest employers, three are from the service sector and nine from the goods sector. Two service sector firms are in health care. In the goods sector, three are in packaging, two in pharmaceuticals, and two in compact discs, videos, or cassettes.

Terre Haute ranks third in the U.S. in retail sales per household. The city has a large geographic retail area, drawing upon a population of approximately 500,000 from 15 counties in Indiana and Illinois. Products include health care, higher education, retail stores, and hospitality facilities. Terre Haute offers a large number and different types of hotel accommodations and dining facilities. The largest hotel is the Holiday Inn, a full-service hotel with 230 rooms. The smallest is the Statesman Inn, with 29 rooms and no other facilities. Of the 17 hotels/motels offering 1672 rooms, 13 are franchise properties. The location of overnight facilities is highly concentrated around the U.S. 41/I-70 interchange. Dining opportunities in Terre Haute include coffee houses, delicatessens, tearooms, steak houses, and, of course, fast-food establishments — over 200 restaurants in all. There are local, well-known favorites as well as national franchise restaurants, and a variety of ethnic cuisine is also available. Considering Terre Haute's 1672 rooms at 17 hotels/motels and over 200 restaurants, the hospitality industry is a significant factor in the city's retail economy. For this reason, the hospitality market is highly competitive.

## Larry Bird's Home Court

With Larry's move in May 1997 from being a Boston Celtics executive to the Indiana Pacers' coach, local interest in the Celtics changed. This provided the Larry Bird's Boston Connection hotel with an opportunity to reposition and further differentiate itself in the market. In the summer of 1998, the owners of Larry Bird's Boston Connection changed the name of the hotel to Larry Bird's Home Court. The new name broadened its appeal and can be identified with any team that Larry has played for or coached. The name change was not the only change being considered. The Gibsons and the Birds looked into seeking a franchise such as Marriott, Ramada, or Best Western. The final decision was made to remain an independent hotel and to focus on their own distinctive image and capabilities.

Renovation has been completed to reflect the new name. Signage at the hotel and roadside billboards has been changed. The lobby parquet flooring and the #33 Boston Celtics silhouette have been removed. A few, less important pictures have been taken off the walls. The gift shop carries only Larry's memorabilia, logo, and novelty items and has discontinued the sale of NBA merchandise. Consideration is being given to changing the name of the Boston Garden Restaurant to possibly just The Garden or The Legend Restaurant, and a name change is also being considered for the Conference Center. No change is planned for the MVP Room and the Bird Nest Lounge, as those names have generic identifications.

The Gibson and Bird (Larry and his siblings) families own the hotel. Executive positions are held by Max Gibson and his son, Greg, and Larry's brother, Mark. Daily operations are managed by General Manager Rick Lundstrom, who is a Terre Haute native and had extensive experience in food and beverage in Florida prior to his current position. The Home Court has six departments, each having a manager who reports to the General Manager: Sales, Food and Beverage (F&B), Kitchen, Front Desk, Gift Shop, and Controller.

The target market for the Home Court is corporate business. This is primarily for hotel rooms, F&B, and meetings. Sports fans are an important segment, as well, particularly for rooms and F&B. The product offered is obviously a full-service, independently owned and operated hotel which has the freedom to develop its uniqueness and to make local decisions. With the name change to Home Court and the return of Bird to Indiana, the hotel is positioned to intensify its marketing of a nationally (and internationally) known sports celebrity.

The Home Court is located on Third Street (U.S. 41), 2 miles north of the U.S. 41/I-70 interchange. Wabash Avenue (U.S. 40 and the city center) is 5 blocks north, and Indiana State University is 6 blocks away. Being located near the city center and ISU (10,700 students and 1760 employees) is an advantage; however, being located 2 miles from the I-70 interchange and its highly developed area is a major disadvantage. Four franchise hotels are located at the interchange, one next to each of the four exit or entrance ramps. Two blocks south of U.S. 41 and I-70 is a 90-store retail mall. Many other retail shops and business offices are also in the area.

The Home Court is competitively priced. Double and king hotel rooms for one person are priced at a rack rate (maximum daily rate) of $65 and $72, respectively. A 10% discount for American Automobile Association (AAA) or American Association of Retired Persons (AARP) members is offered. A flat corporate rate for the same rooms is $58. The three suites range in price from $107 to $150. The Conference Center, with its 320-seat capacity, is priced from $75 to $600 per day, depending on the amount of space or length of time rented. There is no room rental fee if food service accompanies reservation of space in the Center. The food and beverages for the restaurant, lounge, and catering are competitively priced.

## The Competition

The only other full-service hotel in Terre Haute and the primary competitor of the Home Court is the Holiday Inn. Built in the early 1960s, the Holiday Inn has made several additions (hotel rooms, Holidome).

The hotel has 230 rooms, the Sycamore Grove Restaurant, the Apple Club Lounge, indoor swimming pool, and meeting facilities accommodating up to 500 people. The hotel continues to be owned by the original developer, who has ten other properties in Indiana (not all Holiday Inns). The management staff of the Terre Haute hotel have been with the company for many years and know the hospitality industry and local market.

The competitive advantages of the Holiday Inn include their location (U.S. 41/I-70 interchange, a high-traffic area easily accessible from both highways) and franchise affiliation. A large retail mall is located within a 2-minute drive or a short walk. Other shops, restaurants, and activities are in the immediate area. As a franchise hotel, the facility has an international reservation network for referrals (at a fee) and benefits from international advertising (at a fee) for travelers (either transient or arriving at Terre Haute as their destination). In addition, the Terre Haute Holiday Inn uses local print and electronic media for their advertising. The Sales Department makes local, direct calls to promote the hotel accommodations and meeting facilities.

The Holiday Inn is not generally as competitive with their pricing as the Home Court. The premium pricing might be attributed to the hotel's location and by its being a franchise hotel. The daily rack rate for all rooms is $89, with a 10% discount for AAA or AARP members and a corporate rate of $69. The daily meeting room rental rate ranges from $75 to $1000 and is adjusted if functions include a meal. The F&B pricing is competitive in the restaurant and lounge and for catering functions.

## Opportunities and Challenges

Larry Bird's Home Court is entering a new era, just as Larry is. His move from Boston to nearby Indianapolis, his already highly successful coaching career, and his regular appearances in the media should benefit the Home Court. More is needed, however, than just Bird's return to Indiana and a hotel name change to remain competitive in the marketplace. The Terre Haute hospitality market is very saturated and highly competitive. Home Court's location (2 miles from the interstate) is a major disadvantage; however, management has identified the target market as the business (corporate) segment. Focusing its marketing efforts on this business market can provide the Home Court with an opportunity for increased market share and revenue.

This market repositioning allows new alliances with business customers and hotel suppliers. Special amenities for the business guest must be provided, such as a business service facility at the hotel operated in conjunction with a local company (e.g., Office Max) and offering business services at minimal cost. The flexibility of not being a franchise provides an opportunity to customize services for local market needs and to differentiate the Home Court from the Holiday Inn.

With the product (i.e., Larry Bird) moving closer geographically to the hotel (Indianapolis instead of Boston), the market will more easily identify with and should be more aware of the Home Court. This added value must be communicated to the target market. The value of being known as the local business market hotel could be conveyed through direct marketing efforts (e.g., increasing the sales department's role), which should increase market share and revenue. The Home Court has a distinctive image and capabilities and a certain latitude for uniqueness and making local decisions. The challenge for management is to communicate increased customer value and benefits from repositioning the hotel in the marketplace. Having a sports celebrity certainly gives Larry Bird's Home Court a distinctive competitive advantage.

## Questions

1. In Home Court's target market, what role does their sales department play?
2. Recommend ways for Home Court to measure the value of their services to the corporate market.
3. Evaluate the effectiveness of Home Court's repositioning. What role did relationship marketing play in repositioning the hotel?
4. How can the hotel further create and communicate value for their chosen market?
5. What further actions can the Home Court implement to differentiate their product from the Holiday Inn? Explain.

# Case 8. Motorola — Supply Chain Management

I n the late 1980s, the general manager of Motorola's Radio Products Group, along with a plant purchasing agent, attended a supplier business review at a local job shop supplier, Safeway Precision Products. Located approximately 15 miles from the Motorola Fort Lauderdale manufacturing facility, this sheetmetal and machining job shop had won several Motorola supplier awards for excellence in quality and service.

As part of the business review, the job shop offered a customer tour of the facility. An early advocate of statistical process control and automation techniques, this job shop had earned a reputation for fabricating complex designs with high quality and reliable on-time delivery. During customer plant tours, the job shop would proudly point out their manufacturing and design capabilities. For instance, where a competitor might fabricate one unit of output per piece of equipment, the job shop's numerically controlled equipment, using in-house tooling such as custom-designed and -developed pallets, could fabricate multiple units of output.

Following this particular plant tour, the job shop's key managers met with the Motorola representatives to review business issues. After presenting many accomplishments, the job shop's general manager began

* This case was prepared by Les Feldman, Purchasing Manager, Motorola, Inc., Plantation, FL.

discussing what he viewed as a major problem with Motorola and, in particular, the South Florida location — namely, that business with Motorola was on the decline. Regardless of its investments or the supplier awards it was receiving, business had been steadily declining. Furthermore, the job shop was aware that its competitors (that is, other Motorola job shop suppliers) were the recipients of Motorola's growth business.

The Motorola purchasing agent offered his view that the cause of the job shop's failure to grow with Motorola could be attributed to its relatively high pricing practice. Though the job shop was participating in quoting many jobs, their success factor was less than 5%. In contrast, other local job shop suppliers typically achieved a success factor of more than 20%. To make matters worse, the Motorola development engineering community had begun to associate the job shop with a high pricing practice and, consequently, was no longer eager to seek out their quotes on new prototype work.

In response to the Motorola purchasing agent's opinion, the job shop's general manager indicated that Motorola placed too much emphasis on a supplier's price and not enough on quality and service. The purchasing agent pointed out that total cost and not price was the key consideration. Furthermore, as a result of Motorola working partnerships, many of the job shop's competitors were sending their employees to Motorola's quality training classes and were utilizing Motorola's quality and technical resources to upgrade quality and increase productivity. Consequently, the job shop's competitors were making huge gains in quality and productivity.

Accordingly, unless the job shop found a way to get back on track with competitive pricing, future Motorola business would continue to elude them. At the conclusion of the business review, Motorola's general manager made the closing comment that although Motorola is a large company and the job shop is a small one, both have similar problems and opportunities.

In the subsequent years, the job shop would go through management and ownership changes but would never get back on track with Motorola. By the mid 1990s, the job shop was no longer in business, and the building which once employed approximately 70 people was now shuttered.

Lack of competitive pricing and decline in customer satisfaction may or may not have been the cause of why the job shop shut down;

however, it is likely that these two problems contributed heavily to the shop's final decision. In retrospect, what could the job shop have done differently to improve its competitive pricing and increase customer satisfaction? Considering these questions in the context of business effectiveness can yield important insights.

## Business Effectiveness

Let's look at another "textbook" case of relationship marketing. In the late 1970s, Xerox turned to its Japanese joint venture partner, Fuji Xerox, to better understand why Fuji was profitable while other Xerox operations were struggling financially. Upon dispatching a cross-functional team to Japan, Xerox discovered that its Japanese partner carried 6 to 8 times less inventory and half the overhead, and the quality of incoming parts was 99.5%. By comparing its operations with the Japanese partner, Xerox was able to identify and learn the former's competitive manufacturing advantages. This benchmarking approach by Xerox would be combined with participative management practices to form what Xerox would later refer to as its business effectiveness strategy.

Similar to many small businesses, it is likely that Safeway Precision Products did have a financial plan which included return on investment and cash flow analysis. Whether or not it followed a business effectiveness strategy, however, is doubtful for three reasons. First, the practice of benchmarking or investigating "best practices" was not a common practice in the early 1980s. Second, there is a cost associated with benchmarking. Whereas Xerox could easily secure the financial and employee resources to send a cross-functional team to Japan, for many small businesses these benchmarking requirements are not so readily available. Third, many small businesses lack the management skills to utilize benchmarking effectively. This suggests that benchmarking is primarily a strategic rather than an operational issue.

As a joint venture partner, it was certainly to Fuji Xerox's financial advantage to assist Xerox's cross-functional investigative team. Although it is an advantage for a manufacturer and supplier to assist and support each other's growth and profitability, certain business guidelines nevertheless need to be followed. For instance, before a firm can prosper, it first needs to focus on survival. Cash flow is a survival issue. Many small businesses are dependent on their customers to pay bills on time so, in turn, the small business can pay both its bills and employees. In other words, the small business first needs to ensure a sufficient cash flow before it implements benchmarking or a fact-finding study.

Given that a manufacturer treats a small business supplier as a stakeholder and a working partner, what, in addition to a revenue source, can a manufacturer bring to the relationship? To this end, probably a long list of contributions could be developed. Let's focus, however, on a strategic value that the manufacturer can provide the small business — namely, the manufacturer can provide its working partner supplier with competitive information about the supplier's competitor population. Competitive information, or intelligence, can be used by a supplier to focus on areas for continuous improvement.

It is likely, therefore, that such intelligence could have revealed to Safeway Precision Products that its perceptions for possessing competitive advantages in technology and quality were inaccurate. Moreover, its business system was comparatively weak in relation to its competitor population. Accordingly, Safeway Precision Products could have used this intelligence to address how to reduce operating cost and, hence, offer lower prices for its products and services. A mechanism for intelligence collection and subsequent communication is a supplier Quality System Review (QSR). What follows is a discussion of what a supplier QSR is and how standardized scoring is applied.

## Supplier Quality Systems Review and Standardized Scoring

A Quality Systems Review is a formal survey by which the customer evaluates the continuing health of the supplier's quality system. The QSR is intended to lead to continuous improvement and assure that the supplier's quality system is effective in achieving total customer satisfaction. Motorola indicates that the purpose of a supplier QSR is to assess and compare the supplier's quality system to the "ideal system". Continuing, Motorola points out that by reviewing the supplier's quality subsystems it can make known to the supplier its strengths, weaknesses, and opportunities for improvement.

Because a QSR involves quantitative ranking, it follows that the ideal system represents achieving the maximum points attainable. Although scoring based on benchmarking may be less than maximum, nevertheless it establishes a very high performance standard. Furthermore, benchmarking clearly influences determining the ideal system or value of the QSR.

In addition to providing the supplier with information as to how it compares to the ideal system, the supplier's total QSR score as well as each subsystem can be standardized. Consequently, in addition to a comparison to an ideal system, each supplier's subsystem score can be compared to its competitive population. This is accomplished by providing means and standard deviations for each quality subsystem. Because the supplier now has a population mean and standard deviation, it can use a standard normal distribution to determine approximately where each of its subsystems is in relation to its competition. Furthermore, a job shop supplier can use a standard normal curve and $z$-value to determine what future subsystem scores will likely be needed to achieve a desired percentage within its population

## Questions

1. Explain how the job shop could possess competitive advantages in quality and technology, yet receive only 5% of bid work.
2. What did the Motorola general manager mean when he said that both companies had similar problems and opportunities?
3. Will a job shop likely employ the skills necessary to utilize population mean and standard deviation measures for the QSR? How should managers interpret the normal curve and $z$-values in the quality subsystems?
4. What can we learn about benchmarking and business effectiveness from Xerox's experience with Fuji Xerox?

# Case 9. Nantucket Nectars — Perceived Quality*

## Background

N antucket Nectars began rather inauspiciously when two gradu-
ates from Brown University forsook the corporate world and
moved to Nantucket to chart their own course. Shortly after
graduating from Brown in 1989, Tom Scott and Tom First, co-founders
and co-presidents of Nantucket Nectars, started Allserve, a boat business servicing visiting yachts in the Nantucket harbor. Nantucket is a
small island in Massachusetts located 30 miles off Cape Cod. Nantucket
is known for its famous whaling history and rich New England culture.

Watching the daily flow of traffic in Nantucket harbor resulted in
Scott's brainstorm: why not take supplies to the moored yachts on a
boat? To eat, refuel, and restock, boaters needed to make their way from
their boats to the shore to pick up life's little necessities. Everyday chores
of washing laundry, grocery shopping, and buying dinner were a hassle.

Scott envisioned a service that would offer boat-to-boat service in
the harbor. Rather than making the laborious trip to town, boaters

* This case was prepared by William C. Johnson, Professor of Marketing, School of
Business and Entrepreneurship, Nova Southeastern University, and Edward Schwerin,
Associate Professor and Director of Disciplinary Studies, College of Liberal Arts, Florida
Atlantic University.

could radio Scott on his 19-foot, red Sea Way to place their orders. He described the plan to First, and soon the two were in business with their company called Allserve. Allserve began delivering newspapers, laundry, and other necessities not readily available to visiting boatsmen.

The first summer, the partners delivered a lot of groceries, especially ice, because most of the boats did not have adequate refrigeration systems. They went out each morning and served coffee and donuts, and at night they loaded up the boat with fresh lobster dinners from a local restaurant. But Allserve was not just a delivery service. The co-founders were willing to do anything to get the business off the ground, so they cleaned boats and shampooed dogs for visitors who traveled with their pets.

The service became so popular that soon the founders expanded the Allserve fleet to include three boats. The business expanded from its floating store to extending services to land dwellers out of a little shoreside shack that the owners converted into the Allserve General Store, which is still located on the harbor's Straight Wharf.

During their first winter in business, the partners, while mixing fruits in a blender, created a peach juice based on Tom First's memory of a peach nectar he tasted while traveling in Spain. They perfected the peach nectar recipe and planned to offer the Nantucket Nectars juice at both the Allserve General Store and on board the Allserve boats.

Bottling the juice offered a challenge. Because they could not afford a professional bottler, they improvised, using empty milk cartons and soda, beer, and wine bottles. Their juice was an immediate success; however, their business was not. The all-natural juice, although easy to sell, was difficult to store and spoiled quickly. Six months into their venture, having already pooled their combined savings of $17,000, they contracted with an independent bottler in upstate New York to handle the process. Costs for their first batch topped $14,000, and the partners knew they had to sell a lot of juice just to cover their expenses.

## Marketing

The founders quickly discovered that the most effective way to market their juice was to get people to taste it. However, consumers had to be able to buy the juice at their local stores, so this presented a *Catch 22* of sorts. Because the duo spent most of their initial budget on labels and production, they undertook distribution themselves. They met with store owners, took the orders, loaded and unloaded trucks, stocked the shelves, collected the money, and ran the warehouse. In short, they did it all. They soon discovered to their dismay that they were becoming a distribution company instead of a company focused on improving the juice and creating new flavors. In time, they would sell the distribution side of the business and hire outside distributors to sell the product, now available in over half the states, Latin America, France, Korea, Canada, and Britain. Although Nantucket Nectars initially distributed its products through health food and specialty stores, today they sell their line of products in convenience stores and supermarkets.

Early sales figures were encouraging, as customers flocked to the product; yet, the company was losing money. Scott and First eventually identified the problem: they were charging less for a bottle of juice than it cost them to produce it, grossing less than 5% a case. Not only did they learn a valuable lesson in cost accounting, but also that customers "buy quality". The price of the product was not as important as the quality they provided, and that customers are attracted to value, not simply low prices.

The company's promotional strategy was centered almost exclusively on the company's origins, with the founders telling their story in folksy radio spots. Radio was a perfect medium to showcase not only their products but also the unique culture of Nantucket Nectars. Scott and First became almost instant media stars, using a natural, laid-back approach to tell the story of their company and its products. In each of the spots, the founders offer a bit of inside information on the company. For example, in one ad, they talk about the early days of selling the peach nectar off the Allserve boat. The bulk of their advertising is still in radio in cities across the country, although they do a limited amount of print advertising and maintain a website (www.juiceguys.com)

The hallmark of their marketing strategy continues to be the product. The company sells only fruit juice drinks, enabling them to combine soft-drink marketing with rising health awareness. Consumers are looking for high-quality beverages with high percentages of real fruit juice and pure ingredients and are willing to pay for it. To that end, Nantucket Nectars determines to create the best quality product in the juice market. In fact, through their internal program called the Quality Juice Evolution, they follow a strict set of standards to guarantee that each bottle of their juice is of the highest quality and the best tasting it can be. There are now 36 flavors in the Nantucket Nectars Line, including fruit juices, iced teas, lemonades, and the recently introduced line called Super Nectars, which are iced teas and fruit juices containing herbs, vitamins, and minerals to capitalize on the growing "neutra-ceutical" market. The products are mixed and bottled in four different bottling plants located strategically across the country. Each location was carefully chosen to facilitate their distribution network.

While the products represent a key differentiation, so does the company's packaging. Glass plays a big part in Nantucket's strategy, conveying the message of quality. Nantucket uses rather unique proprietary packages, a 12-ounce bottle, a 17.5-ounce bottle, and most recently a 36-ounce bottle. Even the bottle caps are unique. Each purple bottle cap features a real fact about Nantucket Island and Nantucket Nectars. The stories featured on the bottle caps help customers understand the philosophy and character that distinguish Nantucket Island and Nantucket Nectars.

## Corporate Culture

Nantucket Nectars has developed a unique corporate culture, which plays a major role in its marketing success and has shaped its management style and work environment. The corporate culture is reflected in their mission statement and core values, community service commitment, support of environmental causes, and corporate image.

The corporate image is created around the story of the co-founders, Tom First and Tom Scott. Tom and Tom are the Juice Guys, blonde beach boys who represent fun, a laid-back lifestyle, and the Nantucket Island mystique. These Juice Guys wear jeans and T-shirts to work and bring their dogs, Becky and Pete, in to work with them. But, Tom and Tom are also hard-working, free-spirited young entrepreneurs whose core values include providing a quality product and quality service to their customers and a quality work environment for their employees.

As part of the local business community, the Juice Guys wanted to become involved in local environmental issues and to support causes for health and wellness. Therefore, Tom and Tom have recently launched Juice Guys Care, their social responsibility program, by teaming up with the city of Cambridge and donating seven recycling bins to be placed in and around their Harvard Square headquarters.

The corporate image of the Juice Guys and the story of Tom and Tom are communicated to the public and customers via slogans, folksy radio ads, a colorful website, and bottle cap facts about Nantucket lore and the co-founders. Many of the cap facts are simply memories and fun island stories from Tom and Tom's early years on Nantucket. Many of the facts refer to old island legends and characters that make Nantucket unique and colorful. The bottle caps are designed to tell the story of both Nantucket Island and Nantucket Nectars.

While Tom and Tom are the original Juice Guys, they are not the *only* Juice Guys. Customers automatically join the Juice Guy fraternity by enjoying Nantucket Nectars. According to Tom and Tom, if you buy Nantucket Nectars, you are a Juice Guy. If you sell Nantucket Nectars, you are a Juice Guy. If you make Nantucket Nectars, you are a Juice Guy. Women are included, as the term "Juice Guy" is not gender specific, so really anyone can be part of the Juice Guy team.

The Juice Guy story, philosophy, and credo shape Nantucket Nectar's corporate culture and management style. A positive corporate culture is vital to the survival and success of all companies, but this is especially true for startup companies where hard-driving employees typically put in long hours for relatively low pay. The lack of a clearly defined positive corporate culture can keep a new company from ever getting off the ground.

A company's culture should communicate to everyone in the company, from the bottom to the top, what business they are in and who their customer is. A company's culture is reflected in its employees' behavior, values, and expectations. When employees understand and share their company's mission and values, they are more likely to be enthusiastic about achieving the company's goals and the company becomes more prosperous.

A company's culture is typically articulated by its founders early in its existence. At Nantucket Nectars, Tom First and Tom Scott deliberately set out to foster an entrepreneurial, freewheeling corporate culture with no hierarchy, no dress code, and few job titles. Like Tom and Tom, the employees do not wear suits and ties to work, and many of them regularly bring their dogs to work.

According to their mission credo, the stated purpose is "to create a work environment that promotes entrepreneurship, honesty, mutual respect, fairness, orderliness, diversity, and conscientious hard work. Juice Guys will be given a clear definition of their responsibilities and will be expected to meet those responsibilities in a creative, energetic, and timely manner. The work atmosphere should positively impact each of our lives and support, but not intrude upon, our private lives."

The Nantucket Nectar participatory management style combines a dual emphasis on both individual empowerment as well as teamwork and collaboration. Nantucket Nectars tries to recruit "entrepreneurial types" who believe in the American Dream, hard work, and being successful and prosperous.

Employees are empowered by being given the opportunity to make decisions for themselves, to use their judgment, and to make mistakes and learn from them. Employees have a vested interest in the success of the business which stems from being given free rein, creating their departments, and seeing the difference they can make. Tom and Tom regularly communicate their dreams and the importance of setting individual goals, as well as company goals, and of accomplishing them. Constant communication is used to keep employees involved and passionate about the quality of the product and success of the business.

Their participatory management style stresses the importance of teamwork. Weekly staff meetings include employee guest speakers who stand up and talk about their life and what inspires them. The purpose of this exercise is to encourage respect for what other people do and to provide an understanding of who they are and how they are helping the company.

Employees are urged to maintain an even balance between work life and family life. They are encouraged to stay physically active, to continue educating themselves in areas that are of interest to them, to stay informed, and to make suggestions about company policies and procedures. Nantucket Nectar employees are also encouraged to help improve the community by volunteering on a regular basis to work on community issues and problems that are of interest to them. To facilitate community involvement, all employees are given 2 paid volunteer days per year for community service.

One of the biggest challenges currently facing Nantucket Nectars is how to maintain their unique, positive corporate culture during a period of explosive growth. When a company grows rapidly, it becomes more and more difficult to maintain a team atmosphere and to communicate company values and goals to those who work in the field. Now as their juice sales exceed $50 million, Nantucket Nectars is outgrowing its free-spirited fraternity house culture, and Tom and Tom are grappling

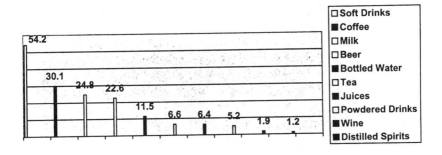

Figure C9.1. 1997 Per Capita Beverage Consumption (Gallons per Person)

with how to manage that growth without destroying the entrepreneurial spirit and participatory management style that have made the company special.

## Industry and Competition

The beverage industry (all beverage categories, carbonated and non-carbonated) continues to grow uninterrupted, growing just over 3% to 30 billion gallons in 1997. Breaking this down in per capita terms, every man, woman, and child consumed 111 gallons of beverages during that year. Juice and juice drinks, the primary market for Nantucket Nectars, represent a small but healthy category of the total soft drink market (see Figure C9.1). Since 1992, the category has averaged nearly a 20% annual growth rate (see Figure C9.2). According to *Beverage Digest,* a leading beverage trade publication, the soft drink industry (including carbonated and noncarbonated alternative soft drinks) grew less than 1% from

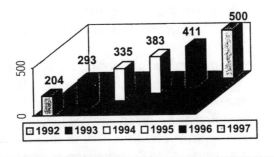

Figure C9.2. 1992–1997 Fruit Juice and Juice Drink Sales (Millions of Cases)

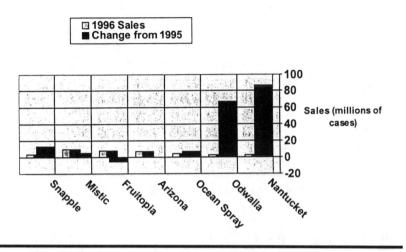

**Figure C9.3. Nantucket Nectars' Competitive Position**

1996 to 1997, while sales of shelf-stable (single-serve glass bottle) juices and juice drinks grew 21.6% during the same period.

The $53 billion soft drink industry is highly segmented according to product type and channel. The major retail soft drink categories include: carbonated soft drinks, ready-to-drink (RTD) teas, sport drinks, bottled water, and juice/juice drinks. With annual sales volume of nearly $34 billion, the carbonated soft drink segment still dominates the industry. Major retail channel segments include supermarkets, convenience stores (C-stores), on-premise (restaurants and bars), vending, club stores, food service, and drug/mass merchandisers. While supermarkets, convenience stores, and health food stores have long carried fruit juices and juice drinks, these products are increasingly available in mass merchandisers, drug stores, and other retail outlets. In 1997, the amount of fruit juice sold through convenience stores increased 7% to 75.1 million gallons. In the drug/mass merchandiser channel, volume grew 3.6% to 72.7 million gallons.

Nantucket Nectars competes directly against other fruit juice and fruit drink (new age) producers such as Snapple, Mistic, Fruitopia, Arizona Iced Tea, Ocean Spray, and Odwalla, just to name a few. Nantucket's revenue growth has far outstripped its chief rivals, however (see Figure C9.3). Profit margins have become increasingly squeezed, especially in the supermarket and C-store channels, where price competition is the norm. In fact, the retail price per ounce of carbonated soft drinks is the same today as it was in 1975, underscoring the nature of price competition in the soft drink industry. Nantucket has been able to maintain premium pricing over its competitors due to the higher juice content and natural ingredients which they offer in their products.

Other product-market competitors include carbonated soft drinks, fresh and juice products made from concentrate, sport drinks (isotonics), iced coffees, smoothies, and ready-to-drink iced tea products. The primary battleground in the soft drink industry continues to be the retail shelf. Failure to secure retail facings and warehouse slots can often doom an otherwise good product. The industry heavyweights, such as Coke, Pepsi, Quaker Oats (Gatorade), and Ocean Spray tend to dominate the retail beverage aisle, often squeezing out smaller rivals. This will become a major challenge to Nantucket as they expand distribution beyond health food and specialty stores to more traditional retail outlets.

## Growth and Performance

Nantucket Nectars has been a true entrepreneurial success story, growing from a start-up delivery business to a company with $50 million in revenues in 1997. The company's early expansion was fueled by the owner's pooled investments; however, additional capital was required when the company wanted to move to the next level. Here is where former Alamo Rent-a-Car Chairman Michael Egan came in, eventually investing $500,000 and taking 50% ownership in Nantucket Nectars. In early 1998, Ocean Spray bought a substantial interest in Nantucket Nectars, essentially replacing Michael Egan as its financial partner. The partnership with Ocean Spray will let Nantucket remain a private company independently run by its founders, Tom First and Tom Scott.

Nantucket Nectars sales have risen steadily; 1998 revenues are estimated at $60 million, making it one of *Inc.* magazine's 20 fastest growing private companies (see Figure C9.4 for annual sales since 1993). The company continues to seek attractive growth opportunities, such as the Nantucket Nectars Fall Harvest creation available in three varieties — Apple Cider, Cranberry Apple Cider, and Peach Apple Cider. Unlike traditional apple juice, these cider products are coarsely filtered to allow more apple into the bottle. The Fall Harvest line-up is 100% not from concentrate fruit juice, and like all Nantucket Nectars, they are pasteurized and all natural with no artificial colors, flavors, or preservatives.

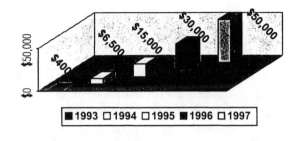

**1993  □1994  □1995  ■1996  □1997**

---

**Figure C9.4. Nantucket Nectars' Revenues: 1993–1998 ($000)**

The new line was slated to be on some market shelves in New Jersey, Pennsylvania, Virginia, Michigan, Illinois, New Hampshire, Vermont, Maine, New York, Connecticut, Rhode Island, and Massachusetts starting in October 1998.

## Questions

1. Suppose you were hired as the Director of Marketing Communications for Nantucket Nectars. Write out a statement which conveys Nantucket Nectars' unique selling proposition.
2. Evaluate Nantucket Nectars' positioning strategy. What is their brand positioning based on?
3. Discuss how Nantucket Nectars has raised the perceived quality for their brand? Does the Nantucket Nectars brand represent a "good value"? Why or why not?
4. What is unique about Nantucket Nectars' corporate image and culture? What are some of the possible advantages and disadvantages of their corporate culture?
5. How has Nantucket Nectars' corporate culture shaped their management style and work environment? Describe their management style in detail. Does this particular style make a contribution to overall customer value?
6. In what ways is corporate culture useful or necessary to the survival or success of a startup company? Of a mature company?
7. As a company grows and develops, how does the corporate culture evolve?

# Case 10. National Association of Small Business Owners — Customer Retention*

J eff Andrews recently applied for the newly created position of Marketing Director at the National Association of Small Business Owners (NASBO). The membership of the association has leveled off at 500,000 members. They have growing concerns regarding member retention, and management is considering restructuring with the objective of increasing member retention and planning for solid growth in the next century. During the interview process, the National Director asked two very critical questions: (1) "What would you do to increase the market orientation of the association?" and (2) "Focusing on a new market orientation and the objective of increasing member retention, in what manner would you restructure the sales division?" Before answering the questions, Jeff spent two days at the administrative offices of NASBO, learning about the association first hand. He knew it was necessary to evaluate the organization as a whole in order to develop a strategy.

Jeff learned that the National Association of Small Business Owners is one of the largest and oldest business organizations in the U.S. The association was formed over 50 years ago for the purpose of advocating

---

* The case was prepared by Pam Hillery, doctoral student, School of Business and Entrepreneurship, Nova Southeastern University.

the concerns of small business to both state and federal lawmakers. The advocacy of small business concerns continues to be the primary objective today. NASBO has lobby offices in every state capitol, as well as in Washington, D.C. Their administrative offices are located in Atlanta, GA.

## A Grass Roots Organization

The National Association of Small Business Owners is proud of its grass roots heritage. This heritage began with the founding charter to advance the interests of small business owners and continues today with the periodic mailing of ballots to the organization's entire membership. The association has a broad membership, encompassing business owners in areas such as farming, construction, and plumbing, as well as doctors, accountants, and lawyers. With a minimum membership fee of $50, each member can determine his own yearly membership dues with participation capped at $1000 per year.

To maintain their grass roots orientation, the association continually polls their members concerning issues currently before Congress that relate to small business. These votes are tallied and reported back to members and also forwarded with members' comments to elected officials. With information from member votes, the staff and some association members lobby and testify before Congress about concerns of small business owners.

Twice a year the association uses the same process to collect information concerning state issues. The association also publishes a monthly magazine that updates members on key legislative issues and provides information on small business operations and management. Last year the association was ranked by the political community as being one of the top ten most effective and powerful lobbies in Washington.

The association's primary competition is the long-established national, state, and local Chambers of Commerce. The national and state chambers function as lobby organizations with legislative agendas, while the local chambers are known for networking among members. The dues participation is a set amount and based upon the type of business and number of employees.

Additional competitive organizations include groups, such as Write Your Congressman, that are aimed primarily at lobbying. They generate memberships from politically active individuals as well as businesses.

Industry-specific associations also compete for the dollars of small businesses. Many association members belong to organizations such as the Farm Bureau, the Board of Realtors, and the National Retail Association.

## Organizational Structure

The association works with a flat organizational structure. There are six division directors who are responsible for their divisions and report to the National Director: the Human Resources Director, the Marketing Director, the Sales Director, the Political Director, the Communications Director, and the Operations Director. Every employee of the association is ultimately responsible for retention of members; however, the Marketing Director, Sales Director, and Communications Director have the most impact.

The Marketing Director is responsible for strategies related to the service needs of the membership. This division is also responsible for producing programs that create public awareness of the association. These programs should both generate membership and increase awareness of small business needs in the political community. They have been exploring partnering programs with large corporate entities that primarily service small businesses. Phone service or computer service companies would be an example.

The Sales Director has responsibility for all membership renewals and new membership sales in the association. The Regional Managers, who are responsible for Area Representatives, and the Membership Renewal Office Manager report to the Sales Director. The association is considering changing the structure so the Sales Division would be part of the Marketing Division. The Communications Director is responsible for all communications concerning political activity. This includes updated political information to the Sales Division. It also includes sending information to members, communications with the political community, and releases to the public through the media.

## Sales Division

The primary objective of the Sales Division has always been to obtain operating funds for the organization. Area Representatives are employees of the association who report to the Regional Manager. They contact small business owners in their areas and enlist their support as members. The principal communication and personal contact with members is through the Area Representative of the association. In most cases, this contact and the voting ballots sent from the Communications Division are the only contacts with a member. Area Representatives are also responsible for managing current members in their areas and arranging renewal of their yearly membership. The Area Representatives may handle renewals one of two ways. They may contact the members themselves or forward the members' files to the Membership Renewal Office (MRO), which will contact the members. Area Representatives are compensated on a commission basis and are responsible for their own expenses.

The Regional Managers are responsible for a state or part of a state. They are compensated with a base salary plus an override on their area's volume. The Regional Manager hires and trains new Area Representatives, who attend training seminars at the administrative office in Atlanta. Three hundred fifty Area Representatives are responsible for approximately 500,000 members. Representatives are trained to pitch each prospective member and renewal exactly the same. They are armed with standard rebuttals for any objection the prospect might give. They are trained to continue pitching until the prospect firmly says no or asks them to leave. Area Representatives are monitored and pressured to perform to a point that often offends members. There are substantial complaints concerning representatives being too aggressive or insisting that a member must renew with increased membership dues. Many members complain that representatives arrive at their place of business without appointments, refusing to leave and creating a difficult situation.

There is a high turnover among Area Representatives. Management views the turnover rate as a problem that results in reductions in the effectiveness of member communications and in turn fewer membership renewals. Because the position entails substantial cold calling, openings are difficult to fill. The association's goal has been to hire professional and dedicated Area Representatives and train them effectively to achieve higher levels of renewals and increases in membership dues, but primarily to add new members.

Sales Division statistics concerning renewals are continually monitored by management. Awards and promotions are based on these statistics. On the average, Area Representatives renew 65% of current members. The Area Representatives generally increase membership dues for 75% of their renewals by an average of $30. Files of the members they are unable to contact and members who are not renewing at that time are sent to the MRO for renewal. If the office is unable to contact the member, the Area Representative is responsible for contacting the member and finalizing the renewal.

## Membership Renewal Office

The MRO for the National Association of Small Business Owners is located adjacent to the administrative office in suburban Atlanta. There are 60 representatives divided into four divisions, each with its own manager. They are part of the Sales Division, and the MRO manager reports to the Sales Director. Their primary responsibility is to contact members that Area Representatives have been unable to reach. Their goal of raising operating funds for the organization is the same as Area Representatives. They contact all types of members, including current members, members who were not renewed on time and must be reinstated, and small business owners who have been nominated for membership by current members. The MRO contacts members forwarded by the Area Representatives. The Area Representatives in turn receive a commission override for each renewal by the MRO.

Representatives employed in the MRO are compensated on a commission basis in the same manner as Area Representatives. The MRO Representatives on the average renew 60% of the current member renewals they receive. They generally increase membership dues for 75% of their renewals by an average of $25. The MRO generated $28 million in revenue for the association last year. The total revenue of the association was $62 million.

There is a long-established rivalry between the Area Representatives and the MRO Representatives. Area Representatives feel they are forced to send member files to the MRO that they could renew themselves and thus receive compensation. For that reason, most files sent to the MRO are perceived as difficult or problem members that the Area Representatives cannot reach or do not want to contact. If there are areas not covered by Area Representatives, due to personnel turnover, the

Regional Manager forwards all member files from that area to the MRO for renewal. The MRO Representatives feel they are often left to "clean up" the problems created by Area Representatives and poor service from offices in the Political Division.

The MRO was started with the idea of contacting members who did not renew their membership with the objective of getting them back "on board". It was viewed as very successful and over a period of years they began contacting current members for renewal as well. With far fewer representatives and lower costs, they are now responsible for securing 45% of the funds raised for the association.

## Member Services

The association realizes that the services offered to members can distinguish them from other organizations and add value to the membership. Many concerns expressed by members have prompted the association to re-evaluate their program with the possibility of value-added services. The diversity of the membership has made it difficult to determine the types of services that are most meaningful to a majority of their members. Members' growing concerns over workers' compensation costs and available health insurance for small business owners have prompted the association to investigate these types of programs. In 35 states, the association has formed partnerships with several insurance providers who work with the association members to provide workers' compensation insurance. Health care insurance programs have been more difficult to put into place and only a few states are up and running. The requests continue for health insurance, and the association is working to make it available in all states.

General information and service are handled through toll-free phone lines at the administrative office. Operators receive and relay information concerning complaints and handle updates on member information, such as address and phone number changes. In most instances, the Area Representative or MRO handles these administrative details when renewing the membership.

The association has established a comprehensive website that supplies general information about the association. It also provides updated political information, voting records, and recommendations on candidates. Members can also vote their ballots on the website.

The majority of member complaints are heard through the toll-free service line or contacts with the Area Representative or MRO. The most common complaints heard by the MRO are (1) "The Area Representative just walked in my office without an appointment and demanded to see me;" (2) "The Area Representative was rude and insisted that I had to renew at a higher dues level;" (3) "I have made several calls to the State Director's office in my state capitol and no one has ever returned a call or responded in any manner;" (4) "I don't have time for the Area Representative, so please do not have them come to my office;" and (5) "I don't do business over the telephone, and the only way I will renew is if the Area Representative comes to me." The MRO Representatives are instructed to write up the complaints on a universal contact form and turn them over to their manager. It is the manager's responsibility to e-mail the Regional Manager or administrative office for appropriate follow-up. In many cases, MRO Representatives feel they are not empowered to resolve problems. They also feel they are not asked to, and in fact are encouraged not to waste time worrying about service. They are there to renew and to encourage members to increase their financial participation.

The management of the association is aware of service problems and has been exploring solutions for better member relations. Recently, they have established a state Member Services Office as a test. This office contacts members periodically in addition to attempting to renew and update members on current legislative issues. The objective for the state Member Services Office is for more day-to-day contact with current members; therefore, the Area Representatives can have more time to develop new memberships. It is too early to evaluate the results. However, to date the new office has failed to renew as many members or obtain as many dues increases as the MRO or the Area Representatives.

## Systems Management

The association realizes that their systems are not technologically up to date. They are a nonprofit organization and have been very cautious about expanding their systems. The initial communication to the MRO is a download of member files for Representatives to contact. The member information is abbreviated, and there is no system available for the Area Representatives and MRO Representatives to contact one another.

If there is a problem, it is up to the MRO Manager to contact the Regional Manager. The MRO Representative has no information concerning past contact and renewal except for the amount of dues for the prior 2 years. Information is often out of date, and it is common for a MRO Representative to be told that the member is deceased or there is a new owner of the business. If there is a problem, MRO Representatives commonly fail to update files and send outdated files back to Area Representatives without any kind of action.

The association is in the process of developing a system that will give the representatives in the MRO better access to member information. In addition, it will give them the ability to interact with the Area Representatives in the field and staff members in the lobby offices. The costs and benefits of making comment sections available are being explored in order for the Sales Division representatives to pass information from members to the lobby and administrative staffs.

## Questions

1. Would you consider NASBO to be market oriented? Why or why not?
2. Evaluate internal marketing at NASBO. How might it be improved?
3. Review the association's strategies for managing and retaining existing members. Discuss current practices that could possibly jeopardize membership.
4. Suggest new ways for NASBO to add value to it members.

# Case 11. Par Value — Enhancing Customer Value*

mateur golf has enjoyed an immense increase in popularity over the last two decades, partly due to increased leisure time and partly due to the exposure that television coverage has afforded it. From 1970 to 1992, the number of golfers grew from 11.2 million to more than 28 million. The number of rounds played annually grew from 266 million to more than 500 million. While the number of golfers and the activity rate have essentially doubled, the number of golf courses in the U.S. has only increased by about 40%, from 10,188 in 1970 to 14,375 in 1992. Figures C11.1, C11.2, and C11.3 illustrate the growth of golf from 1980 to 1990.

This disparity did not escape Edward Moore. Graduated from Yale as an engineer, he recently retired after several highly successful business ventures, his last as a banker. He began to play golf seriously in retirement and noticed that there seemed to be great opportunities in owning and operating golf courses. Aside from the financial potential, he believed that he would enjoy the golf course business: "When most golfers come out to play," he reasoned, "they are relaxed and happy, even if they don't have a terrific score. In so many service business situations, the customer is less than happy. I would like to be able to meet my customers in the more positive setting and think it would be fun."

* This case was prepared by Eldon H. Bernstein, Ph.D., Professor of Marketing, Lynn University.

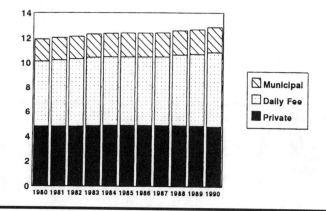

**Figure C11.1. U.S. Golf Courses 1980–1990**

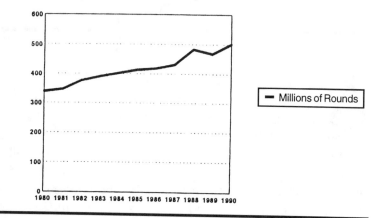

**Figure C11.2. U.S. Golf Activity 1980–1990**

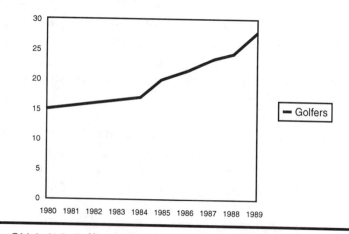

**Figure C11.3. U.S. Golfers 1980–1989 (Millions of Golfers)**

Just before the Thanksgiving holiday, Ed was seated at his desk with three large piles of papers before him. The paperwork represented months of work visiting and investigating golf courses. Now, with a self-imposed deadline only weeks away, he turned to his notes one more time and prepared to make his decision.

## Private and Public Courses

When Ed began his research on golf courses, he noted the first basic difference: private vs. public courses. In the U.S. there are about 5000 private courses and more than 9000 public courses. Private courses can be owned by their members, by a partnership, or by an institution such as a university. They are characterized by stringent regulations regarding the qualifications for membership and restrictions on non-member privileges. Members pay an annual fee, usually for unlimited golfing privileges. Charges for other services such as cart rentals and driving range access are extra.

Public courses are often owned by municipalities, but many are owned by private interests. The public has unlimited access to them by paying daily fees. Many offer annual memberships to the public that allow unlimited playing time. Public courses usually adjust their daily charge, or greens fee, to encourage people to play at off-peak periods, such as weekdays, non-holidays, mid-day, or late day.

Public courses can be divided further into those that serve the general public and those that are owned and operated for transient guests. Golf courses at areas such as Disney World, convention centers, and resort hotels are public but with limited access. Other golf courses are open to any golfer who chooses to pay the greens fee. These courses that target the general public often rely primarily on word-of-mouth advertising. Typically, modest advertising consists of Yellow Pages advertisements in telephone directories, display ads in golfing directories, or billboards located close to the course.

Public courses vary widely in terms of their character. Some courses have been cleverly designed and are challenging, with ample woods, hills, and water hazards. Proper grounds maintenance will be evident in manicured greens, lush fairways, and well-groomed sand traps. Less-attractive courses are uninteresting, often are crowded, cover short distances from tee to green, and might be maintained in mediocre or poor condition.

## Wholesale or Retail

Public courses operate either on a wholesale or retail level. Retail courses target individual golfers; wholesaler courses serve resellers. If an owner elects to operate at wholesale, he or she sells playing time, in bulk, to travel agents and tour operators who include the golfing privileges in the packages that they sell to the public. These blocks of playing time may have to be heavily discounted, but are vital in some areas. In Myrtle Beach, SC, one of the most popular golfing areas in the U.S., there are 88 golf courses. Owners must seek wholesale business to survive. Marketing to intermediaries has great benefits, however. Many golfers who are pleased with the course recommended by a hotel clerk or supplied by a travel agent will choose to return to play that course in the future, often bringing some of their friends to round out foursomes.

## Defining the Offering

As Ed pondered over the alternatives, he decided on several criteria:

- There should be a minimal seasonal component, to avoid dependence on tourists.
- The course should be retail, not wholesale.
- Local golfers should know the course.
- The character of the course should be challenging.
- The physical condition must be excellent, or capable of being restored.
- To increase value, there should be some particular opportunity with the course that can be maximized by innovative management.

## Segmenting the Market

Ed's research and numerous interviews with golfers, owners, brokers, and golf course consultants led him to make several business observations. First, the degree of difficulty and character of the course determine the type of golfer who elects to play it. That profile is an accurate predictor of the amount of money that the golfer is willing to spend on greens fees, carts, food and drinks, and any other services. Those who are willing to play the easier, less-maintained courses tend to be cost conscious, not serious, golfers. He found that segment to be composed in large part of younger, beginning golfers and retirees. Their emphasis was on a low-cost round of golf. The more serious golfer will travel farther to play a course he or she finds more challenging and rewarding, will appreciate the difference, and is willing to pay for it.

## Defining Goals and Objectives

Ed realized quickly that a tee time is a perishable commodity. Once lost, it cannot be resold. Because the costs of maintaining a golf course are fixed and relatively insensitive to the amount of play on the course, he saw his challenge as learning how to fill the tee time, or sending the maximum number of golfers out to play on any given day. If he could maximize the number of golfers playing, he estimated that he would be able to capitalize on the other services golf courses offered: cart rental, lessons, driving range sales, pro shop sales, and food and beverage sales.

The most significant threat to the profitability of a golf course is nature. Rain forces the operator to close the course. Extreme conditions of wet or drought mean extra expenses in maintaining the fairways, greens, and sand bunkers. In northern U.S. climates, play is limited to the temperate months. In northern states, also, even when the course is non-productive during the winter months, taxes, debt service, and the salaries of a few key employees still must be paid. In southern states, revenues may decline in the summer months, but they do not stop entirely as they do in northern areas. Ed decided that he would confine his search for a course to central Florida.

## Pricing Schedules

Public golf courses catering to community golfers in central Florida characteristically derive 50% of their course-generated revenues from greens fees and 50% from cart rentals. While there are some exceptions, fees at reasonably challenging, well-maintained courses are market driven and relatively similar within geographic areas. Several variables affect the fee structure: market areas, nature of the course, and whether it is a resort or non-resort facility. The Disney World-Marriott course might not differentiate weekend from weekday rates because the majority of its

**Table C11.1. Typical Greens Fees, Central Florida, 1997**

|  | Weekends & Holidays | Weekdays | Weekdays (Off-Peak) |
|---|---|---|---|
| Greens fee + cart[a] | $18.00–$22.00 | $15.00 | $12.00 |
| Greens fee only[b] | N/A | $10.00 | $8.00 |

[a]  Assumes two golfers sharing one cart.
[b]  On courses that permit hand carts or carried bags.

players are vacationers. They might give tee time priority to registered guests, however. Some courses cater largely to retirees who can play during the week; those courses do not have a significant weekend premium. A course whose core players are working people needs to have real price incentives or group programs to fill available weekday tee times.

Typically, one half of the play is on weekends, the other half is spread over the other 5 days of the week (see Table C11.1). Most courses also allow discounts for senior citizens and junior golfers. Some courses choose to offer discounts through golfers' associations. For example, the Florida Professional Golfers Association offers a PGA Passport (Figure C11.4) that entitles a golfer to discounted play on more than 250 Florida courses. Non-profit organizations are another source of discount cards (Figure C11.5). The proceeds from the fees that golfers pay directly benefit the sponsoring organization.

# The Profit Centers

Ed felt that his experience as a banker had taught him to look at a business venture in terms of potential profit centers. He recognized that each may have specific features that need to be addressed separately. He divided the golf course business into five specific areas: the course, the pro shop, cart rental, the driving range, and the food and beverage service.

## The Course

To attract and preserve a loyal clientele, a course must be properly maintained. Golfers will excuse an occasional bare spot in a fairway but

**Figure C11.4. PGA Passport**    **Figure C11.5. Discount Card**

have little tolerance for greens that are not in good condition. The course must have an adequate set of signs to indicate the direction to the next hole, accurate yardage of each hole, and the location of any facilities. The tees should have benches, ball washers, and refuse containers. Sanitary facilities and drinking fountains should be placed conveniently.

Daily-fee courses collect the greens fee before each round is played. Some courses offer multi-play coupon books at a discount; others sell seasonal passes. Some have "preferred golfer" programs that allow the golfer a discount from the daily rate and a preferred tee time. Because tee time is perishable, golf course operators strive to keep their courses as full as practical, so they will operate as efficiently as possible. Eighteen-hole golf courses consist of two 9-hole segments. Holes 1 through 9 are referred to as the front nine, or the front side, and holes 10 to 18 are called the back nine, or the back side. Foursomes can be started from both the first and the tenth holes for the first 2 hours of the day when play is usually heaviest. In this manner, more golfers are served at the critical times. During the next 2-hour interval, however, no golfers can start on either side because of golfers continuing to play.

Operators try to maximize the number of rounds played in several ways. Besides varying price to smooth demand, some organize league play, where groups of golfers play on a regular schedule, usually once a week. League membership fees include discounted greens fees and cart rentals. Course operators provide contests, prizes, and other activities. Another common strategy is to package golf outings to business and civic groups. The course operator arranges and schedules special events such as distance driving contests and putting competitions, lunches and dinners, awards programs, and entertainment.

## The Pro Shop

The Pro Shop is a small area, often a small separate building where golfers purchase tickets, arrange for carts, schedule golf lessons, and buy golf-related items. The selection of items ranges from an inexpensive package of wood tees to a complete set of clubs. In resort golf club shops, impulse purchases of high-priced items are common. Items with the resort logo are popular souvenirs. At country clubs, the success of the shop commonly reflects the relationship between the club pro and the golfing members. Pros who devote time developing those ties sell more goods. Pro shops at public courses tend to sell less than those at private courses. They sell modest amounts of balls, hats, visors, and emergency equipment such as umbrellas and rain gear. Most, however, cannot compete with the discounters and "category killers" on clothing, shoes, clubs, bags, and other costly items. Manufacturers sometimes leave sets of golf clubs with pro shops as demonstrators. If the pro shop sells them, they pay the manufacturer and order a new demo set. Course owners typically allow the pro to keep the profit on this type of sale. At a public course, the golf professional is usually paid a modest sum. He receives the proceeds of any lessons and, in some instances, a small percentage of the sales in the shop. While revenues tend to be substantial at private course pro shops, public course pro shop revenues typically account for only 5 to 15% of the course's sales volume. Gross profit on goods sold averages 30%.

## Golf Cart Rental

A considerable amount of revenue is generated from the rental of golf carts. Very few golfers walk the course. The usual method of rental is to charge by the round, whether included in the day's fee or as a separate charge to golfers holding annual memberships. Some courses sell books of tickets, others offer multi-ride packages. Carts are either battery or gas powered. While electric carts are less expensive to maintain, they need to be recharged frequently, limiting their productivity. Gas carts can be refilled quickly but are more complicated mechanically and require more sophisticated service facilities. In addition to recharging or refueling costs, routine maintenance, cleaning, insurance, and general overhauls are significant cost factors.

McKay Associates, the golf course consultants, estimate that in the south a cart should produce 200 rounds per season. They suggest that a cart producing fewer rounds indicates that the course has too many carts or that the fleet is not being managed properly. Their rule of thumb is that the optimum number of carts on an 18-hole course is 55, so that adequate spacing over the course is maintained. Carts coming off of the 18th hole can be sent back out immediately on the first hole. Some estimates, however, suggest that scheduling is precarious with 55 carts and recommend that 72 carts is the optimum number to avoid making golfers unhappy.

Some courses own their carts, while others lease them. In 1996, leasing companies charged between $800 and $900 per cart to course operators. In some instances, contracts allow rental fees to be applied toward the purchase of the carts. New golf carts sell for about $3000. Course operators must be diligent in controlling the use of their carts. Golfers may abuse the carts in a variety of ways — they may damage carts, may rent for 9 holes and play 18, may allow more than two people to use the cart, or may tie the cart up for hours while having lunch. Some public courses permit golfers to have their own carts. In these instances, course operators and cart owners negotiate fees for charging and storing the carts. Fees range from $100 to $400 per year.

## The Driving Range

One area that offers significant potential profits is the driving, or practice, range. Practice ranges attract some people who come only to use the range but do not play the course. The economics of a practice range are appealing. Practice balls cost less than $3 per dozen in bulk. Some are lost, but the number is not great. The range supplies clubs for players who do not have their own, but again cost is not significant. A small "shack" is sufficient to house the equipment and a sales counter. To pick up the balls, an operator can outfit an ordinary golf cart with a screen to protect the driver and a device to gather in the balls for about $700. The balls are returned to the shack and scooped into buckets. Depending upon the type of driving range, a small bucket of balls costs between $1.50 and $3. Jumbo buckets sell from $4 to as much as $10. Like most other jobs at the golf course, the driving range attendant is usually a part-timer, receiving minimum wage and unlimited free golfing privileges.

There are several features that determine whether a range can command premium pricing strategies. While some ranges are simply fields with yardage markers placed in them, others have real golf holes strategically placed at 50, 100, 150, and 200 yard distances as examples. These greens have pins and sand traps so that a golfer who wants to practice approach shots can aim for a very realistic target. Some ranges supply artificial turf as hitting areas, while others use natural grass, which is more appealing. Operators can keep the natural grass in good playable condition by changing the hitting area every few days and replanting the area where the turf has been damaged. Some ranges are lighted for night use, and some are covered to allow use in inclement weather.

An active practice range can have room for 25 golfers to hit simultaneously. It takes a patron about 30 to 45 minutes to hit a large bucket of balls (about 60). Assuming that a range is open 12 hours per day, its maximum usage would be 400 players per day (12 hours ÷ .75 hr/player × 25 spaces). Industry statistics suggest that a typical range operates at a 20% use factor; therefore, a range would be expected to sell 80 buckets of balls at an average of $3 per bucket, or $240 per day. If weather permitted it to operate 300 days a year, the range would realize a gross revenue of $72,000. Ed noted that most recreational golfers tend to go directly to the first tee and begin playing with no warm-up time. Professionals and accomplished amateurs, he pointed out, usually hit a bucket or two of practice balls before starting their round. He planned to promote a practice basket, or what he called "The Stroke Saver".

### Food and Beverage Sales

Food and beverage service at golf courses ranges from vending machine sales to full-service dining rooms. Some courses have "half-way" stands located in a strategic spot on the course. Others have cooler-equipped golf carts that traverse the course selling drinks and snacks. Snack bars usually sell breakfast and lunch items and may remain open at night if the driving range is active. At snack bars, the cost of goods sold is between 25% and 30%. The latest industry statistics indicate that the average golfer spends $30 per round on golf plus $7.50 on food and drinks. To promote snack bar sales, some courses supply menus on the carts. Aggressive marketers provide direct telephone links from the 8th and 17th holes so that golfers can phone in their lunch orders and have them waiting. Snack bar sales tend to be limited to a sandwich and beverage. Snack bar sales fluctuate in direct proportion to the number of rounds played at the course, and it is very hard to generate any sales beyond that formula.

Public courses with full dining service can offer golf outings that provide a full day of golfing activity and conclude with a dinner, often featuring awards for individual golfers. In addition, public courses usually solicit the general public as customers and promote their facilities for private affairs such as weddings, parties, and reunions. Because most public golf course managers are not trained in restaurant management, the majority of the public course restaurants are operated under contracts with professional restaurateurs.

## The Courses

Ed has contacted a golf course broker who has shown him several courses that are for sale, and Ed has narrowed the options down to three of them. The courses are quite different from one another, and he must decide which course, if any, he will buy.

## Twin Cypress Golf Course

Twin Cypress Golf Course is in Polk County, close to Winter Haven. Twin Cypress was built in the late 1950s by Art Singer, who was developing an adjacent parcel of land as residential sites. Singer was an amateur golfer who carved out an 18-hole course from 105 acres of land. Twin Cypress is a "bare-bones" course; the layout is not challenging. It has a lounge with food service and a modest pro shop. A small area in the center of the course serves as the driving range. The driving range has only a few hitting areas with rubber mats for tees. The clubhouse, parking lot, and other general facilities are in need of repair. There are sanitary facilities only on the 5th and 14th holes. The course appeals mainly to retirees and beginning players. Only 3% of the players are women.

Twin Cypress was left in trust to Art Singer's five children. Two brothers are actively involved in managing the course; one is called "The Pro" although he is neither a professional nor an accomplished golfer. All of the employees are retirees who work part time. The two managing brothers pay an annual rental to the Singer Trust. Because they each have a 20% interest in the trust, the brothers are not particularly concerned with how much rent they pay. Intra-family disagreements indicate that it would be better for all concerned if they sold the property. Twin Cypress is conveniently located at the confluence of two major highways and a state road.

Twin Cypress advertises on billboards near the course and offers discount coupons in the sports pages of the local newspapers and shopping papers. They have no annual members. The utilization rate of the potential course capacity is slightly less than 50%. Table C11.2 is a summary of Twin Cypress' operating statements for the years 1994 to 1996.

## Random River Golf Course

Random River is south of Orlando. The original real estate parcel was almost 200 acres. Two 18-hole courses were constructed on the property. In 1987, a land developer bought the property, intending to build condominium housing. The developer sold off half of one of the courses, approximately 50 acres, and condominiums were built on the land. The course employs one full-time greenskeeper and two full-time yardmen.

All other employees are part time. They are paid the minimum wage, but receive unlimited golfing privileges.

It has a challenging and interesting layout but has been neglected over the past few years, so the course condition has deteriorated. The fairways and the sand traps require significant repairs. The parking lot should be resurfaced. The property consists of an 18-hole traditional course named Crest, and a 9-hole executive, or short, course called Challenger. There is significantly more play on the 18-hole course, although previous management has allocated 2/3 of total costs to Crest and 1/3 of the costs to Challenger. There are adequate sanitary facilities around the course, and the modern, full-service snack bar has a beer license. The driving range is located next to the 15th hole. It has grass hitting areas and yardage markers, as well as, at different distances, three greens with traps. At Random River, 30% of the players are women.

The course requires an immediate investment of approximately $30,000 for turf repairs and other maintenance. A well provides the water to irrigate the course. The piping in the system is cast iron but is in disrepair. In the near future, the piping will have to be replaced with PVC (plastic) pipes. Estimated cost to change to PVC piping is $75,000. Random River's operating statements are summarized in Table C11.3.

## West Bay Country Club

West Bay is near Titusville, the closest city to the Kennedy Space Center. The Space Center and the Astronaut's Hall of Fame are strong tourist attractions. West Bay was a private club but is now public. Its touring professional, Bradford L. "Putts" Melamud, retired to become a teaching pro at the course and subsequently bought the course, at which time he decided to convert it to a public facility. West Bay has a challenging layout, and the course and facilities are in very good condition. In 1996, the course had 140 members who paid $1000 annual dues, but the majority of its revenues come from daily fees. Members prefer to play on weekends, so the course provides guaranteed reservation times for them. Women account for almost 50% of the rounds played. There is an area used as a driving range between the clubhouse and the first tee. The range has grass hitting areas and yardage markers but no other improvements. The pro shop provides a positive return, attributable to the fact that Putts has a good rapport with the players.

**Table C11.2. Operating Statement, Twin Cypress Golf Club**

|  | FY 1994 | FY 1995 | FY 1996 |
|---|---|---|---|
| **Sales** | | | |
| Membership fees | 4129 | 2030 | 2567 |
| Greens fees (18 holes) | 148,592 | 138,237 | 173,719 |
| Greens fees (9 holes) | 35,271 | 23,426 | 28,386 |
| Cart rental (18 holes) | 89,662 | 66,185 | 79,961 |
| Cart rental (9 holes) | 19,576 | 11,959 | 13,448 |
| Carts multiway | 23,520 | 40,938 | 51,360 |
| Driving range fees | 5256 | 3449 | 3765 |
| Golf club rentals | 1469 | 1522 | 1525 |
| Pro shop sales | 14,090 | 9360 | 9034 |
| Vending machine sales | 15,039 | 12,111 | 14,025 |
| Lounge sales | 29,851 | 25,075 | 24,984 |
| Londontown fees | 6461 | 4060 | 4714 |
| FCCJ fees | 1206 | 340 | 142 |
| GHL cards/carts | 36,166 | 18,209 | 17,818 |
| Total sales | 430,289 | 356,900 | 425,449 |
| **Cost of sales** | | | |
| Purchases (pro shop) | 8463 | 4028 | 3655 |
| Purchases (vending mach) | 10,386 | 12,248 | 9805 |
| Purchases (lounge) | 13,291 | 10,486 | 10,880 |
| Total cost of sales | 32,140 | 26,762 | 24,341 |
| Gross operating profit | 398,150 | 330,138 | 401,108 |
| **Operating expenses** | | | |
| Advertising | 3885 | 5380 | 3389 |
| Bank charges | 428 | 226 | 304 |
| Car and truck expense | 1750 | 1647 | 1062 |
| Car and truck repair | 488 | 600 | 190 |
| Cart lease charges | 29,564 | 30,037 | 24,404 |
| Cart maintenance | 15,013 | 14,542 | 10,308 |
| Contributions | 72 | 120 | 221 |
| Depreciation | 29,564 | 30,038 | 24,405 |
| Entertainment | 136 | 204 | 291 |
| Dues/subscriptions | 890 | 1150 | 963 |
| Insurance | 25,054 | 27,209 | 29,599 |
| Interest | 15,014 | 14,543 | 10,309 |
| Legal and professional | 4879 | 9556 | 3948 |
| Licenses | 2370 | 10,432 | 34,930 |
| Office expense | 1558 | 1894 | 399 |
| Postage | 336 | 334 | 325 |
| Refuse service | 712 | 960 | 927 |

**Table C11.2. Operating Statement, Twin Cypress Golf Club (cont.)**

|  | FY 1994 | FY 1995 | FY 1996 |
|---|---|---|---|
| Rental of land | 39,900 | 39,900 | 30,000 |
| Repair/maintain carts | 2803 | 1019 | 2992 |
| Repair/maintain clubhouse | 1829 | 577 | 1480 |
| Repair/maintain course | 24,336 | 22,241 | 19,956 |
| Repair/maintain buildings | 917 | 657 | 39 |
| Repair/maintain equipment | 7399 | 3939 | 8969 |
| Supplies (clubhouse) | 3071 | 2020 | 1776 |
| Supplies (pro shop) | 1963 | 937 | 335 |
| Supplies (repair shop) | 373 | 913 | 1489 |
| Taxes (payroll) | 12,873 | 11,958 | 12,067 |
| Telephone | 1929 | 2005 | 1792 |
| Wages (general) | 79,875 | 73,780 | 73,907 |
| Wages (officers) | 78,060 | 73,365 | 74,295 |
| Utilities | 16,967 | 12,833 | 18,926 |
| Sales tax | 5688 | 2594 | 1857 |
| Total expenses | 409,695 | 397,608 | 395,851 |
| **Net operating income** | −11,545 | −67,470 | 5257 |

There are sanitary facilities conveniently placed around the course. The clubhouse has an elegant 7000-square-foot restaurant; however, the restaurant was closed in mid-1994 due to management problems and has not reopened. Vending machines provide the only source of snacks or drinks. There are four Har-Tru-surfaced tennis courts that currently are not being used. There was a swimming pool next to the tennis courts, but the present owners filled it over in 1989.

The majority of West Bay's members live in a residential development of approximately 700 homes adjacent to the golf course. When the area was developed, over 300 of the families were members. Most of those members failed to renew because of management problems at West Bay. About 200 of the 700 homes are occupied by "snowbirds" — people who have residences in northern states and live in Florida only during the winter months.

Putts, the pro, wants to return to the pro tour. He has offered the package valued at $2,000,000, with the provision that he retain 10%, or $200,000. He will grant Ed the right to buy out his $200,000 share in 3 years. West Bay Country Club's operating statements are presented in

## Table C11.3. Operating Statement, Random River Golf Club

|  | FY 1994 | FY 1995 | FY 1996 |
|---|---|---|---|
| **Sales** | | | |
| Membership fees | 64,736 | 57,921 | 61,948 |
| Greens fees (9 holes) | 62,656 | 56,061 | 59,958 |
| Greens fees (18 holes) | 269,631 | 241,249 | 258,020 |
| Cart rental (9 holes) | 27,602 | 24,696 | 26,413 |
| Cart rental (18 holes) | 388,918 | 347,979 | 372,170 |
| Driving range | 43,585 | 38,997 | 41,708 |
| Pro shop | 30,186 | 27,008 | 28,886 |
| Food/beverage | 167,154 | 149,559 | 159,956 |
| Other | 1130 | 1459 | 1560 |
| Total revenues | 1,055,597 | 944,929 | 1,010,619 |
| **Expenses** | | | |
| Advertising and promotion | 8850 | 9350 | 10,000 |
| Association dues | 6875 | 7293 | 7800 |
| Bad debt expense | 2334 | 3671 | 3926 |
| Building maintenance | 6270 | 5610 | 6000 |
| Cart shop/ mechanics | 42,080 | 37,651 | 40,268 |
| Cart rental charge | 71,000 | 71,000 | 71,000 |
| Cart shop /employee benefits | 9924 | 8880 | 9497 |
| Cart shop /supplies | 8679 | 11,052 | 11,820 |
| Course maintenance | 54,456 | 57,489 | 61,486 |
| Course repair | 66,573 | 66,142 | 70,740 |
| Driving range | 28,085 | 25,129 | 26,876 |
| Food/beverage misc. | 15,868 | 14,198 | 15,185 |
| Food/beverage wages | 52,110 | 46,625 | 49,866 |
| Food beverage employee benefits | 10,489 | 9385 | 10,037 |
| Food/beverage cost/goods sold | 62,423 | 55,852 | 59,735 |
| Gasoline | 887 | 922 | 986 |
| Golf payroll | 139,993 | 125,257 | 133,965 |
| Golf payroll taxes | 31,474 | 28,161 | 30,119 |
| General and administrative | 55,639 | 57,269 | 61,250 |
| G&A benefits | 11,275 | 13,249 | 14,170 |
| Insurance | 10,867 | 11,124 | 11,897 |
| Painting and decorating | 1866 | 3422 | 1786 |
| Personal property tax | 568 | 509 | 544 |
| Office supplies | 1615 | 1445 | 877 |
| Postage | 314 | 281 | 300 |
| Professional fees | 3550 | 3740 | 4000 |
| Pro shop benefits | 11,655 | 11,562 | 12,366 |
| Pro shop cost of goods sold | 21,493 | 19,230 | 20,567 |

**Table C11.3. Operating Statement, Random River Golf Club (cont.)**

|  | FY 1994 | FY 1995 | FY 1996 |
|---|---|---|---|
| Pro shop wages | 26,778 | 25,838 | 27,634 |
| Refuse service | 2160 | 2244 | 2400 |
| Real estate taxes | 24,534 | 26,315 | 28,144 |
| Telephone | 8948 | 8006 | 8563 |
| Trade publications | 277 | 281 | 300 |
| Uniforms | 455 | 320 | 342 |
| Utility/electric | 33,234 | 29,736 | 31,803 |
| Utility/water | 2423 | 2168 | 2319 |
| Total expenses | 836,023 | 800,403 | 848,568 |
| **Net operating profit** | 219,574 | 144,526 | 162,051 |

Table C11.4. (Also, see Table C11.5 for projected operating profits for the three competing courses over 3 years.)

## Business Plans

Ed developed business plans for each of the courses. Included in those plans were details on how he intended to increase revenues and to control costs. The projections reflected the degree to which he felt each course could be marketed more successfully and the areas in which expenses would have to be increased or could be reduced. Whichever course he chose, Ed's objectives were to increase the number of rounds played as much as possible without inconveniencing regular players. He expected to tailor promotions to all feasible market segments.

He felt that Twin Cypress and West Bay required upgraded food facilities and a strong marketing program. Random River initially required significant improvements in the condition of the course, followed by a more aggressive marketing program. The features of the three courses are summarized in Table C11.6. Table C11.7 provides selected demographic data for Florida and the three Standard Metropolitan Statistical Areas (SMSAs) where Ed Moore's prospective courses are located. Tables C11.8 and C11.9 present nationwide data on golfers regarding their income, sex, and age.

### Table C11.4. Operating Statement, West Bay Country Club

|  | FY 1994 | FY 1995 | FY 1996 |
|---|---|---|---|
| **Sales** |  |  |  |
| Membership fees | 128,000 | 119,000 | 140,000 |
| Greens fees (18 holes) | 223,593 | 205,095 | 238,347 |
| Greens fees (9 holes) | 87,582 | 65,753 | 77,356 |
| Cart rental (18 holes) | 114,563 | 100,873 | 118,674 |
| Cart rental (9 holes) | 25,376 | 21,791 | 25,637 |
| Restaurant | 156,384 | 73,429 | 0 |
| Pro shop | 91,674 | 72,339 | 97,439 |
| Driving range | 8469 | 7922 | 9320 |
| Vending machines | 12,580 | 11,768 | 13,845 |
| Total sales | 848,221 | 677,970 | 720,618 |
| **Cost of sales** |  |  |  |
| Golf carts | 42,336 | 46,441 | 44,637 |
| Restaurant | 67,453 | 36,285 | 0 |
| Pro shop | 52,345 | 48,669 | 57,846 |
| Driving range | 3128 | 2926 | 3442 |
| Vending machines | 9703 | 9076 | 10,678 |
| Other | 14,305 | 16,445 | 18,759 |
| Total cost of sales | 189,269 | 159,842 | 135,362 |
| Gross operating profit | 658,952 | 518,128 | 585,256 |
| **Operating expenses** |  |  |  |
| Accounting + legal | 3109 | 2909 | 3422 |
| Advertising + promotion | 6674 | 6243 | 7345 |
| Association dues | 591 | 553 | 650 |
| Cart maintenance | 20,060 | 19,411 | 21,071 |
| Clubhouse wages | 34,885 | 32,633 | 38,392 |
| Fertilizer, seed, chemicals | 34,677 | 32,439 | 38,163 |
| Gas and oil | 7147 | 6685 | 7865 |
| Insurance | 10,060 | 9411 | 11,072 |
| Licenses | 500 | 468 | 550 |
| Office expenses | 22,128 | 20,700 | 24,353 |
| Payroll taxes | 29,420 | 23,715 | 17,349 |
| Pro shop wages | 30,129 | 28,184 | 33,158 |
| Real estate taxes | 21,309 | 19,933 | 23,451 |
| Repair/maintain clubhouse | 12,038 | 11,261 | 13,248 |
| Repair/maintain course | 26,808 | 25,078 | 29,503 |
| Repair/maintain equipment | 22,022 | 20,601 | 24,236 |
| Restaurant wages | 45,336 | 23,872 | 0 |
| Telephone | 3109 | 2909 | 3422 |
| Trade publications | 313 | 293 | 345 |

### Table C11.4. Operating Statement, West Bay Country Club (cont.)

|  | FY 1994 | FY 1995 | FY 1996 |
|---|---|---|---|
| Utilities/electric | 25,646 | 23,990 | 28,224 |
| Utilities/water | 7991 | 7475 | 8794 |
| Total operating expenses | 363,951 | 318,762 | 334,613 |
| Total expenses | 553,220 | 478,604 | 469,975 |
| **Net operating income** | 295,000 | 199,366 | 250,643 |

### Table C11.5. Projected Operating Profits for Courses in 3 Years

|  | Twin Cypress | | Random River | | West Bay | |
|---|---|---|---|---|---|---|
|  | Present | 3 Years | Present | 3 Years | Present | 3 Years |
| Sales | 425,000 | 540,000 | 1,000,000 | 1,250,000 | 720,000 | 860,000 |
| Operating costs | 360,000 | 310,000 | 834,000 | 700,000 | 470,000 | 470,000 |
| Operating profit | 41,000 | 230,000 | 162,000 | 550,000 | 250,000 | 390,000 |

### Table C11.6. Summary of Course Data

|  | Twin Cypress | Random River | West Bay |
|---|---|---|---|
| Holes | 18 | 27 | 18 |
| Total acreage | 105 | 153 | 103 |
| Driving range | Basic | Improved | Basic |
| Snack bar service | Lounge | Full | Vending machines |
| Golf cart fleet | 40 | 100 | 75 |
| Cart rental fee | $10 (2 golfers) | $10 (2 golfers) | $10 (2 golfers) |
| Annual rounds[a] | 33,000 | 51,000[b] | 38,000 |
| 1992 sales | $470,000 | $1,000,000 | $720,000 |
| Sales/round[c] | $14.24 | $19.60 | $18.95 |
| Capacity used | 48% | 65% | 55% |
| Fee/off-peak rate | $18/$15 | $18/$15 | $18/$15 |
| Annual members | Negligible | Negligible | 140 @ $1000/yr |
| Operating costs | $330,000 | $834,000 | $470,000 |
| Operating profit | $140,000 | $166,000 | $250,000 |
| Asking price | $1,550,000 | $1,995,000 | $2,000,000 |
| Times earnings | 11.07 | 12.02 | 8.00 |

[a]  Number of paid rounds played.
[b]  41,000 rounds on 18-hole course; 10,000 on 9-hole course.
[c]  Greens fees and food and equipment sales divided by rounds played.

**Table C11.7. Demographics of Selected Florida Standard Metropolitan Statistical Areas**

| | Florida | Orlando | | | Melbourne Titusville Palm Bay | Lakeland/ Winter Haven |
| | | Seminole | Orange | Osceola | Brevard | Polk |
|---|---|---|---|---|---|---|
| **Population** | | | | | | |
| Population, 1990 | 12,937,926 | 287,529 | 677,491 | 107,728 | 398,978 | 405,382 |
| Population estimated, 2000 | 15,988,031 | 392,541 | 843,592 | 145,513 | 533,616 | 504,181 |
| Median age, 1990 | 36.4 | 33.3 | 31.5 | 33.7 | 36.4 | 36.5 |
| % Population age 25–44 | 30.4 | 35.6 | 35.4 | 31.7 | 31.2 | 27.9 |
| % Population age 45–64 | 19.8 | 19.1 | 17.4 | 19.2 | 21.5 | 20.3 |
| % Population age 65–80 | 18.3 | 10.3 | 10.6 | 13.9 | 16.6 | 18.6 |
| Ratio males:females | 47.6:52.4 | 47.9:52.1 | 47.6:52.4 | 48.2:51.8 | 48.9:51.1 | 47.5:52.5 |
| Per capita income | $15,584 | $14,621 | $15,785 | $15,240 | $14,650 | $12,479 |
| **Owner-occupied housing value** | | | | | | |
| Lowest quartile | $56,100 | $70,000 | $62,300 | $59,000 | $58,300 | $43,000 |
| Median | $77,100 | $91,500 | $81,400 | $75,700 | $75,200 | $61,600 |
| Highest quartile | $112,200 | $125,600 | $112,300 | $97,900 | $107,700 | $86,400 |
| **Number of golf courses** | | | | | | |
| Public | 592 | 8 | 23 | 8 | 14 | 7 |
| Private | 460 | 5 | 19 | 0 | 7 | — |
| Total | 1052 | 13 | 42 | 8 | 21 | 19 |

**Table C11.8. Selected Golfer Demographics:**
**Household Income (Thousands of Participants)**

| Activity | Participants | Under $15,000 | $15,000– $24,999 | $25,000– $34,999 | $35,000– $49,000 | Over $50,000 |
|---|---|---|---|---|---|---|
| All sports | 222,551 | 53,397 | 39,253 | 34,476 | 41,507 | 53,917 |
| Percentage | | 23.9 | 17.6 | 15.5 | 18.6 | 24.2 |
| Golf | 23,156 | 2376 | 3221 | 3220 | 5030 | 9248 |
| Percentage | | 10.3 | 13.9 | 13.9 | 21.7 | 40.2 |

**Table C11.9. Selected Golfer Demographics:**
**Age and Sex (Thousands of Participants)**

| Activity | Participants | Male | Female | Age 25–45 | Age 45–65 | Age 65 + |
|---|---|---|---|---|---|---|
| All sports | 222,551 | 108,000 | 114,551 | 80,578 | 46,429 | 30,975 |
| Percentage | | 48.52 | 51.48 | 36.2 | 20.9 | 13.9 |
| Golf | 23,156 | 17,411 | 5745 | 10,329 | 4727 | 2171 |
| Percentage | 10.2 | 75.2 | 24.8 | 46.5 | 21.1 | 10.1 |

# Building the Value of a Course

As he prepared to make his decision, Ed realized that whichever course he chose he would have to design a strategy that built customer value. He was well aware that each of the three courses would have to become more market oriented. As he studied the characteristics of the individual courses, he realized that the customer-development program for each would have to be quite different. Each one appealed to a different customer segment, and the customers on each course had differing sets of values. He wondered how he could build value in each of them, and how he might be able to measure the customers' satisfaction with the new features. Only after he completed that analysis, would he feel comfortable in making this major decision.

## Questions

1. Discuss the key service quality indicators for a typical public golf course.
2. Propose how customer satisfaction might be measured when adding the new features.
3. Develop a value statement for each of the three public golf courses mentioned in the case.
4. What value-creating strategies would you suggest for each course?

# Case 12. Pizza Hut® — A Customer Loyalty Program

can't figure it out," Rick, the Pizza Hut delivery area manager, admitted to Jean, an area manager on the dine-in side of the business. "I've got stores with double-digit sales growth. Their bottom lines are as strong as they've ever been. Yet, the managers of these stores aren't meeting their quarterly bonus targets so they're quitting. In the past few months, I've lost many of my best managers. Some have gone to work for Papa John's and one now works for Domino's. Two of them have even taken voluntary demotions to become delivery drivers, saying that driving pays more than managing. All because their customer loyalty scores are not very good."

"I've got the opposite problem," replied Jean. "My dine-in restaurants are showing negative sales growth, yet have very high customer loyalty scores. My managers are happy because they're making their quarterly bonus targets; however, my boss is breathing down my neck wondering where the sales growth and profit are."

"It wasn't like this in previous years," Rick said. "In those days, all the management bonuses were based on store profitability. If you weren't making a profit, you weren't getting a bonus. Then, in 1995, the company began their customer satisfaction/loyalty initiatives. The company was jazzed about it. All my managers were jazzed about it. Instead of

---

* This case was prepared by Alan Seidman, doctoral student, Nova Southeastern University.

receiving bonuses based on their stores' financial statements, managers now qualified for bonuses based upon how loyal and satisfied their customers say they are when surveyed. It seems to make sense. Loyal customers were going to patronize us more and tell their friends about us. That meant extra business. Extra business meant extra profits."

"And extra profits would mean big bonuses for the managers," agreed Jean. "But somehow that never happened. Somewhere, somehow, the system broke down. Maybe we can figure out why."

## Overview

In 1958, the Carney brothers in Wichita, KS, borrowed $600 from their mother and opened the first Pizza Hut restaurant to great success. Within a year, the first franchise was opened. By 1977, it had grown to nearly 3200 units and was acquired by PepsiCo. With over 12,300 units, Pizza Hut has become the largest pizza restaurant chain in the world, operating in 84 countries and territories.

Providing carry-out, dine-in, and delivery service, Pizza Hut features a variety of pizzas as well as pasta, salads, sandwiches, chicken wings, and other food and beverage items. Its list of awards includes being chosen as the best pizza chain in America in a survey conducted by *Restaurants & Institutions* magazine, as well as being named the best pizza chain in America by *Consumer Reports* in January of 1997. Its recognition is tremendous, and there is hardly anyone left in the U.S. who has not tried a Pizza Hut pizza at one time or another.

In 1986, the company began offering delivery service. Special Pizza Hut delivery units were constructed, separate from the traditional "red roof" restaurants. Because of their relatively low cost and easy construction, delivery units began to proliferate in strip malls and other centralized locations, competing directly with Domino's Pizza, the leading pizza delivery company in the country at that time.

Although delivery was a huge success, the company continued to search for new products and ideas that would keep Pizza Hut at the forefront of an increasingly competitive pizza delivery segment. In 1993, Bigfoot™ pizza was introduced, followed by Stuffed Crust pizza in 1995 and Triple Decker Pizza in 1996. All three pizzas were instrumental in providing short-term increases to sales; however, they lacked the ability to increase sales over the long term.

In 1996, worldwide system sales exceeded $7.4 billion. Although this was a record sales figure, it was due primarily to system growth. Same store sales in the company-operated stores decreased 4%, reflecting fewer transactions within each store. In the first half of 1997, same store sales of company-owned restaurants dropped an additional 7%. Clearly, the company was headed in the wrong direction.

Pizza Hut's role as a PepsiCo subsidiary ended in 1997 when the parent company spun-off its three major fast-food holdings (Pizza Hut, KFC, and Taco Bell) in an effort to concentrate solely on its beverage and snack food (Frito Lay) business. By consisting solely of fast-food restaurants, the new company, Tricon Global Restaurants, focuses solely on the needs of its three restaurant holdings. The major challenge facing both Pizza Hut and Tricon is trying to remain competitive in today's global environment by keeping old customers happy while trying to attract new ones.

## Customer Loyalty

In response to increasing competition and declining sales, Pizza Hut began a comprehensive customer loyalty initiative in 1995. Through marketing research, the company aimed to improve guest satisfaction and unit-level execution at over 3700 company-owned stores and about 200 franchised restaurants. By presenting restaurant managers with weekly feedback from their customers, Pizza Hut hoped the feedback would strengthen operations within the control of each restaurant manager. The plan itself was comprised of two components: a customer service 1-800 number and a customer satisfaction/loyalty survey.

### 1-800 Customer Service Number

For the first time in its history, Pizza Hut introduced a customer satisfaction hotline. The 1-800 number was visibly posted inside stores and on individual pizza boxes and was designed to address all questions, problems, and/or complaints a customer might have about the product or service. Because many issues and concerns were now being handled by an outside marketing agency, the hotline was able to reduce the time managers spent handling customer complaints, thereby giving them more time to devote to running their stores. Additionally, the hotline operator was able to listen and respond to each situation from a neutral perspective.

The customer service hotline provided another benefit. It became a forum for those who chose not to complain to a store manager or employee during a face-to-face encounter. Many customers who normally do not like to complain now had an opportunity to do so. This was very important for Pizza Hut. Consider the following findings from *Consumer Complaint Handling in America*, a study by Technical Assistance Research Programs, Inc. (TARP):

- About 50% of the time, customers who have a problem with a product or service are not likely to tell the company about it.
- Nine out of 10 of these "silent critics" will probably take their future business to a competitor.
- Even when a customer does complain, one out of every two will not be thoroughly satisfied with the company's efforts to solve the problem.

These findings have a large impact for Pizza Hut, as well as all other service firms. Because dissatisfied customers typically tell between seven to nine other people when they had an unsatisfactory experience with a company, it is imperative that companies do all they can to get a dissatisfied customer to complain. If a customer's concern goes unresolved, the likelihood of that customer returning is greatly diminished.

When a call was made to the hotline, the operator would try to find out which Pizza Hut was in question (landmarks and other relevant information could be used to help identify individual stores in case a customer was unsure). The operator would make notes of the incident and send the customer free pizza coupons as an apology. All incidents were sent to each affected store manager and area manager via a computerized download. More severe incidents would be presented to people further up the chain of command. These incidents did not affect a manager's bonus opportunity in any way. The customer service hotline was merely a tool for Pizza Hut managers to listen to customers who might not normally complain. It was a great resource for both the customer and the company.

## Customer Satisfaction/Loyalty Survey

Identifying loyal customers has become a necessity for many service businesses. In the early 1990s, articles in the *Harvard Business Review* detailed the impact loyal customers can have on a business. Simply stated, if a customer is satisfied with the product and service, he or she stands a good chance of returning to that business. Keeping the customer loyal to your business has obvious implications. A loyal customer will return to your business time and time again. Often times he will bring other customers along. Almost certainly, he will tell other people about the good experiences he had. Such positive word-of-mouth will bring other customers. Over time, they, too, become satisfied and loyal, telling their friends as well. Over time, the business becomes more profitable, having been driven by the repeat business and positive word-of-mouth of loyal customers.

The questions asked in Pizza Hut's survey were constructed in such a way as to analyze the relationships between repeat customer visits and the operational components within each restaurant that would affect customer loyalty. Such components included product quality, service quality, and overall restaurant appeal. Each interview was done by an outside marketing agency. Brief telephone interviews were conducted only with customers who had purchased a Pizza Hut pizza within the last 36 hours. After that time, it was deemed that the survey results would lose some degree of accuracy. Because delivery stores and dine-in restaurants had unique customer relationship characteristics, separate survey processes were developed for each, as described below.

## Delivery Restaurants

Capturing and quantifying loyalty is by no means an easy task for any business. Pizza Hut (in the delivery side of the business) did have a distinct advantage. Carry-out and delivery customers were kept track of on an in-store database. Each database contained the customer's name, address, and phone number, as well as a record of what they had ordered in the past. The satisfaction/loyalty initiative for the delivery stores worked as follows. A name at random would be drawn from the store's database and contacted by the marketing research representative. The customer was asked if he or she had ordered and eaten the pizza within the last 36 hours. If the answer was "yes", the following questions would be asked (in this order):

1. On a scale of 1 to 5, if you had a chance to return to this Pizza Hut in the next 90 days, would you do so? (1 = definitely not;

2 = probably not; 3 = may or may not; 4 = probably would; 5 = definitely would)

2. Did you have any type of problem with your last order? (yes or no)
3. Did you receive the correct order? (yes or no)
4. How valued did we make you feel as a customer? (felt valued or didn't feel valued)
5. On a scale of 1 to 7, how would you rate the topping amount on your pizza? (1 = hardly any toppings; 7 = toppings were plentiful)
6. On a scale of 1 to 7, how would you rate the temperature of your pizza? (1 = very cold; 7 = very hot)
7. On a scale of 1 to 7, how would you rate the appearance of your pizza? (1 = didn't look appealing at all; 7 = looked very appealing)
8. On a scale of 1 to 7, how would you rate your overall experience? (1 = terrible, 2 = unsatisfactory; 3 = average; 4 = above average; 5 = good; 6 = very good; 7 = excellent)

On average, nine customers per store, per week were polled, regardless of the store's volume. Generally, delivery stores would range from about 800 orders a week up to 2000 orders a week.

Survey data were then brought into Pizza Hut's mainframe computers, where they were organized, analyzed, and sent or downloaded to individual stores. Each delivery store manager and area manager (as well as every other level of management up the chain of command) received a tabulation of these scores on a weekly basis. Tabulations were kept on a running 4-week basis. In other words, all scores and data were the reflection of 4 weeks of customer surveys (approximately 36 surveys). When results from a new week were downloaded, the earliest week's scores would drop off, meaning that the scores reflected the last 4 weeks' worth of surveys.

Questions 1 and 8 determined customer loyalty. It was hoped that a customer would answer the first question with a 5 (definitely would return to this store in 90 days) *and* either a 6 or 7 (very good or excellent) for Question 8 (dealing with his overall experience). If Question 1 received a 5 and Question 8 a 6 or 7, Pizza Hut considered the respondent a loyal customer. The percentage of loyal customers was regularly tabulated and considered to be the leading index of that store's performance. For example, if 36 customers were surveyed in a month and of the 36, 20 answered Question 1 with a 5 *and* Question 8 with a 6 or 7, that store would have a loyal customer reading of 56%.

## Dine-In Restaurants

The dine-in restaurants, or "red roofs" as they are euphemistically known, did not have the computerized database information that the delivery stores did. As a result, the "red-roofs" had a different approach toward the survey process. In these cases, loyalty/satisfaction measurements were based on voluntary surveys taken by customers. At random, certain customer receipts were issued that asked the customer to participate in a loyalty survey. The customer was to call a special 800 number (within 36 hours after his visit), give a coded identification number (provided on the receipt), and answer questions about the quality of food and service identical to the delivery customers' questions. The only question that might differ was one dealing with a lunch buffet, if applicable.

Customers were encouraged to participate by being given incentives described on the receipt. Such incentives included a free soft drink or free order of breadsticks with future purchases. Whereas the questions were basically the same between delivery and "red roof" stores, the one major difference was that the dine-in surveys involved the customer calling the survey company, while the survey company called the delivery customers.

# The Bonus Program

All company-owned Pizza Hut store managers' weekly salaries were competitive with the salaries of fast-food managers of other companies. Every 3 months (quarterly), however, all store managers became eligible to receive a bonus. Bonuses generally ranged from $0 to $4000 per store manager a quarter. The bonus program was a major incentive for all store managers.

Traditionally, store bonuses were based on a store's sales growth and profitability. With the advent of the customer satisfaction/loyalty initiatives in 1995, that index was changed. Bonus potential for store managers now depended solely on his or her overall quarterly customer loyalty percentage. The minimum percentage a manager needed to achieve to receive a bonus was 60%. A loyalty rating below 60% meant that the manager was automatically out of the running for a quarterly bonus.

Managers who received a bonus were given a flat dollar rate for each loyalty percentage point they received. Managers scoring between 60 and 64% loyalty would receive one amount. Those scoring between 65 and 69% would receive a larger amount, while those scoring 70 to 75% would warrant a bigger bonus, and so forth. Pizza Hut perceived that there would be a direct relationship between a store's overall operational strength and its percentage of loyal customers.

## Today

Phil Crimmins, vice president of customer satisfaction for Pizza Hut and founder of its loyalty program, claims the loyalty initiatives made many positive inroads. "About a year ago, we noticed our ratings on the abundance of toppings weren't where they should be," Crimmins recently told a group of restaurant operators at a multi-unit technology conference in March 1998. As a result, the company added $50 million to its food costs by adding more toppings to each pizza. Since then, Crimmins claims, topping amounts are no longer an issue.

Crimmins also claims that the customer loyalty initiative helped Pizza Hut identify underperforming stores. By visiting and studying the stores with high loyalty scores and comparing them to the underperforming stores, Crimmins and his team were able to develop a blueprint for success. Many underperforming stores were slowly transformed from "marginal" or "breakdown" stores into "excelling" or "standard" stores. Today, over 60% of its participating stores are now considered to be "excelling" or "stable", as opposed to only 40% when the loyalty process started in 1995.

Unfortunately, their have been some setbacks. High loyalty scores did not always translate into high-performing stores. Conversely, many low-loyalty stores continued to be extremely profitable. Area managers and store managers alike continue to discuss and evaluate the system and its deficiencies. Pizza Hut has listened to such discussions and continually strives to improve the process by making modifications. Both the pros and cons of the customer loyalty initiative continue to be evaluated. (See Table C12.1 and Figure C12.1.)

## Questions

1. In what ways did Pizza Hut benefit or not benefit from its customer satisfaction/loyalty initiatives?

### Table C12.1. Pizza Hut's U.S. Market Share Among the Top Five Pizza Chains[a]

|                  | 1995 | 1996 | 1997 |
|------------------|------|------|------|
| Pizza Hut        | 4700 | 4927 | 5300 |
| Domino's         | 2480 | 2300 | 2100 |
| Little Caesar's  | 1375 | 1400 | 1450 |
| Papa John's      | 868  | 619  | 459  |
| Sbarro           | 422  | 400  | 395  |

[a] U.S. system-wide foodservice sales (in millions of dollars).

*Source:* Rubenstein, E. (1998) Research prompts Pizza Hut to listen to its customers, *Nation's Restaurant News*, April 6, p. 8.

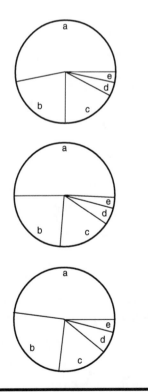

**Market Share 1995**
a = Pizza Hut **(54.6%)**
b = Domino's **(21.6%)**
c = Little Caesar's **(14.9%)**
d = Papa John's **(4.7%)**
e = Sbarro **(4.1%)**

**Market Share 1996**
a = Pizza Hut **(51.1%)**
b = Domino's **(23.8%)**
c = Little Caesar's **(14.5%)**
d = Papa John's **(6.4%)**
e = Sbarro **(4.1%)**

**Market Share 1997**
a = Pizza Hut **(47.7%)**
b = Domino's **(25.2%)**
c = Little Caesar's **(14.0%)**
d = Papa John's **(8.8%)**
e = Sbarro **(4.3%)**

**Figure C12.1. Pizza Hut's Market Share**

2. In your opinion, what were the causes behind the issues mentioned in the previous question?
3. Identify the breakdowns in the process as they affected both delivery restaurants and dine-in restaurants.
4. Where was the breakdown in the quarterly bonus program? What changes (if any) would you make to the quarterly bonus system?
5. What else can Pizza Hut learn from its customers using their marketing research/loyalty process?
6. Evaluate the wisdom of introducing the loyalty programs the way they were and the "law of unintended consequences" which soon followed.

# Case 13. Publix Super Markets — Customer Intimacy*

**P**ublix Super Markets, Inc., is a Florida-based grocery chain which has about 120,000 employees; operates over 600 stores in the states of Florida, Georgia, South Carolina, and Alabama; and serves over one million customers every day. There are no immediate international expansion plans. Publix, named after a chain of motion picture theaters, is one of the largest employee-owned companies in the world, with annual sales of approximately $12 billion. It was the first supermarket chain to install electric-eye doors, Muzak, fluorescent lighting, and air conditioning in its stores. Publix was also one of the first companies to have water fountains, self-service shopping, shopping carts, and computerized scanning technology. Publix has been rated as one of the best companies to work for in America by *Fortune* magazine and other sources.

At Publix, everything they do revolves around pleasing the customer; this is why they have enjoyed the kind of success they have had since the 1930s. Publix's goal is to make every customer feel personally valued in such a way that they see themselves as one in a million. This profile focuses on the company's customer intimacy philosophy and

---

* This case was prepared by Bahaudin (Dean) Mujtaba, DBA. Dr. Mujtaba is a management development specialist at Publix Super Markets, Inc., Lakeland, FL. The information herein is based on the opinions of the author and do not necessarily represent the views of Publix management.

how Publix satisfies and delights its customers daily, helping the company become the "premier quality food retailer in the world."

## Background and Company Philosophy

In 1997, Publix opened 33 new stores and ended the year with 563 stores operating in Florida, Georgia, South Carolina, and Alabama. In 1998, Publix added 30 more new stores to its 458 stores in Florida, 86 stores in Georgia, 16 stores in South Carolina, and three stores in Alabama. Also, from 1991 to 1996, Publix's return on investment outperformed the S&P 500 Index and the customer Peer Group Index, which includes A&P, Albertson's, American Stores, Bruno's, Food Lion, Giant Foods, Hannaford Bros., Kroger, Safeway, Smith's Food & Drug, Weis Markets, and Winn-Dixie.

The key differentiating factor in Publix's success formula can be attributed to the philosophy of its founder, George W. Jenkins, who stated that, "Some companies are founded on policy. This is wrong. Philosophy, the things you believe in, is more important. Philosophy does not change frequently ... and is never compromised. ... We attempt to adapt a philosophy in such a way as to allow ordinary people to achieve the extraordinary ... to reach higher ... to look upon average with disdain." The philosophy of caring for people has been embedded in Publix's corporate culture throughout its stores in the four states. Publix associates understand that they are not just in the grocery business but are also in the people business. Therefore, taking care of associates, customers, suppliers, and community members is important to Publix people and the communities which they serve.

George Jenkins once told employees that, "Publix will be a little better place to work or not quite as good because of you." A philosophy of employee appreciation has been embedded in the culture of the organization, so when the upper echelon visits retail stores, especially during appreciation week, they make it a point to personally see and thank every associate. They understand that people need recognition and sincere thanks for their hard work and commitment to the company. According to Howard Jenkins, Chairman and CEO of Publix, "Growth is the end result of a simple equation. As each of us continues to please our customers, more customers will look to Publix for their shopping needs. We must never lose sight of exactly what those needs are."

Publix associates are encouraged to interact with their customers on an hourly basis. Publix associates constantly attempt to keep their fingers on the pulse of the customer in order to get immediate and local feedback. One of the district managers in the central Florida region used to encourage, and in some cases require, his department managers to learn at least two customers' names every day through face-to-face introductions and interaction. This is important because Publix employees serve their own communities and through this face-to-face interaction they can determine customers' needs, wants, and desires faster than any research firm could ever do. Also, research shows that nearly 75% of supermarket shoppers shop and visit supermarkets on a weekly basis. So, building a relationship with customers is a necessity as opposed to a luxury in order to stay aware of their needs and expectations.

It is through these types of programs and committed people that Publix is able to offer its employees an environment "where *working* is a pleasure" and its customers an environment "where *shopping* is a pleasure." Publix's success with customers originates from their belief that no sale is final or complete until the meal is eaten and fully enjoyed. Only then have they made a positive and lasting impression. Publix's guarantee, of which every associate is aware, states: "We will never knowingly disappoint you. If for any reason your purchase does not give you complete satisfaction, the full purchase price will be cheerfully refunded immediately upon request." These are not just words to live by but are moral imperatives for retailers and have made Publix the successful and innovative giant it is today.

## Focusing on Business, Products, Customers, and Training

There is strong competition in the supermarket industry. For example, Wal-Mart is opening major supercenters throughout Florida. However, Publix is not willing to concede their customers to the competition. Bill Fauerbach, vice president of the Miami division, said, "Only we can give our customers a reason to shop elsewhere. As long as we take care of our customers better than anyone else, we will defeat our competition." The new generation of Publix leaders understands that complacency is their number one enemy; therefore, they continue to focus and improve on factors which have made them successful in the past.

They further understand that delivering superior customer value is a race without a finish line in today's fast-paced world. Therefore, they never lose sight of caring for people, delivering quality products and service and excellence in everything they do. In 1995, during his first year in the office, the president of Publix, Ed Crenshaw, introduced four success drivers for the company: knowing the business, knowing the product, knowing the customer, and continuously training people. Every department has implemented different means of doing a better job with these four success drivers.

Publix has instituted a world-class training program for its perishable departments, such as deli, bakery, produce, and seafood. The goal of getting to know the customer has made Publix better than ever with regards to understanding customers and fulfilling their needs in a timely fashion. Publix's customer intimacy program has enabled managers to keep their fingers on the pulse of the customer on a daily basis. This focus on customers has encouraged management to gather feedback not only from their own customers but also from their competitors' customers. They gather data and feedback from satisfied as well as dissatisfied customers, because they understand that using biased data to make generalizations regarding all customers is more dangerous than not using them at all.

## Industry Rankings

Publix was ranked at the top of the list of supermarket chains in August of 1997. Publix had topped the same list in 1993, the last time supermarkets were reviewed. With a score of 83 out of 100, Publix tied California-based Raley's, but edged them out in price satisfaction. According to the survey, Publix was recognized for having clean stores, helpful staff, and superior meat and produce. Publix was also credited with high rankings for their bakeries and delis and for having specials in stock. In the list of 35 supermarket chains, Albertson's was 10th with a score of 75 and Kroger placed 19th with a score of 73. Food Lion was 30th with a score of 70, and Winn-Dixie was 31st with a score of 68.

For the third consecutive year, Publix ranked the highest among its competitors in *Fortune's* (February 16, 1998) American Customer Satisfaction Index (ACSI). The ACSI was based on a survey of how U.S. customers rate a wide range of products and services. The questions

### Table C13.1. Publix and Competitors — A Comparison

| Company Name | No. of Stores in 1996 | 1996 Revenues[a] | 1995 Revenues[a] | 1994 Revenues[a] |
|---|---|---|---|---|
| Kroger Co. | 2067 | 25,170.91 | 23,937.80 | 22,959.12 |
| American Stores Company[b] | 1695 | 18,678.13 | 18,308.89 | 18,355.13 |
| Winn-Dixie Stores, Inc. | 1174 | 13,218.72 | 12,955.49 | 11,787.84 |
| Food Lion | 1112 | 9005.93 | 8210.88 | 7932.59 |
| Safeway, Inc. | 1052 | 17,269.00 | 16,397.50 | 15,626.60 |
| Albertson's Inc.[b] | 826 | 13,776.68 | 12,585.03 | 11,894.62 |
| Publix Super Markets | 534 | 10,525.97 | 9470.71 | 8742.49 |
| Bruno's, Inc. | 218 | 2899.04 | n/a | 2869.57 |
| Eagle Food Stores, Inc. | 92 | 1014.89 | 1023.66 | 1015.06 |
| Kash 'n' Karry Food Stores | 135 | 1021.67 | 1026.00 | 1065.17 |

[a] Revenues in millions of dollars.
[b] Albertson's announced their acquisition of American Stores in 1998.

touched on perceptions of the value of quality service, how well the products or services lived up to customer expectations, and how willing customers were to pay more for it. The National Quality Research Center polled more than 50,000 customers on 200 companies. The University of Michigan measured the responses according to six quality indexes and scored the companies on a 100-point scale. Publix received a score of 80 points, while its closest competitor on the list, Albertson's, received a score of 77. In another ranking by *Fortune*, Publix moved up to the number two spot in the Food and Drug Store Industry for America's Most Admired Companies. Walgreen's took first place. While Publix has had its share of success and recognition as a tough competitor, the fact remains that it is still relatively small compared to other supermarket giants in regard to the number of stores and yearly revenues (see Table C13.1).

## The Publix Style: Service With a Smile

The late Bill Schroter became a legend within the Publix culture as the author of the slogan "Where Shopping Is a Pleasure." This statement replaced an older slogan, "Florida's Finest Food Stores," which according to Schroter was self-congratulatory and offered no promise to customers. The current slogan tells Publix employees that their customers want more than just groceries. Publix people know that customers want good quality, excellent prices, and a good shopping experience. While quality products and good prices are very important to creating customer value, they are not enough to keep customers coming back to their stores. Therefore, Publix associates receive training on relationship-building techniques in order to better understand customers and quickly take care of their needs.

Publix's mission statement clearly states that Publix is passionately focused on customer value. While their competitors can offer good prices and quality products, Publix wants to stand out in the customer's mind for providing a delightful customer service in every shopping experience. This is why Publix associates closely align their daily work habits to stay focused on customers. Publix people understand that they cannot be casual about achieving customer intimacy. They realize that customer intimacy requires a professional, thorough, consistent, and disciplined method of serving customers that will become a normal way of doing business. You cannot just satisfy and delight customers one time; customers must be satisfied, delighted, and excited every time they visit or shop at the store.

In 1994, Publix introduced the goal of building customer intimacy in all of its stores. Publix associates are taught that customers are their most valued assets whom must be welcomed, cherished, and appreciated for choosing to shop at their stores. In most retail training sessions, associates are asked to reflect on some of the following facts about customers:

- The average customer spends $5000 on groceries each year and lives in one geographic area for about 10 years (total spending = $50,000).
- Attracting a new customer costs companies five to six times more than keeping one who already shops with them.
- Of the customers who complain, 95% will continue to do business with the company if you take care of their problems properly and resolve those problems on the spot.
- Of the customers who quit shopping at a store, 68% do so because they feel the company or an associate was indifferent to a problem they expressed.
- One dissatisfied customer tells eight to ten potential customers about a problem or bad experience that was not addressed in

the store. It has been said that each of these eight to ten potential customers is likely to tell at least five more people about the problem or bad experience.

Publix associates understand that if they cannot satisfy customer's requirements and meet their demands, the customer will cease doing business with them and will shop with other retailers. They remember that if they, as Publix associates, do not offer a great shopping experience for their customers then someone else will. This also means that customers are never lost; they simply take their business elsewhere. So, it is extremely important to take advantage of every opportunity and serve customers with delight in order to keep them coming back.

## Concluding Remark

Publix's history shows that they bought seven Grand Union stores in Miami in 1959 and 19 All American stores in 1945 to expand their market share. According to Publix leaders, currently there are no plans for mergers or acquisitions. However, Howard Jenkins is not against the idea of acquiring another company that fits Publix's culture and philosophy: "If the right opportunity came up we could acquire another company. ... We may or may not find another company we like." Jenkins added that, "We believe in internal growth, building our own stores." Publix's current strategy is to steadily grow from within and to expand the Publix culture throughout its stores.

## Questions

1. What factors are currently involved in successfully competing in the supermarket industry, and how will these factors change in the next 10 years?
2. What can Publix do to strengthen its market position in regard to its suppliers, customers, competitors, and employees?
3. What are the values of Publix's organizational culture, employees, customers, shareholders, suppliers, and competitors? Which ones do you consider to be value adders and which ones do you see as value destroyers, as Publix attempts to become the premier quality food retailer in America?

4.  What factors are currently influencing a customer's decision to shop at Publix? Why haven't competitors been able to duplicate such success factors successfully? How will these factors change in the next decade?

# Case 14. Rubbermaid — Market Orientation*

Rubbermaid is a multi-national company that manufactures and markets a wide array of houseware, recreational, infant, commercial, agricultural, and institutional products. It also sells office furniture and accessories, indoor and outdoor casual furniture, and Little Tikes traditional preschool and juvenile products. The company continues to be one of most successful and admired American companies. In fact, it made *Fortune* magazine's list of one of America's ten most admired corporations for 3 consecutive years during the early 1990s. In 1993, it won the coveted number one spot in *Fortune's* Survey of America's Most Admired Companies. Rubbermaid has succeeded in a market made up of "humdrum" products. The company is now in its 42nd year of record sales and 56 years of profitable performance. Its stock has also richly rewarded its shareholders. Anyone investing $10,000 in Rubbermaid in 1980 would have realized $180,000 in 1990! See Table C14.1 for a 7-year summary of Rubbermaid's financial performance.

## Background

In 1920, five local businessmen formed the Wooster Rubber Company in a rented building in Wooster, OH, to manufacture the Sunshine brand toy balloon. Horatio Ebert and Errett Grable then purchased the company in the mid-1920s. During the early 1930s, while shopping at

---

* This case was prepared by William C. Johnson, Professor of Marketing, School of Business and Entrepreneurship, Nova Southeastern University.

**Table C14.1. 7-Year Summary
of Rubbermaid's Financial Performance**

| Date | Sales ($000) | Net Income ($000) | Earnings Per Share |
|------|------|------|------|
| 1997 | 2,399,701 | 142,536 | 0.95 |
| 1996 | 2,354,990 | 152,400 | 1.01 |
| 1995 | 2,344,170 | 59,772 | 0.38 |
| 1994 | 2,169,354 | 228,126 | 1.42 |
| 1993 | 1,960,207 | 211,413 | 1.32 |
| 1992 | 1,805,332 | 184,207 | 1.15 |
| 1991 | 1,667,305 | 162,650 | 1.02 |

a department store, Grable noticed a line of houseware products that had been developed by James Caldwell. Caldwell's product line, which he named Rubbermaid, included rubber dustpans, drainboard mats, soap dishes, and sink stoppers. Grable contacted Caldwell, and the two men agreed to combine their businesses. In 1943, Wooster Rubber began producing Rubbermaid brand products.

During the 1950s, Wooster Rubber produced its first plastic product, a dish pan, along with a line of commercial goods aimed at hotels, restaurants, and institutions. The company went public in 1955, and 2 years later changed its name to Rubbermaid. It was during the decade of the 1980s when Rubbermaid experienced phenomenal growth; sales increased fivefold from just over $300 million to over $1.5 billion. Rubbermaid also went on an acquisition binge, acquiring Con-Tact (decorative coverings) in 1981, Little Tikes (plastic toys) in 1984, Gott leisure and recreational products in 1985, SECO floor products in 1986, Microcomputer Accessories in 1986, and Viking Brush (cleaning supplies) in 1987. Rubbermaid then formed a joint venture with the French company Allibert in 1989 to produce resin furniture and, the following year, established a joint venture with the Curver Group (whom they purchased in late 1997) of the Dutch chemical company DSM to market housewares in Europe, Africa, and the Middle East (Rubbermaid ended the joint venture with DSM in 1994).

Growth through acquisition continued in the 1990s with Rubbermaid's purchase of EWU A.G., a Swiss floor-care supplies company. They also acquired Eldon Industries, a producer of office accessories, and formed a joint venture with the Hungarian Group CIPSA, the number-one housewares company in Mexico. In 1992, Rubbermaid purchased Iron Mountain Range, a manufacturer of playground equipment. One of Rubbermaid's newest acquisitions, Carex, Inc., is a producer of walkers and canes, giving Rubbermaid a toehold in the home healthcare market. In order to shore up its juvenile products business, Rubbermaid recently acquired the stroller maker, Graco Children's Products. Finally, in late 1998, Rubbermaid agree to be acquired by Newell Co., a housewares concern specializing in sales to discount retailers, for $5.8 billion. Newell sells a range of household products from pencils and combs to window blinds. Newell is known for acquiring attractive brands, squeezing costs, and then boosting profit margins.

Rubbermaid has begun to extend its highly respected brand name through a series of licensing agreements. Beginning in early 1997, Rubbermaid signed a licensing agreement with Town & Country Living to manufacture a new bathroom accessory line. The new bath products collection, to be known as Rubbermaid Bath Coordinates, will consist of shower curtains, curtain rings, liners, tension rods, and bath rugs. This move will allow Rubbermaid to expand its presence from retailers' housewares departments into their home textiles departments, which will carry Rubbermaid's new bath products line. Moreover, this agreement is part of Rubbermaid's strategy to offer consumers a "total room" approach. Key retail customers for this line include K-Mart, Wal-Mart, and Target. The company also entered into a licensing agreement with Amway Corporation in late 1997, whereby Amway will market food storage containers made by Rubbermaid.

## Performance

During the 1980s, Rubbermaid has routinely posted double-digit growth in sales growth. For the year ending 1997, Rubbermaid recorded $211 million in profit on sales of nearly $2.4 billion (see Figures C14.1 and C14.2). In 1996, Rubbermaid earned $152 million, or $1.01 per share. Currently, over 80% of Rubbermaid's revenues are earned in the U.S.; by the year 2000, they project that foreign revenues will constitute 25% of Rubbermaid's overall sales. The bulk of Rubbermaid's revenues is derived from three divisions; the Home Products division contributes the largest share, followed by the Commercial Products division, and Infant/Juvenile division (see Figure C14.3).

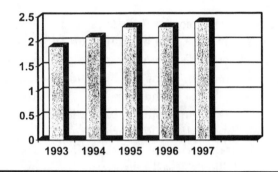

**Figure C14.1. Rubbermaid Revenue (Billions)**

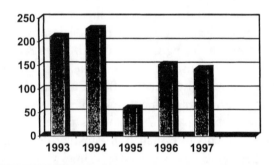

**Figure C14.2. Rubbermaid Income (millions)**

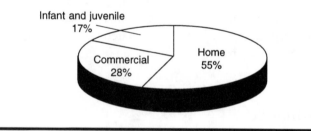

**Figure C14.3. Major Businesses (Percentage of Sales by Segment)**

Rubbermaid's total market capitalization in 1993 was $4.8 billion, delivering a return on shareholder equity of 18.7%. Its price-earning ratio was 23 in 1993; it fell to 22 in 1995 but then rose again to 24.5 in 1996 (see Table C14.1). Rubbermaid has also grown through the years by using a surprising low level of debt. Their long-term debt as a percentage of total shareholder's equity in 1992 was only 3% as compared to an average of 61.4% for all U.S. manufacturers.

## Environment

Rubbermaid has responded to changing public attitudes regarding the environment by using recyclable plastic whenever possible and designing its containers for easy recycling. It recently introduced a "litter-less" lunch box that can carry food and drink without the need for throw-away sandwich wrappings, paper bags, and juice containers. Rubbermaid annually conducts surveys of the needs and preferences of consumers and recycling coordinators before designing new products. They also send out recycling kits to retailers and recycling-related educational materials to public schools and use product labels to inform consumers about the environmental benefits of using recycled goods.

## Technology

Rubbermaid continuously invests in state-of-the-art equipment in order to remain a high-quality, low-cost producer. Rubbermaid uses a chemically advanced mixture of polyethylene as well as an intricate injection molding process for their plastic products. Between 1980 and 1991, Rubbermaid invested over $600 million to expand manufacturing and distribution facilities, modernize equipment, install process control systems and automatic packaging systems, upgrade tooling for new products, and increase capacity for producing new products. In 1992, Rubbermaid invested over $132 million to purchase molds for new products, to expand production capacity, to add new equipment, and to keep facilities efficient and productive. Rubbermaid is also upgrading computer systems to track inventory and improve service to retailers.

Rubbermaid has relentlessly pursued quality. Stanley Gault, the former CEO for Rubbermaid, visited several retail stores weekly to see how Rubbermaid products were displayed and to inspect the quality of workmanship. Gault once remarked, "No one surpasses our quality ... we use more and better resin ... we don't buy cheap resin ... and we use a thicker gauge."

## Strategy

Before retiring in 1991, Rubbermaid's CEO Gault outlined six basic strategies for "leap" growth: (1) develop new products, with 30% of their revenues to come from products introduced in the previous 5 years; (2) enter new markets every 18 to 24 months; (3) acquire new companies; (4) diversify through joint ventures with outside partners; (5) establish stronger bonds with its suppliers; and (6) create specialized goods for their customers.

Creating high-quality, functional plastic products for the housewares market, as well as the office, industrial, and farm markets, represents a great deal of Rubbermaid's success. Part of Rubbermaid's success is due to continuous improvement of the design of existing products, such as revising the design of its ice trays to make the cubes easier to remove or the company's recently introduced Lid-Access Tool Box, which delivers added convenience by providing compartments built directly onto the lid, allowing a person to keep the parts for a project in reach. Yet, Rubbermaid's genius lies in its ability to satisfy customer needs precisely and to make the small changes they demand, as well as their ability to imbue otherwise ordinary kitchen and household products with fashion. Rubbermaid has recently diversified by producing storage for clothing, videocassette tapes, and computer disks. Rubbermaid makes nearly a half-million different items, boasts an amazing 90% success rate on new products, and obtains at least 30% of its sales each year from products less than 5 years old. Rubbermaid is practically a "new product development machine" that cranks out 400 new products a year.

Most of Rubbermaid's new products come from cross-functional teams, each with five to seven members (one each from marketing, manufacturing, R&D, finance, and other departments, as needed). Each team focuses on a specific product line so that someone is always thinking about key product segments. Yet, innovation at Rubbermaid is not limited to teams. Individual employees are focused on creating new products, as well. Rubbermaid has taught its employees to think in terms of letting new products flow from the firm's core competencies, encouraging managers to find out what is happening in the rest of the company by continually looking at processes and technologies. Employee brainstorming sessions can yield up to 200 to 300 product ideas in one sitting.

Yet, Rubbermaid's new product strategy ultimately begins with the customer, thus the company is market driven rather than technology driven. Rubbermaid relies extensively on focus groups and consumer marketing research to assess customer needs and to identify new product opportunities. Customers phone, fax, write, or e-mail more than a dozen or so new product ideas daily. Recently, researchers at Rubbermaid began to conduct "home visits", 2-hour inspections of randomly selected consumers' homes in which they photograph closets and ask about how people live. These visits have yielded about 100 new product ideas.

Another part of Rubbermaid's marketing intelligence also includes studying their competition. Rather than benchmark their competitors, though, they benchmark against the standards set by their customers. They run focus groups to test color and style preferences and confirm those preferences by conducting surveys in shopping malls.

Rubbermaid also obtains a great deal of feedback from customer complaints. Each complaint received from either comment cards or their toll-free number is documented by marketing and is widely distributed, even to the company's executives. Rubbermaid makes good on every customer complaint, as well, replacing products without charge to the customers. The company also runs a day-care program that allows researchers to observe children having problems with toys and to test Rubbermaid's new toys. This input from the customer is then used to modify existing products or develop totally new products.

New products are launched at Rubbermaid with record speed, sometimes within 20 weeks of the birth of the idea. New product, cross-functional teams, consisting of a product manager, an R&D manager, a manufacturing manager, and a financial analyst, manage the entire process from spotting a need to commercialization. These product development teams, which have considerable autonomy and authority to carry out their objectives, are also rewarded based on achieving those objectives. Rubbermaid bypasses traditional test marketing because of their careful homework with customers to develop the right product and their wish to avoid exposing their new products to competitors.

Rubbermaid has recently moved away from a product and price focus in its ads toward pitching its products as problem solvers in a myriad of areas — homes, offices, backyards, gardens, and playgrounds. According to current CEO Wolf Schmitt, "Ours is the only product portfolio that literally spans from cradle to cane." Rather than focus on selling individual items, such as garbage cans, Rubbermaid increasingly is trying to sell "solutions". Rubbermaid recently began promoting an 89-page book — *1001 Solutions for Better Living* — which offers tips on how Rubbermaid's products can help consumers deal with problems in their homes and home offices. The book, which is free with three proofs-of-purchase of Rubbermaid products, also comes with coupons having a face value of as much as $101 for the company's products. Several of the booklet's tips are practical, such as putting a Rubbermaid Ultra Grip plastic liner under a computer keyboard to keep it from slipping or using a Rubbermaid ice cream scoop to fill cupcake tins with cake or muffin batter. Others are more blatantly aimed at increasing sales, such as a suggestion to use laundry baskets in different colors for sorting whites, darks, and delicates.

As far as pricing, Rubbermaid's prices tend to be higher than those of its competitors. Rubbermaid products command a 5 to 10% premium over competitors, due to their stellar reputation and the high-grade plastic that it uses in the manufacture of its products. However, rising resin costs are creating added pricing pressures; for example, there was a 50% rise in the cost of resin in 1996.

Rubbermaid's products are marketed primarily through mass merchandisers and home center stores such as Home Depot, although the company has recently moved to find new ways to sell its products using specialty stores and the Internet. Rubbermaid teams up with their trade partners, such as K-Mart and Wal-Mart (Wal-Mart accounts for 15% of Rubbermaid's annual sales), to develop displays, merchandising plans, promotions, and logistics. In fact, Rubbermaid has already redesigned many items to make them easier for retailers to handle (e.g., the plastic picnic tables produced by Little Tikes are now collapsible). Rubbermaid also provides generous allowances to retailers to help support price promotions and co-op advertising in local markets. Finally, Rubbermaid has shown its trade partners how to increase Rubbermaid sales by displaying Rubbermaid products in their "Best Practices Room" in Wooster, OH. Retailers who visit this center can see how Rubbermaid products can be most effectively merchandised.

Rubbermaid's field salespeople are organized around categories instead of products, allowing them to work closely with retailers to decide what goes on the shelves. For example, Rubbermaid is working with fast-food concern McDonald's to look at how their products could be used in commercial kitchens. Rubbermaid believes that this channel specialization allows for more intensive management involvement with their trade customers. It seems to be paying off, as Rubbermaid has increased penetration of its served retail market from 60,000 outlets in 1980 to over 100,000 outlets in 1993.

For promotion, Rubbermaid supports its products with national television and radio ads. It also supports its products at the local retail level with trade allowances and co-op advertising. Rubbermaid recently partnered with its retailers in a project called Earth View which sponsors programs geared to retail management that reinforce Rubbermaid's long-standing commitment to both recycling and utilizing recycled materials in its own products. Rubbermaid also showcases its products on the Internet, where visitors to their website can click on an image of a kitchen and see "before" and "after" pictures of how Rubbermaid products can be used to organize a refrigerator or that space under the sink.

## International Operations

Currently, an increasing share of Rubbermaid's sales is coming from their foreign operations. The goal of management is to increase foreign revenues from international operations to 30% by the year 2000, compared with 18% in 1995. Rubbermaid plans to achieve this goal by establishing a strong brand image and developing extensive distribution networks in its international markets. Moreover, foreign assets represented 13% of the company's total assets in 1993. Rubbermaid has recently begun shifting more production to lower-cost locations, including Korea, Hungary, Spain, and Mexico.

Rubbermaid appears to be moving away from a strictly export-based strategy to one of direct foreign investment. For example, Rubbermaid entered a joint venture with French company Allibert to produce resin furniture in 1989. Rubbermaid also formed a strategic alliance with Sommer-Allibert of France to manufacture and distribute resin casual furniture in the French market. In 1990, they established a joint venture with Curver Group of the Dutch chemical company DSM to market housewares in Europe, Africa, and the Middle East, and they purchased Curver, Europe's leader in plastic housewares, in late 1997. Other acquisitions in the 1990s included their purchase of EWU A.G., a Swiss floor-care supplies company. In 1992, Rubbermaid acquired CIPSA of Mexico, a leading plastics and housewares company. In 1994, Rubbermaid formed a joint venture with Richell of Japan in which they currently hold a 40% equity interest. Rubbermaid formed another joint venture with Royal Plastics Group, Ltd., of Canada for the manufacture and marketing of modular plastic components and kits to build storage sheds for consumer, commercial, and industrial markets. Also in 1994, Rubbermaid broadened their portfolio further by acquiring Ausplay, an Australian maker of playground equipment.

Rubbermaid is making a significant effort to boost its presence in Europe. The company recently opened a new retail concept called "Everything Rubbermaid" in key European cities. They are also working more closely with host country partners to more effectively gear their products to European tastes. For example, when Rubbermaid saw that European parents were not buying novelty children's beds, such as Rubbermaid's sports-car-shaped bed, they found out that the standard European mattress did not fit the beds. The company then approached a European company to design an appropriate mattress. Rubbermaid is also trying harder to attract top European retailers, bringing them to its Wooster, OH, headquarters to showcase its ability to design efficient product displays for retailers' store shelves.

## Questions

1.  Discuss how Rubbermaid is market oriented. Address customer orientation, competitor orientation, and interfunctional coordination in your response.
2.  How does Rubbermaid use quality function deployment in their new product development?
3.  How does Rubbermaid practice "relationship marketing"?

# Case 15. The U.S. Newspaper Industry — Changing Markets*

**N**ewspapers traditionally were a mass medium. While large general audiences remain its core market, progressive newspaper publishers have realized the need for targeted sections, specialized publications, and non-print products. Market-driven decisions based on information and feedback from the target markets (readers and advertisers) are critical for effective strategic planning in this dynamic business environment. A market profile of the industry is shown in Table C15.1.

Changing industry forces (e.g., competition, technology, consumer desires, and advertiser needs) have necessitated reexaminatin by newspaper executives of the very nature of their business. This market redefinition has meant that newspapers are no longer just in the "news business". The industry has been reshaped from a print media business for mass audiences to an information/entertainment provider for targeted audiences. The American newspaper industry in the late 1990s faces three major pressures which threaten its existence as a dominant media force. Specifically, newspaper executives must cope with market share erosion due to competing media and new technologies, the struggle

---

* This case was prepared by Art Weinstein and is extracted from his book, *Defining Your Market: Winning Strategies for High-Tech, Industrial, and Service Firms* (Haworth Press, 1998). These ideas were presented to the California Newspaper Publishers Association.

## Table C15.1. U.S. Newspaper Industry Profile

| | |
|---|---|
| Industry receipts | $46 billion |
| Total advertising revenues (retail 48%, classified 40%, national 12%) | $38 billion |
| Daily sales/readers | 36 million sales, 78 million readers |
| Sunday readership | 91 million readers |
| Daily/Sunday readership (by age) | 18–34 (46%/59%)<br>35–44 (59%/70%)<br>45–54 (65%/73%)<br>55+ (70%/75%) |
| Daily newspaper websites | 500+ |

Top 10 newspapers based on average daily circulation (millions):
*Wall Street Journal* (1.84); *USA Today* (1.66, exclusive of bulk sales); *New York Times* (1.11); *Los Angeles Times* (1.07); *Washington Post* (.82); *New York Daily News* (.73); *Chicago Tribune* (.66); *Newsday* — New York (.56); *Houston Chronicle* (.55); *San Francisco Chronicle* (.49)

Top 10 newspaper companies:
Gannett Co., Knight-Ridder, Newhouse Newspapers, Times-Mirror Co., The New York Times Co., Dow Jones & Co., Thomson Newspapers, Tribune Co., Cox Enterprises, and Scripps-Howard

*Source:* Newspaper Association of America, 1997 (www.naa.org) and Bureau of Circulation, 1997.

to maintain and attract new readers (e.g., the youth market), and the challenge of being responsive to demanding advertisers. Successful newspaper publishers must invest in research, product development, and promotion. A new mindset and marketing philosophy are mandated.

# Information: Expanding the Market

While daily newspapers remain the primary business for newspaper publishers (at least in the near future), the new market environment of the late 1990s calls for a variety of niche products (information-based) designed to appeal to specific market segments. Such specialized offerings include targeted newspaper sections/inserts, magazine-like supplements, audiotext services, fax services, online products, and other forms of information delivery. An industry observer noted that, "Readers do

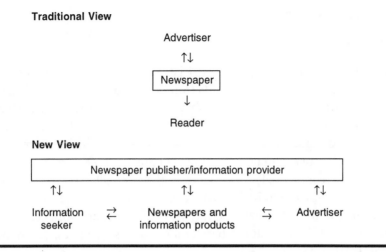

**Figure C15.1. An Expanded Business/Market Definition of Newspapers and Information Products**

not merely buy newspapers but solutions to individual problems." Hence, to combat declining readership and static advertising revenues, an expanded business/market definition is needed to find new revenue-producing opportunities. Robert J. Hively, president and CEO of The Knoxville (Tennessee) News-Sentinel Co., illustrates progressive thinking by stating: "Our philosophy is to be an information company, and an information company distributes information through newspapers, fax papers, campus papers, zoned editions, and audiotext."

The traditional and new views of the newspaper industry are depicted in Figure C15.1. As the top of the figure shows, newspapers historically were product oriented and served two prime markets — everyman (the reader) and general advertisers (newspapers considered advertisers' needs to a lesser extent than their own). The new market-oriented view (see Figure C15.1, bottom) reveals that there are still two prime markets; however, companies must now redesign the core product (newspapers) based on two-way input from diverse information seekers in a segmented market and from focused advertisers trying to reach carefully targeted markets. Interaction and strategic partnerships play key roles in the new era of newspaper publishing. Furthermore, just as Coca-Cola cannot satisfy everyone with its flagship brand, newspaper publishers must diversify their product lines to fulfill the needs of niche markets.

# Niche Markets

## Niche Opportunities

According to the Newspaper Association of America (NAA), newspapers still earn 90% of their profits from traditional sources. While paper and ink will remain with us for many years, the statistics are declining annually. Aggressive newspaper publishers must search for new revenue streams to maintain and enhance their presence in highly competitive markets. There are literally thousands of potential niche products available to entrepreneurial newspaper executives. Initially, companies should explore a limited number of niche concepts, with the goal being to find one or two immediate winners; additional promising profit centers can subsequently be introduced based on the firm's resources, capabilities, and market position.

Knight-Ridder, a newspaper conglomerate that publishes 29 newspapers, utilizes different strategies in its various markets. Here are two examples: (1) the *Miami Herald's* TeleHerald service offers more than 200 categories of information (business, entertainment, news, and sports) via a touch-tone phone, and (2) the *San Jose Mercury News* is accessible electronically to more than 10 million subscribers of America Online.

## Researching Newspaper Niches

The "ABCD" rule of marketing research stands for "Always Be Collecting Data". A dozen low-cost research techniques useful for uncovering and exploiting newspaper and information market niches are detailed in Figure C15.2. Niches can be found in many places. A checklist of market opportunities for newspaper publishers/information providers is offered in Table C15.2. This checklist provides a strategic springboard for developing a marketing plan.

# Market Guidelines For Management

The following seven-point program provides newspaper executives with a framework for coping with changing market forces:

1. *Listen to your customers.* Information providers can benefit from a multitude of research techniques to find their market. Consumers and advertisers should be targets of this market intelligence effort.

| | |
|---|---|
| **Secondary data:** | Use census data, statistical abstracts, Chambers of Commerce, *American Demographics* magazine, etc. |
| **Syndicated data:** | Purchase industry reports and demographic/ lifestyle data. |
| **Do-it-yourself:** | Use in-house talent, assign project teams, work with consultants/small firms to supplement efforts, conduct co-op research. |
| **Ongoing customer panels:** | Implement quarterly insight sessions. |
| **Low cost surveys:** | Utilize telephone surveys, subscriber inserts, and field intercepts; piggyback research efforts. |
| **Qualitative research:** | Conduct focus groups and in-depth interviews. |
| **Input, suggestions, and complaints:** | Listen to the voice of the market; encourage calls, letters, faxes, and e-mail. |
| **College students:** | Tap cheap but good services via marketing research, advertising, entrepreneurship, and journalism students; set up internships. |
| **Monitor the marketplace:** | Attend trade conventions, read trade journals, study competition and market forces |
| **Concept tests/test marketing:** | Evaluate competing niche concepts, and do small-scale product rollouts. |
| **Lead users:** | Find innovators with needs ahead of the general marketplace. |
| **Marketing information system:** | Create and use a database. |

**Figure C15.2. How To Research Newspaper/Information Niches**

2. *Involve the customer.* As part of the interactive process and consumer-driven focus, contemporary newspapers/information products should be editorially relevant, reader friendly, and time cognizant and should encourage user input/feedback.

3. *Test new niche concepts.* There are dozens of print and electronic niche opportunities (see Table C15.2). Qualitative (strategic) and quantitative (financial) screening criteria should be developed to assess new information products. Examples of the former set include, but are not limited to, the nature of the businesses preferred by top management, strategic synergy with existing operations, market trends, and level of competition. The latter group consists of sales and profit potential, return on investment/payback period, and projected market size and growth.

### Table C15.2. Newspaper Niche Opportunities

| Marketing Implications | Niche Opportunities |
|---|---|
| **Reader/information seeker** | |
| Age demographic | Generation X products |
| Ethnic demographic | Non-English language editions |
| Gender demographic | Working women, health issues |
| Household composition demographic | Single vs. family life |
| Geographic | Regional editions |
| Psychographic | Activities/interests sections |
| Usage | Delivery frequency variations |
| **Advertiser** | |
| Relationship marketing | Joint promotions, long-term "deals" |
| Special promotions | Custom promotions, advertorials |
| Value-added services | Market research, targeted ads |
| **Technology-driven** | |
| Database marketing | Customized and personalized products, tailored promotions |
| Delivery/packaging | Fax service, on-line products |
| Interactivity | Telephonic and computer-based, menu-driven products |
| **New products** | |
| Information services | Educational products/reprints |
| Research services | Business/market/legal research |
| Total market coverage | Preprints, special publications, non-subscriber products, piggyback delivery |

4.  *Develop business partnerships.* Long-term commitments and/or joint ventures with compatible advertisers and other business service organizations (e.g., online information providers, sales/distribution companies, "competing" media, etc.) are the keys to success in the age of relationship marketing. Value-added events, tie-ins, and co-op promotions are effective tactics for building beneficial alliances.

5.  *Invest in technology.* Information providers can use new technologies to expand their offerings and market coverage. While costly and still not perceived as a mainstream delivery option, developments in audiotext, databases, fax services, and online products have generated profits for scores of newspaper publishers, and their market presence is gaining daily.

6. *Be unique/different.* Newspapers will remain a viable product for many years to come. Successful publishers are able to effectively differentiate their products from the pack. This is accomplished by providing substance and quality and responding to market needs. The temptation for formula journalism and corporate conformance (note the chain influence in the industry), however, is a potential threat to fulfilling newspapers' missions.
7. *Grow via planned change.* Information providers should seek careful, planned change, not radical transformation. Change means challenges and a reexamination of the basic operating assumptions for doing business. But, change also means great opportunities for newspaper publishers/information companies that adapt and respond to the new market environment.

## Questions

1. Market redefinition implies a change in at least one of the following: customer groups, needs, and technologies. How should advertisers cope with such market changes?
2. The new market view of the industry is depicted in Figure C15.1. Explain the relationships among the three principals in the model: the publisher, the information seeker, and the advertiser. How can advertisers use newspapers/information products to add value and enhance customer relationships?
3. Describe how a small, independent publisher can use the research techniques in Figure C15.2 to find niche opportunities shown in Table C15.2 (identify three viable niches). How might your response differ if you consulted for a top-ten newspaper?

# Case 16. StatePride Industrial Laundry — Value Chain Analysis[*]

The rental laundry industry is highly competitive and in the midst of consolidation. Laundries generally rent industrial uniforms and entrance mats along with the service of periodically (once or twice a week) picking up the dirty uniforms and mats, which are then laundered and returned clean. To survive and generate a reasonable profit, locally owned StatePride Industrial Laundry must outperform the larger national chains. The general manager, Don McDonald, wants to develop a market advantage. He believes that value chain analysis is the correct tool to help him provide customers the benefits they want at prices that are reasonable. If StatePride can do this analysis effectively, the firm will discover the basis for a competitive edge.

## What Is Value?

McDonald first needs to understand how customers such as the local Ford dealership, dairy plant, or plumbing supply firm perceive the value of StatePride's offerings. Each of these companies purchases goods and

---

[*] This case was prepared by Dr. Hilton Barrett, Chair, Division of Business and Economics, Cumberland University, Lebanon, Tennessee.

services on the basis of the value they believe their companies receive. There is a simple mathematical formula that expresses this: Value = Benefits ÷ (Price + Associated Cost).

Let's explore the customer value formula in more detail. The potential customer looks at the benefits he receives from products — not the physical characteristics. The customer does not rent a uniform or a mat. He pays a service fee to reduce the maintenance costs of keeping his workers and workplace clean, healthy, and presentable. The entrance mat fiber description "Nylon 6,6" has little or no meaning to the customer, whereas the words "clean", "presentable", and "healthy" have a great deal of meaning. If the mat is at the entrance to a laboratory, the customer receives little additional benefit from a mat with the company's logo, but, if the mat is at the front door of a car dealership, the customer may perceive a large additional benefit from the positive image generated from a logo mat. Thus, increasing the benefits increases the value — if it helps the customer. However, simply providing more product features does not necessarily mean the customer places an increased value on the additional offering. The objective is to meet customer requirements or needs. The customer will expect to pay for benefits that satisfy needs, but nothing more.

The product is more than the mat itself. It includes the mat's cleanliness, timeliness, and service delivery, as well as StatePride's response to requests for additional mats or replacement of dirty mats in an emergency. Furthermore, "product" also means office functions such as invoicing and flexibility in regard to contract responsibilities. It also includes the attitude and helpfulness of the laundry's customer service representatives and the clarity of communications between these people and the customer.

The emphasis today is on total costs and long-term relationships. This is more than simply the price paid to StatePride. It includes associated costs. Associated costs are costs incurred by the customer using this service. For example, these costs may include the square footage within the customer's facility required for uniform lockers. After all, the area devoted to lockers cannot be used for production machinery or related profitable activities. Associated costs include normal business functions such as personnel time needed to check-in product and account for returns, accounting department time to process invoices, or workers' time to fill out repair tags. Often, neither the customer nor the supplier recognizes the various associated costs. The key to success is to drive down total costs. If a customer's total costs over the long term are reduced, the resulting value to StatePride is increased.

Price can be confusing. The uniform rental price may be quoted per change, but normal pricing within the rental laundries can include loss and abuse charges, wastewater surcharges, name and emblem charges, or setup charges. The customer is relatively unconcerned about StatePride's costs. He simply wants a viable, profitable supplier who can provide a long-term, ongoing solution to his needs. He is concerned only about the invoiced price coupled with his company's associated costs and the supplier's continuing ability to provide the required quality level of service.

The value formula math is simple and straightforward: increase the benefits and increase the value. Decrease the price paid and/or associated costs and increase the value. The customer will pay up to the perceived value — not a penny more! And, if the price paid is less than the value received, so much the better.

## Creating Value: The Value Chain Analysis

Value chain analysis is a powerful management tool used to understand how to drive down costs, provide greater benefits to the customer, and understand the generation of value. This technique is the most useful weapon in the marketing arsenal for increasing the value of StatePride's products to its customers. A value chain follows the generation of value from design through operations to the final product/service delivered to the customer. It can then be expanded to include development of StatePride's suppliers and delivery of their goods/services, and finally into the customers' systems as the products are used. Each phase of the chain provides an opportunity to increase a customer's benefits or to decrease costs. As shown earlier, either increasing benefits or decreasing costs, or both, can increase the value of StatePride's offering as perceived by the customer. Remember, value, quality, and beauty are in the eye of the beholder (the customer)!

Michael E. Porter, an economics professor at Harvard Business School, discusses the value chain concept in his book *Competitive Advantage* (Free Press, 1985). A generic value chain is shown in Figure C16.1. At this stage, the core question to be answered is what activities add value within your firm? To use value chain analysis fully, the generic

Design → Materials Management → Operations →
Marketing and Sales → Distribution → Service

---

**Figure C16.1. The Generic Value Chain**

chain needs to be expanded and redefined to include your suppliers, firm, and customers. Let's follow the value chain for a StatePride Laundry uniform rental program for a regional plumbing company, DownEast Plumbing.

Three separate levels of activity are depicted in Figure C16.2. In value chain analysis, the middle phase is always the analyst's firm. If a uniform manufacturer performs the analysis, the supplier might be a textile mill and the customer might be a rental laundry. By tracing the activities of each phase and the generation of value, management can evaluate possibilities for increasing benefits and lowering costs within each of the phases. These possibilities are shown in the figure by the comments given under the various activities.

The more the analyst understands the processes and real needs within the customer's internal value chain, the easier it is to develop products and related support services that increase the benefits or drive down the associated costs. Value chain analysis is a multipurpose tool. It can be used in numerous applications, as listed in Figure C16.3.

## Applying Value Chain Analysis

DownEast Plumbing is a large regional firm with many service vehicles. Its major competitor is a national franchised firm with a similar number of service vehicles in the targeted market. Competition is intense (where is it not today?). DownEast's marketing tactics emphasize the professionalism of its people and its service response time. Management wants company personnel to wear appropriate uniforms, and to wear them appropriately, to enhance the company image. StatePride's salesperson is working with DownEast on developing an image-oriented program. The uniform will be basic navy pants and a striped work shirt that is unique for DownEast Plumbing. The uniform program is an important part of DownEast's marketing activities. A series of local cable television

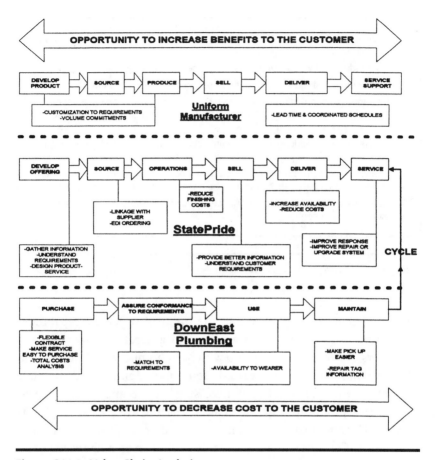

**Figure C16.2. Value Chain Analysis**

commercials is built around their friendly and professionally uniformed plumbers.

McDonald's initial use of value chain analysis is to examine the activities within his firm. This evaluates the intra-firm or horizontal linkages between value-generating activities. The first step is to review possible alternatives for increasing value by increasing benefits or lowering costs. For example, more durable uniforms will increase StatePride's initial purchasing costs but will lower the replacement, repair, and average weekly costs.

Next, McDonald assesses the inter-firm or vertical linkages between the supplier, StatePride, and the customer. What are the requirements of each within the process? The greater the understanding of buyer

1. Cost reduction through reengineering your processes (changing the way you run the business)
2. Cost reduction through reengineering processes with suppliers
3. Cost reduction through reengineering processes with customers
4. Developing a competitive advantage by restructuring the value chain (supplier-firm-customer) to offer greater benefits, lower total costs, and increase the value of your goods and services
5. Including benchmarking in your value chain (for example, FedEx is often benchmarked for its world-class logistics systems)
6. Analyzing strengths and weaknesses of key competitors — competitive analysis — a learning experience that can help you find a unique market advantage
7. Objectively critiquing the performance of business strategies and tactics — evaluation and control

**Figure C16.3. How To Use Value Chain Analysis**

needs and requirements as well as the uniform supplier's capabilities and requirements, the better the ability to generate greater value for customers. A working relationship with both supplier and customer will allow evaluation of capabilities and requirements and provide possible alternatives with the objective of increasing benefits and reducing costs.

DownEast wants to emphasize comfort as much as appearance for its personnel. It anticipates redefining the image of its workforce in about 18 months. On the basis of StatePride's salesperson's knowledge and support from the uniform manufacturer, this could lead to a proposal for 100% cotton shirts and pants. While these garments do not last as long as 65/35 fabrics, the plumbing firm does not need the longer wear life, nor does such a fabric increase the benefits of StatePride's products for them. Further discussion may indicate that wrinkle-resistant cotton shirts and pants provide an acceptable appearance. The laundry can then forego pressing and decrease labor and energy costs. Such savings can be passed on to its customer.

StatePride can work with the uniform manufacturer on a shirt unique to DownEast, possibly using a base fabric already in stock by the manufacturer. McDonald can work with the manufacturer to look for ways to reduce his costs while still meeting the objectives of DownEast Plumbing. Good manufacturing suppliers welcome the opportunity to work with their customers on this objective. Hence, value chain analysis helps the manufacturer in the same way it assists StatePride. A shirt that is over-engineered may be a great shirt, but, remember, StatePride will only pay for a shirt that meets its requirements, and nothing more.

McDonald can easily use value chain analysis to evaluate his marketing options. It is typical for a manufacturer to require a volume commitment and a lead-time commitment. The value chain shows once again that this is an area of opportunity. Working with the customer, StatePride can develop forecasts for the customer's uniform needs. This benefits the production planning for the manufacturer and leads to a delivery schedule agreed to in advance by all participants. It reduces inventory vulnerability by all concerned — another cost reduction. These "win-win" solutions benefit all parties.

Communication is the key to success in the development of any value chain analysis program. What are DownEast Plumbing's requirements for the uniform and servicing? What are the uniform manufacturer's requirements for volume and lead-time? What are the laundry's requirements for receiving garments so as to provide adequate time for preparation for initial placement? Every participant in the transaction has its own requirements and capabilities. Armed with value chain analysis knowledge and understanding, the process of supplying uniforms, from uniform manufacturer through laundry to customer (and the service cycle back through the laundry), can be evaluated. Properly assessed, the opportunities for increasing benefits, lowering costs, and increasing value are readily apparent. Successfully implemented, satisfied customers receive greater value, and StatePride builds customer loyalty and retention and increases profits.

## Questions

1. What are some ways that StatePride can reduce the price paid without changing their regular list prices for services?
2. How can StatePride's advertising campaign affect a customer's perceived benefits and resulting perceived value?
3. Explain how service firms should apply value chain analysis to create, deliver, and maximize customer value.

# Case 17. Southwest Airlines — Value-Added Services*

Southwest Airlines commenced service in 1971 with three Boeing 737 airplanes serving Dallas, Houston, and San Antonio. In July 1998, Southwest had 72 Boeing 737 airplanes serving 52 cities all over the U.S. (see Figure C17.1). The airline provides primarily single-class, short-haul transportation between pair cities. Southwest's strategy has been effective; their net profit margin in 1994 was 6.9%, while the rest of the industry broke even. The company has achieved an average of 50% market share in pair cities due to rapid turn-around times, congestion-free airports, utilizing a single type of aircraft, and simple yet frequent scheduling. The philosophy of the airlines is best summed up from Southwest's 1994 Annual Report:

> Southwest Airlines is the nation's low fare, high customer satisfaction airline. We were built from the ground up to save our customers time and money. Our vision is to keep productivity high and fares low. Maintain a young, pure jet fleet, provide triple crown service, and let the Southwest spirit come shining through.

Southwest's 26,000 employees currently operate over 2300 flights a day. For the year 1997, Southwest offers such fun facts about the airline

---

* This case was prepared by Donald J. King and Art Weinstein. The authors thank Linda Burke Rutherford, Manager, Public Relations, Southwest Airlines, for editing and updating the case.

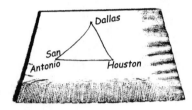

## 1971

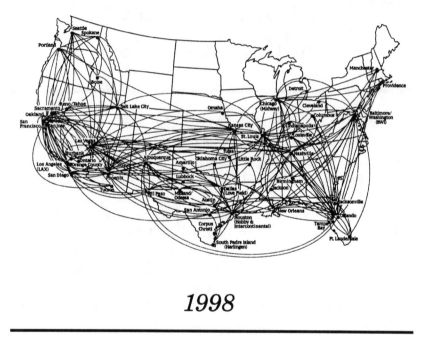

## 1998

**Figure C17.1. Southwest Airlines' Growth Chart**

as the company answered 83 million reservation calls, served 87.4 million bags of peanuts, received 105,583 job applications (with 3006 new employees hired), utilized approximately 65.6 million gallons of jet fuel, and employed over 993 married couples.

## Value-Added Services

Southwest Airlines provides many value-added services, but most are not promoted. Southwest's spirit is thought to be a major part of their success. Comedic comments and gestures distinguish Southwest as being more fun and personal than other airlines. Flight attendants have been known to put the oxygen cup on their head and do their best imitation of the pet monkey of Aladdin in Disney's recent smash cartoon. Pilot's comments such as "Whoa, boy!," as the plane lands lowers stress for some flyers.

Herb Kelleher, the CEO of Southwest, even uses "high school" machismo to settle would-be lawsuits. Several years back, another local company felt that Southwest had stolen their advertising campaign. Kelleher challenged the president of the other company — not to a court battle, but to an arm-wrestling contest. Herb lost, but the other company decided to let them use the campaign anyway. Listed below are other services that may add value for Southwest:

- Southwest completed negotiation of a contract for installation of "heads-up displays" (HUD) in the cockpits to provide greater landing and takeoff capabilities in adverse weather conditions.
- Southwest designed, developed, tested, and went nationwide with "ticketless" air travel.
- Southwest was the first major airline to offer online booking via an Internet website.
- Southwest won the triple crown for best baggage handling, best on-time performance, and fewest customer complaints per customers carried from 1992 to 1996.
- Southwest placed first (twice) in airline quality rating statistics.
- Southwest negotiated a contract with the state of Arkansas and city of Little Rock for a 900-agent reservations center.
- In 1996 alone, Southwest operated over 780,000 flights, carrying 50 million customers in perfect safety; it is one of the few worldwide major airlines never to have had a crash.
- Southwest began the first profit-sharing plan in the U.S. airline industry more than 21 years ago. Through this plan, employees own about 10% of the company stock.
- The average age of the company fleet is only 8.1 years.
- Southwest was the first major airline to utilize an efficient no-seat-assignment boarding process to facilitate quick turn-arounds (60% of its planes turn around in 15 minutes or less).

### Table C17.1. Sample Fare Comparison: Dallas-Houston

|  | Southwest[a] | Continental[b] |
|---|---|---|
| 2 week advance before 7 p.m. | $51 | $41 |
| 2 week advance after 7 p.m. | $44 | $41 |
| 1 day advance before 7 p.m. | $79 | $156 |
| 1 day advance after 7 p.m. | $59 | $41 |

[a] One-way prices; Southwest had a tag-along promotion for which the first fare was $158 round-trip for the first person and $50 for the second.

Round-trip prices, subject to the availability of lowest fares. Continental has 13 different fare classes. The 1 day advance price of $41 is based on a sales promotion.

## Challenges

While the Southwest "formula" has been extremely successful, the airline has recently been experiencing more competition. MetroJet, Delta Express, and the United Shuttle are just some of the companies trying to overtake Southwest as the low-cost, low-airfare leader. Southwest has for over 27 years never had an accident; however, reaction to the accident involving discount airline, ValuJet, puts pressure on Southwest to maintain its perfect record.

Delta, United, US Airways, and the other major airlines are starting to compete with Southwest. The largest advantage the major airlines have is being able to connect easily to hundreds of cities and overseas locations. Unlike Southwest, the majors have assigned seating, will transport pets, and offer first-class service. Major airlines provide movies and food on long flights, amenities expected and more important for long hauls. The majors are also able to reduce their price structure to compete head to head with Southwest, as shown in Table C17.1. Continental had repetitive 50%-off sales, and the United Shuttle opened service in the strong Oakland market. Competitive pressures are affecting Southwest, as the United Shuttle has taken away 10% of Southwest's passengers.

Delta Airlines' "Leadership 7.5" program is a series of cost reduction measures that will lower Delta's operating expenses per average stage mile (ASM) to 7.5¢ by 1997. Southwest's expenses per ASM are 7.1¢. Competition? Kelleher thinks not: "People forget that Delta's average stage is 901 miles, compared to Southwest's 506. Therefore, Southwest's ASM would be 4.6¢ when compared directly to Delta's average stage length."

Southwest is constantly instituting cost-reduction programs. The airline's employees deserve a bow in helping reduce costs. Southwest has a very extensive profit-sharing program, and pilots recently chose profit-sharing programs over traditional raises.

Over-expansion trouble? In 1994, Southwest's fourth quarter earnings were $20.3 million compared to $38.4 million for the fourth quarter in 1993. The principle cause of the decline was the 30% growth in capacity and 20% growth in available seat miles, all in new markets; also, technical problems in their reservation system upset some customers and caused them to go to other airlines. At the time, Southwest management predicted that the reduced loads, lower earnings, and smaller yields would continue until second quarter 1995, at which time Southwest would have effectively penetrated the new markets. Figure C17.2 shows 4 years of financial data from 1994 through 1997. Overall, Southwest establishes within 5% of the market penetration they will succeed based on past flight traffic patterns. Southwest lowers its fare structure by the percentage it is higher than competition. Southwest feels it has created a market of 400,000 passengers a year; by adding six additional on-time trips, the market expands to 500,000. For example, their Oakland to Burbank route soared from being the 179th largest passenger market to the 25th largest.

## Future

Southwest Airlines' planning specialists have planned for potential expansion in 2003 and have determined that Southwest requires 212 additional aircraft. CEO Kelleher feels that it is a little too ambitious, especially because some routes are over 80% loaded, so additional flights could be added. Southwest leaders realize that they must make money while expanding, but they have been successful at that for over 25 years straight.

## Questions

1. What value-added services does Southwest offer? Should these services be promoted? How?
2. What value-added services do the other airlines offer? Should these services be promoted? How?

SELECTED CONSOLIDATED FINANCIAL DATA [1]

| (IN THOUSANDS EXCEPT PER SHARE AMOUNTS) | 1997 | 1996 | 1995 | 1994 |
|---|---|---|---|---|
| Operating revenues: | | | | |
| Passenger | $ 3,639,193 | $ 3,269,238 | $ 2,760,756 | $ 2,497,765 |
| Freight | 94,758 | 80,005 | 65,825 | 54,419 |
| Other | 82,870 | 56,927 | 46,170 | 39,749 |
| Total operating revenues | 3,816,821 | 3,406,170 | 2,872,751 | 2,591,933 |
| Operating expenses | 3,292,585 | 3,055,335 | 2,559,220 | 2,275,224 |
| Operating income | 524,236 | 350,835 | 313,531 | 316,709 |
| Other expenses (income), net | 7,280 | 9,473 | 8,391 | 17,186 |
| Income before income taxes | 516,956 | 341,362 | 305,140 | 299,523 |
| Provision for income taxes [1] | 199,184 | 134,025 | 122,514 | 120,192 |
| Net income [1] | $ 317,772 | $ 207,337 | $ 182,626 | $ 179,331 |
| Net income per share, basic [1] | $ 1.45 | $ .95 | $ .85 | $ .84 |
| Net income per share, diluted [1] | $ 1.40 | $ .92 | $ .82 | $ .82 |
| Cash dividends per common share | $.03310 | $.02932 | $.02667 | $.02667 |
| Total assets | $ 4,246,160 | $ 3,723,479 | $ 3,256,122 | $ 2,823,071 |
| Long-term debt | $ 628,106 | $ 650,226 | $ 661,010 | $ 583,071 |
| Stockholders' equity | $ 2,009,018 | $ 1,648,312 | $ 1,427,318 | $ 1,238,706 |

CONSOLIDATED FINANCIAL RATIOS [1]

| | | | | |
|---|---|---|---|---|
| Return on average total assets | 8.0% | 5.9% | 6.0% | 6.6% |
| Return on average stockholders' equity | 17.4% | 13.5% | 13.7% | 15.6% |

CONSOLIDATED OPERATING STATISTICS [2]

| | | | | |
|---|---|---|---|---|
| Revenue passengers carried | 50,399,960 | 49,621,504 | 44,785,573 | 42,742,602 [3] |
| RPMs (000s) | 28,355,169 | 27,083,483 | 23,327,804 | 21,611,266 |
| ASMs (000s) | 44,487,496 | 40,727,495 | 36,180,001 | 32,123,974 |
| Load factor | 63.7% | 66.5% | 64.5% | 67.3% |
| Average length of passenger haul | 563 | 546 | 521 | 506 |
| Trips flown | 786,288 | 748,634 | 685,524 | 624,476 |
| Average passenger fare | $ 72.21 | $ 65.88 | $ 61.64 | $ 58.44 |
| Passenger revenue yield per RPM | 12.84¢ | 12.07¢ | 11.83¢ | 11.56¢ |
| Operating revenue yield per ASM | 8.58¢ | 8.36¢ | 7.94¢ | 8.07¢ |
| Operating expenses per ASM | 7.40¢ | 7.50¢ | 7.07¢ | 7.08¢ |
| Fuel cost per gallon (average) | 62.46¢ | 65.47¢ | 55.22¢ | 53.92¢ |
| Number of Employees at yearend | 23,974 | 22,944 | 19,933 | 16,818 |
| Size of fleet at yearend [4] | 261 | 243 | 224 | 199 |

(1) The Selected Consolidated Financial Data and Consolidated Financial Ratios for 1992 through 1989 have been restated to include the financial results of Morris Air Corporation (Morris). Years prior to 1989 were immaterial for restatement purposes
(2) Prior to 1993, Morris operated as a charter carrier; therefore, no Morris statistics are included for these years
(3) Pro forma for 1992 through 1989 assuming Morris, an S-Corporation prior to 1993, was taxed at statutory rates
(4) Excludes cumulative effect of accounting changes of $15.3 million ($.07 per share)
(5) Excludes cumulative effect of accounting change of $12.5 million ($.06 per share)

---

**Figure C17.2. Selected Consolidated Financial Data**

3. What pricing strategy and promotions do you recommend for Southwest?

4. What pricing strategy and promotions do you recommend for other airlines to compete with Southwest?

5. Perform a SWOT analysis of Southwest.

6. Extend the financial analysis of Southwest by 2 and 5 years. How do you propose Southwest achieve those results?

# Case 18. Teleplaza — Competitive Orientation*

ROI Teleservicing, Inc., is a call-center consulting firm which assists telemarketing companies in finding new clients, growing their existing businesses, and improving operations. ROI helps clients employ better and more experienced people, manage business processes, and utilize technology to enhance corporate performance in various areas. Companies hire consultants to organize and present information they do not have the time or resources to acquire. Teleplaza, a division of ROI, was designed to assist call-center management in finding such resources. The explosive growth of the Internet led to the creation of Teleplaza websites; by making these resources available via the Web, Teleplaza provides a marketing service for companies who have the products and services (solutions) to assist Teleplaza visitors. This is the unique nature of Teleplaza — meeting an unfilled need by reducing the time it takes to research companies who provide specific resources or solutions to help individuals improve their call-center operations.

---

* This case was prepared by Jim Moylan, President of Teleplaza, Dania, FL. The company's website can be found at www.teleplaza.com.

# Business Description

Teleplaza is an Internet directory, similar to Yahoo! and specializing in providing information for the call-center, telemarketing, and customer service industries. Teleplaza creates value for professionals looking for industry-specific resources by organizing, categorizing, and indexing call-center information available on the Internet. Companies selling products and services list their firm on Teleplaza where people looking for resources to improve their telemarketing and customer service results can quickly find these businesses and review their offerings.

In general, when looking for information before the Internet was widely used, the more specific the need, the higher the cost to acquire it. Conversely, the easier the information was to acquire, the lower the cost. The Internet and World Wide Web have made it easier to locate information, so that information that was expensive prior to the Web is becoming less so. Teleplaza is a perfect example of this. The cost to market a firm to the call-center industry has been significantly reduced.

Unlike many competitors, Teleplaza provides services on a pay-for-performance basis. Offering an Internet marketing service that charges on a per-visitor basis allows customers to more easily measure the performance of their listing on Teleplaza. Combining the pay-for-performance pricing strategy with all of the advantages of the Web in terms of one-to-one communication opportunities and the reduced cost of acquiring information opens the marketing gates for companies of all sizes to promote their products and services effectively via the Internet.

The Web is still an emerging medium; therefore, there is no proven method for comparing how it performs as a marketing tool vs. more traditional marketing methods. By offering its services on a per-visit basis with a cap on the maximum dollar amount spent in one year, Teleplaza provides an incentive for companies to try this new marketing medium.

# External Changes

## *Economy*

Over the past decade, business has become much more global with diminishing international trade barriers. IDC/Link Resources notes that there are approximately 32.2 million households with in-home offices operating in the U.S., and this number is growing approximately 10% annually. People are sending more information via telecommunications vehicles rather than through the U.S. mail or courier services. The service economy and its focus on customer service departments are increasing the demand for call-center and related teleservicing services.

## Technology

Technology has changed how business will be conducted in the 21st century. The Internet has been the source of the greatest change. Electronic commerce allows products and services to be ordered and billed through the Internet or some other form of telecommunications vehicle. IDC predicts that goods and services purchased online by businesses will grow from $1.3 billion in 1996 to over $176 billion in 2001. Interesting Internet facts include:

- Approximately 47 million people have access to the Internet.
- There are 6.6 million host computers connected to the Internet.
- The fastest growing portion of the Internet is the World Wide Web.
- The Internet created approximately 1.1 million new jobs worldwide in 1996.
- There are approximately 85,000 new domain name registrations added per month.

## Regulatory Environment

There is opposition to the telemarketing industry, primarily due to the enormous amount of fraudulent activities and sales practices. In 1994, President Clinton signed the Consumer Protection Telemarketing Act, which strengthened the authority of the Federal Trade Commission to protect consumers in connection with sales made over the telephone. This act is primarily directed at preventing abusive practices by unscrupulous businesses, but it also affects the way legitimate telemarketers conduct business and the cost of doing business by telephone. In spite of the poor reputation of the telemarketing industry, telemarketing is not going away anytime soon. When used properly, telemarketing has proven to be a viable and profitable business tool to enhance customer relationships.

# Industry Forces

## Availability of Substitutes

The Teleplaza Jobs Section is an advertising medium, a way to bring buyers and sellers together. Other forms of advertising that might be suitable for businesses requiring telemarketing and/or call-center services employees are trade magazines, local and national newspapers, direct mail, and other Internet advertising sites.

All of these substitutes, with the exception of the Internet, are temporary in nature. In contrast, a listing on Teleplaza's Job Section is accessible 24 hours a day, 7 days a week, for two months. Teleplaza, like direct mail and trade magazines, is targeted specifically to those looking to hire individuals specifically in the telemarketing industry. Local newspaper advertising does not reach enough potential prospects, and national print advertising is considerably more expensive. Teleplaza provides more words per advertisement, allowing employers to define position qualifications more narrowly.

## Bargaining Power of Buyers

For most advertising sources, prices are non-negotiable. The prices are usually set according to the popularity and number of people the medium reaches. The more people (not necessarily prospects) the advertising reaches, the more expensive it is. Internet job directories, while very popular, are still offering "special deals" to increase their market share. The Internet as an advertising medium for job postings is still in its infancy, giving buyers bargaining power. The industry is struggling to develop measurement tools for determining the number of people the medium actually reaches.

## Bargaining Power of Suppliers

Suppliers for Teleplaza are the Internet service providers (ISPs) who provide website hosting services and Internet access. Although ISPs have been experiencing fierce competition for subscribers, there are few firms really qualified and good at fulfilling website design services. Creating a partnership with an ISP is a good idea; however, they may not share the common goal of creating superior customer value.

## Entry and Exit Barriers

Barriers to becoming an Internet jobs directory service are practically non-existent, as is the case for most website-based businesses on the Internet. Exit barriers are also minimal, unless time-contingent service contracts have been signed with customers. Because doing business on the Internet has such low barriers, competitive differentiation and positioning are very important in offsetting these threats.

## Competitive Rivalry

Internet job listing services are increasing, yet the competition in the specific telemarketing and call-center services arena is limited (currently there are three key competitors). C@ll Center Solutions has a strategy of promoting its magazine (*C@ll Center*) and three yearly conferences via their website. The Telem@rket website, created by *Teleprofessional Magazine*, is a more direct competitor, as it appears to have a similar goal of delivering information to visitors. Both firms are private and do not disclose financial information. The *C@ll Center* magazine reaches about 60% of the first two competitors' market. Their companion magazine, *Computer Telephony*, targets call centers as well as businesses utilizing computer telephony equipment. Overall, their audience has a circulation of over 100,000.

The magazines have strengths due to their experience in the industry, access to current advertisers, and their wealth of published information gathered over the years. The weaknesses they may face are sharing a similar customer base and managing websites like trade journals — revolving around advertising revenues. Teleplaza's competitive strategy is to treat the resource as a direct marketing vehicle rather than as an advertising vehicle.

# Teleplaza: Strategic Considerations

## Teleplaza Mission Statement

Teleplaza organizes, categorizes, and indexes call-center industry resources and business know-how available on the Internet. It makes business techniques accessible to millions of business people utilizing the telephone to facilitate their business. It provides users with a resource for researching the business tools available to improve call-center performance today and take advantage of the Web as a new source of revenue in the future. Teleplaza provides a rewarding work environment and fair compensation to its employees, a fair return to its owners, and a fair marketing return on investment for its customers.

## Service Description

Teleplaza publishes its information exclusively on the Internet. The Internet term that best describes the site is an "e-zine" or electronic magazine. The company provides quality information via links on its website to industry-relevant information available on the Internet. The e-zine will be the most comprehensive web-based resource for call-center information, reaching operations, sales and marketing, and human resources professionals. At the same time, the site offers firms marketing to the call-center industry an opportunity to talk directly to a specific audience to communicate the benefits of their products and services.

## Market Segmentation

The market for client customers is divided into distinct subsets right on the Teleplaza site. The Tele-Directory has 42 product and service categories for companies to list their services. Each group has the same need to reach the call-center marketplace that led them to respond in similar ways to the product/service offerings and the strategic marketing program. The Tele-Relevant and Tele-Classifieds sections provide segmentation in a similar fashion.

Teleplaza is a niche-based, Internet media company that reaches two types of customers. It offers: (1) call-center professionals an information resource via the Internet to locate relevant industry information to help them make their businesses more competitive, and (2) companies across all industries the ability to target call-center personnel to deliver a message about their products and services.

## Marketing Strategy

Via targeted lists and related association memberships, Teleplaza's management believes it can effectively serve a clearly defined market.

Teleplaza's value proposition revolves around building a strong brand image. By targeting a narrow niche in the call-center industry, Teleplaza plans to use its resources to provide quality content, exceptional customer service, and a good price.

Pricing offers a competitive advantage. Although supplying Internet marketing services is a new concept, the idea of paying only for what is received is intriguing to clients. Annual commitments, which are traditional in publishing (may exceed $10,000 a year for some clients), are not required. Pricing strategy adaptations are an important marketing tool to ensure that Teleplaza is listening to their customers.

By evaluating visits to particular categories on the site, Teleplaza can determine what products, services, and specific information are most in demand. Teleplaza's solid network of Web links, including American Express, *Inc.* and *Success* magazines, the U.S. Small Business Administration, Yahoo!, Netscape, and the Mining Company, among others, adds value to their customers.

Prospects and core customers are contacted through a series of strategically planned letters and telephone calls. A database of over 2500 firms in the call-center sector has been developed over the past 3 years. This database is used to move leads from C prospects (never been contacted) to B contacts (expressed interest in Teleplaza) to the prime A accounts, which will be closed by the internal sales force. Sales will keep in contact with upwards of 400 targeted companies (B+ leads) per month via a combination of direct mail, e-mail, and telephone follow-up. Postcards are sent to C leads, sales kits go to B leads, and personal phone calls are made to A leads.

Sales efforts are focused on firms already embracing the Web as a marketing tool. Teleplaza works on building positive, long-term relationships with new and core customers. Public relations efforts utilize the Internet media to develop site listings, gain a positive image of the company in the telemarketing industry and community, and attract the best people and customers.

## Questions

1. Critique Teleplaza's strategic marketing plan. What changes would you suggest management consider to improve their competitive position?

2.  What impact will the environmental factors (i.e., external changes and industry forces) have on Teleplaza's strategy and its business performance?
3.  Is Teleplaza market oriented? Why or why not?
4.  How does Teleplaza create value for its customers?
5.  If the Internet community embraces the concept of advertising over direct marketing, competition may be difficult to overcome; however, if the Internet favors a direct marketing approach, Teleplaza has an excellent chance to succeed. Comment on this statement.

# Case 19. Time Insurance — A Study of Process Quality Improvement*

A longtime industry leader in providing health insurance to individuals and small groups, Time Insurance Company had always enjoyed an excellent reputation with its network of independent agents. But, increasing costs, added product complexities, and uncertainty in the health-care industry threatened Time's ability to maintain its track record of profitable growth. In the second and third quarters of 1992, the company's management undertook a fundamental review of its business strategy, which included a 6-month reengineering effort in the individual medical underwriting unit. Dramatic improvements in quality were achieved through a combination of strategic context, methodology, teamwork, and commitment.

## Forming a Team

The company's main challenge was to increase effectiveness in dealing with an increasingly uncertain and changing environment where local

* This case was prepared by John Feather, Partner, Corporate Renaissance, Inc., and William C. Johnson, Professor of Marketing, School of Business and Entrepreneurship, Nova Southeastern University.

| Phase I | Phase II | Phase III | Phase IV |
|---------|----------|-----------|----------------|
| Planning | Analysis | Design | Implementation |
| 0.5 months | 2 months | 2.5 months | |

**Figure C19.1. Phases of the Project**

and regional differentiation requires rapid and flexible competitive actions. This meant that the organization had to become more nimble in identifying and taking marketplace initiatives, while at the same time achieving substantial improvements in operating costs and service. A critical element involved the identification and redesign of Time's key business processes to simultaneously minimize cycle time and waste while providing superb quality service to policyholders and agents.

It had become quite apparent that Time's medical underwriting department was in trouble. Policy issuance for the last 2 years remained flat, units costs were increasing, and policy reissues had reached an alarming 10%. Moreover, help-desk calls for application-related problems were increasing 50% a year. Incremental improvement would not help; instead, radical change was needed.

A project team was formed with nine Time employees and two consultants. The two consultants acted as reengineering czars, providing project management guidance while facilitating process analysis. The team was charged with developing and testing a new process design. Figure C19.1 illustrates the phases of the project and the approximate time spent on each phase.

## Planning the Project

First, an organizational readiness assessment was conducted to determine the company's climate for change. The assessment was done by the consulting firm using a questionnaire and interviews. The results indicated that the organization was change ready, meaning that most employees recognized the need for and welcomed change. Next, biweekly divisional meetings were held to inform and include the entire organization in the project. Monthly communication forums were also established, as were daily mechanisms for employee involvement, including a newsletter, an electronic mailbox for questions and ideas, a suggestion box, and a "living list" which included ideas that employees thought should be incorporated into the design.

## Analyzing the Situation

As part of the analysis, the team developed a customer segmentation analysis (needs assessment by customer type), a workload profile (volume and mix of work), activity-value analysis (steps in the process that add value for the customer), design specifications (specific customer demands, such as 24-hour turnaround), and design options (range of options used to customize the design). It then constructed a business process map that detailed work flow to the customer.

From the start, the team felt it needed to look at the new policy issue process from the perspective of its customers: the agents. To gain this outside-in view, it developed a business process map. In this map, the flow of work required to issue a new policy was described in terms of blocks of activity. For example, as applications go through the process, each underwriting request gets quote sold, processed, delivered, and serviced.

By mapping work flow, the team uncovered startling information about the underwriting process. First, it learned that contact between the company and the customer was minimal, with lengthy gaps between each intersection. At the time, the process required the underwriter to wait for requirements to arrive, and it took an average of 37 days of internal processing time to issue a policy. Often as much as 60 days had elapsed by the time the policyholder received the policy.

Mapping the existing process also revealed that a new policy application went through 284 process steps, and only 16 of these actually added value for the customer. These 16 steps accounted for only 9% of the process time (the actual hands-on time that a person spends working on the application being processed). About 95% of the time not defined as hands-on was attributed to work waiting in queue.

In addition to mapping the existing process and quantifying the workload, the project team performed a documentation of customer specifications and a documentation of design options. Questions about service were developed and circulated to gather broad input from agents. This survey was supplemented by a series of customer focus groups. The data collected by the team were categorized by four performance dimensions: quality, delivery, cycle time, and cost. From this research, a set of process specifications was developed to guide the process redesign.

# Designing the New Process

There were two stages to the design of the new process: high-level design and detailed design. In the initial high-level design, team members strove to think out of the box to create a conceptual model that would exceed the already ambitious design specifications. The driving specifications for the design were a dramatic improvement in responsiveness to customer needs and a drastic reduction in cycle time.

Sub-teams worked in parallel to design the new business. The best attributes of each sub-team were integrated into one cohesive vision of the new process and supporting structures. The resulting high-level design envisioned a work-team approach. Each work team would be aligned regionally with agents. Some of the key features of the high-level design concept were that the high-level conceptual design provided guidance for designing the details, the Time team created a new detailed business process map as the primary documentation of the new design, and the new process contained only 85 process steps, with more than 60% of these adding value for the customer.

# A New Organizational Structure

The new process called for new roles and responsibilities throughout the organization, where the traditional vertical organizational structure with first-line supervisors was replaced with a flatter organizational structure. Considerable responsibility was assumed by teams under this new organizational structure. Employees were then matched with the skills required in the newly identified roles, and intensive training began. The entire division participated in planning and implementing the transition to the new process. A new organization was to be structured around core teams regionally aligned with agents. A technical resource center would be used to train people continually. Teams would pull resources from the technical resource center when trends indicated a higher volume of work or, if the volume were high enough, new teams would be formed.

## Successful Results

The new design has resulted in significant process improvements, which have in turn had a substantial impact on Time. The process improvements have increased quality and delivery to agents while reducing Time's unit cost and cycle time. Revenue growth has been significant due to the exceptional service given to the agents. The increased flexibility with the new team structure gives the company a competitive advantage and also permits quick changes to regulatory constraints along with providing Time with a solid base for transition in the new health-care environment. Other results are shown below:

- 60% reduction in policy reissuances
- 50% increase in measured customer satisfaction ratings
- 10% reduction in cost per policy issued
- 80% reduction in process cycle time for fast-track applications
- Significant increases in revenue from higher customer retention

## Questions

1. Using the Deming cycle, evaluate Time Insurances's process improvement efforts.
2. What are some other quality tools that Time Insurance could have used to better understand and improve their service levels?
3. What were the key success factors in this case, particularly as they have to do with process re-design?
4. Discuss the relationship between process improvement and customer-added value.

# Part 3. Customer Value Applications

# Customer Value Applications

## Exercise 1. Value Recipes of Restaurants — Sizzler or Fizzler?

The restaurant industry provides a market laboratory with respect to developing a customer focus and creating value for target markets. As an example, Sizzler recently filed for bankruptcy protection because its menu and dining experience could not keep up with stronger competitors and changing consumer tastes. Sizzler's problems included the following: buffets required lots of space and turnover, cafeteria-style service was provided (not fast food, not table service), the decor was dated, inferior quality meat was used, and the chain had a relatively poor steakhouse image.

### Discussion

1. As marketing consultants to Sizzler, briefly outline a plan to management for saving the company (discuss customer value issues such as image, service quality, and pricing in your response).
2. Explain how *two* of the three restaurants in each group (below) have fallen behind, are adapting to changing market desires, or have assumed a leadership position in their respective niche.
   - *Decliners:* Steak & Ale, El Torito, Shoney's
   0 *Adapters:* Denny's, Red Lobster, International House of Pancakes
   + *Stars:* Outback, Roadhouse Grill, Rainforest Cafe

a. How do these restaurants create value for their customers?
b. What is their competitive advantage in the marketplace?
c. What value-based strategies should these restaurants use for repositioning and/or future growth?

# Exercise 2. Analyzing Market Orientation for the U.S. Post Office

Based on *Fortune* 500 rankings, the U.S. Post Office, an independent government agency, is the ninth largest company in America, with revenues of more than $58 billion (1998 profits are projected to be $500–600 million). The Post Office delivers more than 200 billion pieces of mail annually, up 20 billion from 1995 and more than twice the 1971 rate. Currently, 93% of local first-class mail is delivered overnight (a 1% increase from 1997). As the largest employer in the country (776,000 personnel), the Post Office's goal is to evolve into a premier provider of 21st century postal communications products and services and to be recognized as the best value in America. (Visit www.usps.gov for further details on this organization.) Realize that customer value is determined by an organization's market orientation; this in turn is impacted by changes in the business culture and strategies adopted to be customer responsive.

## Discussion

1. What is value? How does the U.S. Post Office create value for its customers?
2. Analyze the components of a market orientation:
   a. *Customer orientation*: Who is the Post Office's customer? What does the customer value?
   b. *Competitive advantage*: Who are the competitors? What are their strengths/weaknesses?
   c. *Interfunctional coordination*: How is the Post Office organized? How do the departments interact?
3. Discuss how product mix, new product development, and perceived quality impact the market orientation of the U.S. Post Office.
4. What changes should the U.S. Post Office implement to improve its market orientation?

# Exercise 3. Using Total Quality (TQ) Tools For Improved Decision-Making

## Application A

The raw data below represent complaints from a recent study conducted among customers of a large car rental firm based on their most recent car rental experience. Suppose you are called in as a consultant in order to isolate the most critical factors so as to improve service quality in the future. Construct a pareto diagram from the raw data below and make recommendations based on your analysis.

| Long Lines at Counter | Popular Models Unavailable | Priced Too High | Vehicle Not Clean |
|---|---|---|---|
| / / / / / | / / / / / | / / / / / | / / / / / |
| / / / / / | / / / / / | / / / / / | / / / / / |
| / / / / / | / / / / / | / / / | / / / / / |
| / / / / / | / / / / / | | / / / / |
| / / / / / | / / / / / | | |
| / / / | / / / / / | | |
| | / / / / / | | |

## Application B

Naturally Yours, a small health food producer in the midwest, was facing a severe decline in profits. The company packages and sells wholesome snack foods, such as potato chips, salsa chips, pretzels, and crackers, to name just a few. Naturally Yours' two plants are responsible for producing the total product line, consisting of 42 snack-related items, most of which carry a premium price due to the higher quality ingredients used. The company president recently remarked, "Profitability will only result from running our plants at capacity. Adding new products to utilize our excess capacity will allow us to spread our costs over a greater volume."

Most of the company's products are distributed through national and mom 'n' pop health food stores. The company has a line-forcing policy, requiring any store wanting to carry its snack foods to be willing to carry the entire Naturally Yours product line. Many of the smaller health food stores refuse to carry the company's line because of this stocking policy. Average retail inventory turnover for the company's snack line is 22 times vs. the industry average of 25. Naturally Yours uses limited trade magazine advertising and attends one trade show annually. The company employs 11 salespeople who either call on the national chains, such as GNC, or natural food brokers who service the smaller health food stores. (Note: Many of the large national chains are beginning to stock and promote their own labels.) The company president issued a terse memo concerning inadequate market coverage of their products, blaming this failure on the salespeople. The company has very little leverage with their suppliers, given their relatively low volume of purchases. You are called in as a consultant to this firm. Your task is to identify the problem and symptoms facing this company. Use a fishbone diagram to guide you in formulating your response.

## Exercise 4. The "Love Bug" Rides Again (Value Proposition)

Volkswagen recently reintroduced the VW Beetle in the U.S. The Beetle or "love bug" was the smash economy car in the 1960s and '70s and the most successful model of any car ever produced. More than 21 million Beetles were produced at plants in Germany, Brazil, and Mexico.

The stylish, new "bug" complies with required anti-smog and safety legislation. Several aspects of the older model were changed. These oddities included that fact that it came with an AM/FM radio only, air conditioning and heating were not offered, the car could only fit four adults under 5 foot 9 inches comfortably, and the engine performed from 0 to 60 mph in 12 seconds with a maximum speed of 75 mph.

Management feels that success in the auto industry is based on providing the highest value to the most appropriate market segment. Management has split the marketing department into four sections (teams) based on market segments. Each segment must determine the appropriate marketing value strategy for their segment. The challenge is for each team to choose a marketing strategy that maximizes the value proposition of the new Beetle.

Value Proposition = Price + Service + Quality + Brand Identification

## Discussion

Determine a value-based pricing, quality, service, and brand-identification strategy. The options provided here are provided for reference; teams may determine others. (Go to key questions.)

- Team 1: Create a value strategy for the aging baby boomer (mid-life crisis, re-living their childhood) segment.
- Team 2: Create a value strategy for the high school/college student market segment.
- Team 3: Create a value strategy for the young, just starting out couples segment.
- Team 4: Create a value strategy for a specialty segment (such as a low-rider, convertible, and/or small sports car segment).

|  | *1999 Volkswagen Beetle GLS 2 Door Hatchback — Dealer Invoice* (Kelley Blue Book) |
|---|---|
| Base model (loaded) | $15,535 |
| Destination charge | 525 |
| Emission equipment (California, northeast) | 98 |
| Automatic transmission | 856 |
| Accessory packages | |
| Luxury package (power, wheels, moon roof) | 873 |
| Partial leather package | 742 |
| Alloy wheel package | 270 |
| **Other options** (you set these prices) | |
| Dealer advertising campaigns | — |
| Dealer incentives or premiums | — |
| Extended warranty (2 year, 24,000 miles standard) | — |
| Service program (may include guaranteed fast service and free loaner cars) | — |
| **Other pricing issues** | |
| Pricing structure — set prices or negotiations | |
| Recommended profit margins 15–30% | |

## Key Questions

(Apply these questions to your team's particular market segment.)

1. What is the value-based pricing strategy? What options will be incorporated to meet the needs of the targeted audience? At what price will the product be marketed?

2. What is the value-based services program strategy?
3. What (if any) is the value-based quality strategy?
4. How will the Beetle brand be successfully identified and submitted to the targeted market? What are the promotion and advertising activities recommended?

## Exercise 5. Managing Moments of Truth

Buyer-seller interactions (service encounters) are used by customers to assess the functional quality of the firm's service offerings. *Moments of truth* are the times and places where the service provider demonstrates the value of its performance effectiveness to the customer. It may begin with a customer inquiry and end when the service experience is consummated.

When patronizing an organization, customers experience a series of moments that will impact their relationship longevity with that service firm. For example, one service cycle for a drug store visit might include: (1) parking the car, (2) entering the store, (3) getting a shopping basket, (4) selecting a few over-the-counter remedies, (5) requesting help from a clerk, (6) waiting in line at the pharmacy, (7) talking to the pharmacist about the medication, and (8) paying for the items selected.

### Discussion

1. Identify the relevant moments of truth in a specific service organization. What are the three most critical service encounters?
2. How do these key interactions impact ongoing customer relationships? (In your response, consider what the customer values and the concept of critical incidents.)
3. Develop marketing/business strategies to effectively manage the moments of truth.

## Exercise 6. Value Pricing Strategies for Services

The definition of value is the ratio of perceived benefits divided by the perceived sacrifice. The largest and most common sacrifice is monetary;

therefore, it is important to have a value-based pricing strategy appropriate to the market orientation desired by the company. The purpose of this exercise is to determine value-based pricing strategies for the following "new" service products: (1) prepaid cellular phone service, (2) bilingual Internet websites, (3) take-out food delivery service, (4) premium cable television service packages, and (5) other — design your own service offering. For each service, respond to the following five questions.

## Discussion

1. What are the perceived service attributes (i.e., search, experience-based, and credence) that affect price strategies?
2. What is the perceived value of alternative (competitive) services?
3. Define the value-based pricing strategy. Discuss brand identification/image, advertising/promotion, and service quality in your response.
4. What are the transaction costs, life-cycle costs, and risk factors that may affect purchasing decisions for the service offering?
5. Would you recommend using a satisfaction-based, relationship-based, or efficiency pricing strategy?

# Exercise 7. Adding and Promoting Value via Differentiation

Successful companies stand out from the pack; they are perceived as being unique and better than their competitors. This can be accomplished through one of three marketing strategies.

1. *Differentiation*: minor difference based on product and/or image positioning (e.g., Cherry Coke, a brand variation/line extension)
2. *Moderate incongruencies*: product discrepancies within a product market that are valued and interesting (e.g., Slice, a soft-drink with real fruit juice)
3. *Strong incongruencies*: major product discrepancies that lead to the creation of separate submarkets or new niches in an industry sector (e.g., Gatorade, a sports drink)

## Discussion

Choose one of four product categories: consumer good, consumer service, industrial service, or industrial good. Next, select an "appropriate" market to analyze.

1. Building on your "basic" product (e.g., laptop computer, overnight package delivery service, etc.), explain how you can apply the above concepts — differentiation, moderate and strong incongruencies — to gain a competitive advantage for this offering.
2. How will you add value based on your three product-augmenting strategies?
3. As promotional consultants, devise an ad theme (unique selling proposition) for your moderate or strong incongruency. What type of headline, graphic elements, and key selling points would you recommend for this new product?
4. How could you incorporate your advertising plans into an integrated marketing communications program to promote value effectively to your target market?

# Exercise 8. Building Loyalty, Customer Retention, and Relationship Marketing

Marketing management seeks to create product, service, and company loyalty. The increased interest in relationships and long-term marketing recognizes the significant value of a customer. Furthermore, it is less expensive to keep (and upgrade) customers than to attract new ones (estimated to be five times more costly!).

## Discussion

Identify approaches that companies can use to retain customers and build long-term relationships in the late 1990s.

1. List appropriate strategies for:
   a. High-tech companies
   b. Industrial goods distributors

    c.  Business service firms

    d.  Consumer service firms

2. Rank your top five strategies for the aforementioned companies.

3. Estimate the value of an *average* customer to your company.

4. How should your company measure long-term customer satisfaction, loyalty, and retention?

# Part 4. Customer Value Abstracts

# Customer Value Abstracts*

## Abstract 1. Customer-Accelerated Change

(Band, William A. *Marketing Management*, Winter, pp. 47–58, 1995.)

### Contribution

The author suggests a framework to cope with customer-accelerated change. This framework consists of two sets of variables: the enterprise system and a set of strategic questions. The integration of these sets provides tools that leverage the voice of customers.

### Summary

Band proposes that the rate of change in customer expectations is increasing faster than the ability of companies to respond. This can result in lost market share and lower profit margins. Companies can compete in the "value decade" via a framework for change that helps them connect with their customers. Leverage for such change resides in the "linkages" among the individual elements of the enterprise system: (1) leadership, (2) organizations, (3) customer, and (4) process. A series of questions drives customer-accelerated change within the four elements of the enterprise system. For significant change to take place

---

* All abstracts were prepared by Norapol Chinuntdej under the direction of Art Weinstein.

which truly creates customer value, a firm should ask these five questions for each of the enterprise elements:

1. What is our vision?
2. What is our current reality?
3. What are our leverage points?
4. How do we operationalize?
5. How do we sustain change?

To determine the firm's leverage points, Band suggests the use of a customer value deployment matrix, a grid that shows how core processes relate to each customer attribute to determine how effectively the process is being performed. Companies that seek greater customer alignment not only need to better understand their customers' requirements but they should also assess their own organizational culture and climate. For example, identifying hindrances that employees experience when trying to provide exceptional value is crucial to achieving customer alignment. Finally, sustaining customer-accelerated change requires the use of well-designed metrics to provide managers with a balanced summary of business performance.

### Customer Value Implication

Managers will find this framework useful for understanding the customer expectations and then delivering the correct customer value. Also, this framework helps managers review and improve their firms' business performance.

## Abstract 2. Capture and Communicate Value in the Pricing of Services

(Berry, Leonard L. and Yadav, Manjit S., *Sloan Management Review,* Summer, pp. 41–51, 1996.)

### Contribution

This article details the relationship between customer value and price in the service industry. The key to success in services is to clearly relate the price that customers pay to the value that they receive. The three pricing strategies proposed — satisfaction-based pricing, relationship pricing, and efficiency pricing — contribute to the collection of marketing tools that provide customer value.

## Summary

The authors emphasize the importance of linkage between customer value and price in the service industry. They explain that services differ from goods in the degree to which they possess search, experience, and credence attributes. Products that can be evaluated before purchase and use have search attributes; products that can be evaluated only after they have been used have experience attributes; and others that cannot be fully evaluated even after use have credence attributes. Services tend to have higher degrees of experience and credence attributes. Based on such characteristics, customers are likely to wonder if the service they buy is worthwhile. Three pricing strategies are developed to capture, communicate, and provide value to the customers:

1. *Satisfaction-based pricing strategy:* recognizes and reduces customers' perceptions of uncertainty in purchasing services. Implementation of this strategy includes service guarantees, benefit-driven pricing, or flat-rate pricing.
2. *Relationship pricing:* encourages the development of profitable and long-term customer relationships. This strategy can be implemented through long-term contracts and price-bundling.
3. *Efficiency pricing:* passes cost savings on to customers. Implementation of this strategy is cost-leader pricing.

By applying these strategies, companies can expose and exploit the vulnerabilities of competitors' traditional pricing practices because these new pricing strategies consider customer value as their focal point.

## Customer Value Implication

Price is a major component of the value proposition. This article clarifies three important pricing strategies that can be effective in service markets. Managers can use these insights to provide value to their customers.

# Abstract 3. Seven Pillars to Future Success

(Anon., *Chain Store Age,* Aug., pp. 9A–15A, 1996.)

## Contribution

This article examines and suggests that seven main factors lead to the success of retail stores. Hence, we can clearly see that the value concept is not simply quality divided by price; it is a multi-dimensional proposition designed by "in touch" marketers.

## Summary

The article shows how retail stores can survive in a highly competitive industry. The seven pillars framework is suggested to meet such a goal:

1. *Value* — retailers must thoroughly understand the definition of value. Value means price, quality, time, convenience, and service.
2. *Dominance* — allows retailers to stand out from the flock. Dominance can be developed in several areas: assortment, inventory depth, store size, store locations, store design, among others.
3. *Marketing* — retailers will have to understand their customers' needs and make sure that they have whatever their customers desire in their store.
4. *Technology* — everything retailers need to serve their customers must be assisted effectively by technology (e.g., computer-aided design, customer databases, etc.).
5. *Entertainment* — retail stores will have to change a boring shopping experience into an enjoyable one. Also, the selling experience can be developed to be a main theme for the stores.
6. *Electronic shopping* — retailers will have to help customers enjoy shopping via home television, telephone, or Internet options.
7. *Globalization* — because growth in the U.S. market is limited, retailers need to seize the faster-growing opportunities in the international market.

## Customer Value Implication

The article stresses the new definition of customer value. Customer value includes several attributes: price, quality, time, convenience, and service. The article also suggests that retailers need to apply these value-creating elements in their stores. Technology can be used to support these customer value activities.

## Abstract 4. Move It Fast ... Eliminate Steps

(Dawe, R.L., *Transportation & Distribution*, September, pp. 67–74, 1997.)

### Contribution

The author proposes that companies should adopt supply-chain management to increase customer value while maintaining low prices. Merge in transit (MIT), which is a tool of supply-chain management, is also detailed.

### Summary

According to the author, customer demand for value-added services comes in various forms: (1) product line variety, (2) shorter order cycle time, (3) faster speed, (4) demand for high quality, (5) customer return policy, (6) globalization of product or service, and (7) flexibility/agility. However, this increased customer demand never means that customers are willing to pay more. It means that companies must increase customer value while maintaining low prices. The author suggests supply-chain management (SCM) as a solid management tool for companies to survive in this value decade. SCM is the integration of inbound, in-process, outbound, and after-sales service flows. SCM can be viewed as a continuum — companies acquire inbound materials (with the integration of procurement), convert them in the process (with the integration of production), deliver them to customers (with the integration of marketing), and finally provide after-sales service to customers (with the integration of procurement, production, marketing, and finance). The integration of logistics and SCM enables companies to provide superior service to customers. Some new SCM logistics techniques include just-in-time (JIT), quick response (QR), efficient consumer response (ECR), vendor-managed inventory (VMI), and continuous flow. All of these highly focused customer services will create operations in a high degree of speed, control, quality, flexibility, and efficiency. Undoubtedly, this provides customer value. The author then discusses merge-in-transit, which is one example of continuous flow. MIT collects shipments from multiple origin points and consolidates them into a single delivery to the customers. For example, Dell Computer manufactures the processing unit but outsources monitors and keyboards. UPS merges the shipments of processors, monitors, and keyboards for Dell from different sources at one of their facilities and then delivers the entire system intact.

### Customer Value Implication

Because customers demand value-added services, companies need speed and flexibility in their operations. Supply-chain management is one of the solid management strategies which companies should adopt in their operations. Merge-in-transit, an application of supply-chain management, is useful for companies in this value decade.

## Abstract 5. Customer Value Change in Industrial Marketing Relationships: A Call for New Strategies and Research

(Flint, D.J., Woodruff, R.B., and Gardial, S.F., *Industrial Marketing Management*, March, pp. 163–175, 1997.)

### Contribution

This article offers a major contribution to the understanding of the forces that drive customers' perceptions of value that change. The authors develop a customer value change theory. They propose a general model which is mainly constructed by three relevant trigger events and three forms of value.

### Summary

According to the authors, relationship marketing is linked primarily to how to retain customers. Customer retention involves understanding: (1) what the customers value, (2) customers' satisfaction with suppliers' responses, and (3) factors that drive customers' perceptions of value to change. The authors intend to fill the gap in understanding the third issue. They propose that different types of events will trigger different value changes and eventually will result in different levels of customer satisfaction. They propose a general model which explains the relationship among relevant trigger events, customers' perceptions of value, customer satisfaction, and customer retention. They define a trigger event as "a stimulus in the customer's environment that is perceived by the customer to be relevant to his/her goals, which results in some form of change in values, desired value, and/or value judgments" (p. 165). There are three types of trigger events: supplier-located, customer-located, and environment-located. Supplier-located events would be changes in products (e.g., product performance or pricing), changes in service (e.g., service quality or management procedures), and interpersonal (e.g., personal turnover or quality). Customer-located events are changes in the customer's organization. There are three classifications of these events: strategic events (e.g., ownership or focus), operational events (e.g., management team or finances), and tactical events (e.g., point of contact or equipment). Environment-located events occur outside of both the customers' and suppliers' organizations. They represent a macroenvironment (e.g., regulatory issues or technology), customer's competitors (e.g., product or service innovation), and customer's channel members (e.g., new suppliers or new alliances). Such trigger events will affect customers to varying degrees depending upon their predictability and strength. The authors clarify that the relevant forms of value (change in customer's perception of value) that trigger events are likely to drive change in three forms: (1) value — the implicit beliefs that guide behavior, (2) desired value — what customer wants to happen, and (3) value judgment — assessment of what has really happened. The triggered value change model is offered to show how each trigger event will impact on each value. The change in customer satisfaction will be linked to the change in customer's perception of value through disconfirmation. If the customers feel that value received exceeded what was expected or some standard, the customer is satisfied (positive disconfirmation). Eventually, customer retention which is an outcome of customer satisfaction, will rise.

## Customer Value Implication

The article offers a process to understand better how customers perceive value, after which managers can set up an appropriate strategy to respond effectively to customers. Finally, customer satisfaction and customer retention will emerge.

## Abstract 6. Beyond Customer Satisfaction

(Fredericks, J.O. and Salter, II, J.M., *Management Review,* May, pp. 29–32, 1995.)

### *Contribution*

Fredericks and Salter's framework for building customer loyalty is a noteworthy contribution. It states that price, product quality, service quality, innovation, and image are the factors that create what the customer perceives to be superior value. It also explains systematically how these components will be found and by which process these components will be delivered to customers. Moreover, this framework contributes to the appreciation of customer value by pointing out that each process stems from customer requirements. Also, it considers the important linkage between customer value and shareholder value.

### *Summary*

Satisfying the customer is no longer the ultimate business virtue. Companies need to look for ways to create and increase customer loyalty. The key to this new loyalty-centered approach to customer relationships is creating and managing the "customer value package" — the combination of factors (price, product quality, service quality, innovation, and company image) that creates what the customer perceives as superior value. The authors explain how companies can create customer loyalty based on these factors. Five steps are recommended:

1. *Clearly define and communicate your objectives.* The company needs to make sure that every stakeholder clearly understands the importance of creating and delivering customer loyalty and knows how to make it possible.
2. *Let customers define, in their own words, their criteria for quality, price, image, and value.* The company needs to distinguish between basic requirements and loyalty builders. Meeting the basic requirements will get the company on the approved vendor

list, but generating loyalty will encourage a customer to stick with the company during difficult times.

3. *Conduct a critical need and value assessment.* The company must set priorities among important customer requirements and determine the relative importance of these aspects of the customer value package.

4. *Develop an action plan and move to implementation.* This turns management of customer loyalty into a way of doing business. The company must make sure that the voice of the customer becomes the principle around which the business processes are organized.

5. *Monitor the marketplace and organization results.* Managing customer value is not a one-time effort, so all of the loyalty-building components of customer value have to be monitored regularly with a focus on the relationship between customer value, customer loyalty, and financial performance.

### Customer Value Implication

Customer value consists of the correct combination of price, product quality, service quality, innovation, and company image. This leads to the building of customer loyalty. Customer loyalty must be considered in the context of a financial perspective, as well as a marketing perspective.

# Abstract 7. Customer Retention Begins With the Basics

(Geller, L., *Direct Marketing*, Sept., pp. 58–62, 1997.)

### Contribution

The author states the underlying reasons why firms need to focus on customer retention. She offers 15 customer-retention strategies for survival in this value decade.

### Summary

Ninety-five percent of the profits in some companies comes from long-term customers, and it costs three to seven times more to get a new customer than to retain a current one. Customers are a company's most valuable assets. The author explains the importance of customer retention by using a direct-marketing case. Companies are likely to fail in their first efforts in direct advertising, as the fixed costs are in the upfront marketing; they will not reach the payback period until after several purchases. However, customers can easily switch purchasing from current companies, as there are many companies that offer a variety of products simultaneously; hence, it is not surprising that companies will lose customers after only one purchase if they do not have a customer-retention program in place. The author offers these important customer-retention pointers: (1) deliver a high-quality and high-value product; (2) make every single contact count and make sure that the customer's first impression is an invaluable experience; (3) know your customers and build a marketing database to record customers' sales patterns; (4) know when your customers defect — your marketing database should help you know when your customers' spending drops off; (5) keep your company at the top of your customer's mind — treat your customers the way they should be treated; (6) modify your product/service mix and update your offers; (7) always close the loop in your marketing programs by evaluating and fine-tuning your programs; (8) deliver excellent customer service, which is still one of the most important elements of any retention program; (9) keep your customer-retention programs human by treating customers on a person-to-person, not company-to-person, basis; (10) use partnerships to build customer retention — the partnership between VISA card and an airline company for frequent flyer miles is an example; (11) do the unexpected and treat customers way beyond their expectations; (12) use your database to maximize the personalization of offers; (13) identify the timing and frequency of customer promotions — based on the database, you can offer the product/service to customers at the appropriate time; (14) utilize retail and catalog synergies — retailers can offer current customers special discounts via their mailing catalogs; and (15) use on-line marketing, as it helps customers shop effectively. The author reminds us of the two key pitfalls in customer retention: ignoring the customer after the sale and over-investing in new prospects at the expense of old customers.

### Customer Value Implication

The above fifteen tips favorably impact customer-retention programs. Customer-retention strategies enhance customer value and lead to increased profitability.

# Abstract 8. From Marketing Mix to Relationship Marketing: Towards a Paradigm Shift in Marketing

(Gronroos, C., *Management Decision*, 32(2), pp. 4–20, 1994.)

## Contribution

Gronroos proposes the possibility of establishing a general theory of marketing based on the new relationship marketing school of thought instead of the traditional marketing mix concept.

## Summary

According to the author, today's environment has been changing, and several new concepts in marketing have been emerging— the globalization of business, customer retention, market economies, and relationship marketing, among other trends. He feels that marketing theory which is based on the marketing mix which emerged in 1950s should be changed to a new concept for approaching marketing problems in today's environment. Relationship marketing is suggested as the new marketing paradigm or core concept for this new marketing theory. The author argues that the four P's of the marketing mix are no longer suitable to fulfill the requirements of the marketing concept. The marketing mix is a production-oriented paradigm, but the paradigm has already been shifted to a customer or market orientation. He also reviews the evolution of three theories of marketing after the emergence of the marketing mix: the interaction/network approach to industrial marketing, the marketing of services, and customer relationship economics. He points out that both the interaction/network approach and service marketing view marketing as an interactive process in a social context where relationship building is a cornerstone. He defines relationship marketing as marketing designed (p. 9) "to establish, maintain, and enhance relationships with customers and other partners, at a profit, so that the objectives of the parties involved are met. This is achieved by a mutual exchange and fulfillment of promises." He suggests that establishing a relationship can be divided into two parts: attracting new customers and building a relationship with these customers. Moreover, there are two integral elements of the relationship marketing approach: promise concept and trust. To develop the customer relationship, we could not depend on only the marketing mix; however, the author accepts that the marketing mix is still necessary in some perspectives. To establish the right approach or strategy, he offers the marketing strategy continuum. This continuum places relationship marketing at one end and transaction marketing at the other end. Various types of products and services will be placed along this continuum. For example, consumer packaged goods are on the transaction marketing side, whereas services are on the relationship marketing side. This strategy continuum also shows the differences in characteristics between transaction marketing and relationship marketing: short-term focus and long-term focus, marketing-mix function and interactive marketing function, monitoring by market share and monitoring by the customer base, etc.

### Customer Value Implication

The author suggests that relationship marketing should be the foundation for marketing theory and practice in today's service-oriented economy. The marketing strategy continuum can be employed by researchers and practitioners in developing the proper strategy in this value decade.

## Abstract 9. Walking the Talk of Customer Value

(Heard, E., *National Productivity Review*, Winter, pp. 21–27, 1993/1994.)

### Contribution

To survive in this value era, Heard suggests that firms concentrate on improving four key business processes: designing, making, marketing, and supporting. Customer value is maximized when product, order, and experience — which are outcomes of the first three processes — are correct, timely, appropriate, and economical.

### Summary

The author suggests that we are moving into the value era and firms will no longer survive if they simply focus on price and product features. Several non-price factors are thought to have great influence on customers' perceptions of value received: (1) the length of customer lead times; (2) variation from promised delivery dates; (3) condition of product on arrival; (4) sales call and order initiation procedures; (5) credit, billing, and collection procedures; (6) effectiveness of after-sales support; (7) product documentation; (8) product performance; (9) product downtime frequency and duration; and (10) maintenance cost and difficulty. There are four key business processes responsible for creating better customer value: (1) design — integrating the "voice of the customer" when building the product; (2) making — getting key inputs from suppliers and transforming them into other components or finished products leading to filled customer orders; (3) marketing — transforming sales leads into sales calls, sales orders, service calls, and sales support which lead to completed service transactions; and 4) support — those activities and tasks that serve internal customers. In addition, Heard suggests that the four key business processes must be reengineered and firms should strive for: (1) simplicity — provide the required variety of outputs at low cost and with minimum capital intensity; (2) focus — customer and supplier processes should be treated as the same process; (3) energy — employees should be empowered and also have problem-solving skills; (4) continuity — processes must have extensive improvement and refinement; (5) linearity— subprocesses within each process must be linked together and be customer driven; and (6) dependability — strong customer-supplier relationships assure the success of each process.

### Customer Value Implication

The article provides guidance to managers looking for ways to improve their organizations' processes in this value decade. Managers need to go beyond offering the customers good prices and good products. They need to think thoroughly about their organizations' processes and how they deliver value to customers.

# Abstract 10. Application for the Lifetime Value Model in Modern Newspaper Publishing

(Keane, T.J. and Wang, P., *Journal of Direct Marketing*, Spring, pp. 59–66, 1995.)

## Contribution

The authors show that the lifetime value model (LTV) can be applied to the newspaper industry. The model helps analyze and quantify the value of customer segments or zones. This provides maximum benefit to customers and better use of budgeted resources.

## Summary

In today's competitive publishing environment, marketers need to segment and target readership to meet advertising and circulation goals. Newspaper publishers face a number of business challenges: (1) customers must buy the newspaper continuously, (2) the newspaper must keep the cost of subscriptions low while maintaining high market-penetration levels, and (3) the newspaper must maintain a high volume of advertising revenues. The lifetime value model (LTV) can assist in meeting such objectives. Briefly, LTV is the "calculation of the cost of attaining and servicing customers and weighing that cost against the customer's likelihood to remain or grow loyal over time." It is based on the premise that customers are not created equal and as such have different value to the company based on demographics and cost of retention and attainment. LTV in this case consists of various key components: (1) the zone — the lowest level of customer segmentation; (2) penetration — number of subscriber households compared to the total of number of households in the zone; (3) sales per customer — divided into zoned and non-zoned sales; (4) average circulation revenue per year — total income per year for each zone; (5) average annual churn costs — cost of persuading a current subscriber to renew a subscription; (6) total sales per customer — the average sales to each customer within the zone; (7) average customer lifetime — how long the customer remains a subscriber before quitting permanently; (8) most current acquisition cost — how much it costs to obtain a customer; (9) total sales — calculated within each zone; (10) 5-year net present value based on average life — based on years of subscription, circulation, and advertising revenue and the churn and customer service costs; and (11) percentage of total 5-year net present value and percentage of total subscribers. In addition, the authors use inflation in the calculation of acquisition cost, price, and total direct costs. Cash flow is calculated at the final stage.

## Customer Value Implication

Managers should find this model to be a handy tool to analyze a firm's investment. It helps managers allocate their budgets more efficiently. The model also serves as a guide to increase zone sales to attract more advertising, to segment zones further to make them more attractive to advertisers, and to identify unprofitable zones. This model helps managers serve customers better, which increases customer value.

# Abstract 11. Welcome to the Experience Economy

(Pine, II, B.J. and Gilmore, J.H., *Harvard Business Review*, July/Aug., pp. 97–105, 1998.)

## Contribution

The authors suggest that the service economy has been changed to an experience economy. This experience economy provides a new economic distinction which any firm requires to design new strategies to compete successfully. This article provides the four realms of an experience and identifies five key experience-design principles. A newly designed strategy ensures that firms will strengthen their performance in the customer value era.

## Summary

According to the authors, our economy has gone through an evolution of three stages — an agrarian economy, an industrial economy, and a service economy — to a fourth kind of economy, the experience economy. This new economy provides new economic distinctions. For example, whereas an economic function of service economy is "deliver", delivery is a "stage" in the experience economy. The service economy treats a buyer as a "client", but in the experience economy the buyer is a "guest". Service may be tangible; however, experience is "memorable". This new experience economy has been spreading beyond theaters, restaurants, or theme parks. Even the high-tech firms are adopting this new concept. Firms need to create new strategies to play in this new ballpark. The authors are convinced that it is reasonable to charge customers for receiving the experience. By charging, such a firm will be encouraged to provide the best memorable experience to customers. The authors propose the framework of four realms (educational, entertainment, esthetic, and escapist) of an experience. This framework is constructed on the concepts of customer participation (active participation and passive participation and connection), absorption, and immersion. Firms need to ask themselves what specific experience their firms will offer. The authors suggest that firms need to treat experiences the same way as they do for goods or services. Experiences must meet customer demand, deliver, etc. The authors also identify five key experience design principles: (1) theme the experience, (2) harmonize impressions with positive cues, (3) eliminate negative cues, (4) mix in memorabilia, and (5) engage all five senses. Finally, the authors suggest that firms still need to understand laws of supply and demand — for example, not overpricing the experiences.

### Customer Value Implication

Because goods and services have become commodities, experiences have emerged as a new competitive arena for providing superior customer value. Twenty-first century companies are likely to excel at services marketing by embracing the experience economy.

## Abstract 12. Exploiting the Virtual Value Chain

(Rayport, J.F. and Sviokla, J.J., *Harvard Business Review*, Nov./Dec., pp. 75–85, 1995.)

### Contribution

The virtual value chain is a marketing tool creating customer value. This concept offers a powerful linkage between the physical value chain in the evolving services and information-based economy — the difference is a new locus of value creation. Based on the combination of these two chains, any company can apply these ideas to create and deliver superior customer value and enhance business performance.

## *Summary*

Today's business competes in two worlds: a physical world of resources that we can see and a virtual world of information. The new information world is the marketspace, and the physical world is the marketplace. Management must understand thoroughly how companies can create value in both the physical and virtual worlds. In other words, management must collect raw information in the virtual world and then integrate this into the physical world. By doing so, companies can be successful. However, the authors argue that the process of creating value differs for the physical and virtual worlds. In the physical world, the value chain refers to the physical stages and processes necessary to create finished goods for customers, and information plays a supporting role in the value-adding process; it is not a source of value itself. In the virtual world, however, the information itself is a source of value. Creating value in any stage of this virtual value chain involves a sequence of five activities: gathering, organizing, selecting, synthesizing, and distributing information. Companies need to adopt value-adding information processes in three stages:

1. *Visibility.* In this stage, companies acquire an ability to see physical operations more effectively via information. Companies need to invest in technology systems to manage and control activities (e.g., production, distribution, financing, etc.).

2. *Mirroring capability.* Once companies have such systems, they can begin to implement value-adding steps in the marketspace. They should consider such issues as what value-adding steps currently performed in the physical value chain might be shifted to the mirror world of the virtual value chain. In this step, the companies should find some activities that can be set up in the marketspace to provide customers with greater value.

3. *New customer relationships.* Companies must do more than create value in the marketspace. The authors encourage the companies to extract value from the marketspace, as well. Companies might try to use customer databases to better serve specific needs of customers or stay in touch with customers via the Internet.

## Customer Value Implication

The authors advise us to think in terms of a combination between a virtual value chain and a traditional physical value chain. The two chains must be managed distinctly but also in concert. Companies can seek more opportunities for creating and extracting value than they would have by considering the business just from the viewpoint of a traditional physical value chain.

# Abstract 13. Follow the Value Chain to Superior Performance

(Reidenbach, R.E., *The Bankers Magazine*, Nov./Dec., pp. 48–52, 1996.)

## Contribution

This article provides three main contributions. First, it explains that customer value is not only the usual benefits companies deliver to customers but is also the price that customers pay for such benefits. Second, the proposed value chain strengthens our understanding that customer value creates customer satisfaction, which is a link to the ultimate goal of any business — high shareholder value. Third, it suggests that the value matrix shows the relationship between access to problem solving (benefits) and perceived cost. This framework makes it easier to analyze customer value.

## Summary

According to the author, it is necessary for banks and other financial service providers to move past customer satisfaction and begin to focus on customer value. However, there is an underlying question — how can we effectively measure customer value so that we can create the right customer value? Customer value is the relationship between the benefits provided and the price that a customer pays. The linkage among customer value, customer satisfaction, customer retention, profitability, and shareholder value is developed via the value chain. To measure customer value, managers first need to understand two characteristics of benefit: qualifying benefits, which are the benefits that customers use in deciding to include a company and its product into a choice set, and determining benefits, which are those benefits that win business for the company— these are the benefits used in the value calculation. The author suggests three steps to measure and ultimately manage customer value: (1) identify key benefit components which must be defined from the customer's point of view, (2) separate such benefits into qualifying benefits and determining benefits, and (3) identify cost components associated with each product. Once a company identifies the benefit and perceived cost, it can develop the value matrix. The value matrix is a tool developed to identify the different value propositions offered by competing organizations. By examining each position in this value matrix, a bank or other service firm can evaluate its overall performance and then can improve its customer value strategy.

### Customer Value Implication

The article provides guidance to managers in measuring customer value by considering the relationship between benefits and the costs of such benefits under the value matrix framework. When managers examine their customer value position, they know when and how to improve their business performance.

## Abstract 14. Developing a Customer Value-Based Theory of the Firm

(Slater, S.F., *Journal of the Academy of Marketing Science*, 25(2), pp. 162–167, 1997.)

### Contribution

The author proposes a framework to illustrate the relationship between the firm focused on customer value and that firm's environment. He suggests that the environment has been changing due to fragmented markets and hypercompetition. Companies should have market-oriented cultures: continuous learning about customers, a commitment to customer innovation, and a process-focused organization.

### Summary

Although the foundation for a theory based on customer value of the firm was laid decades ago by researchers, customer value does not receive adequate attention in the theory of the firm today. The creation of customer value must be the reason for a firm's existence and certainly for its success. Firms face an increasingly turbulent and complex competitive environment. Moreover, customers are very demanding. Markets have fragmented into numerous segments, and each has its own unique value equation. Companies need to respond to such changes. Slater proposes that a firm should have a market-oriented culture, which consists of three components:

1. *Continuous learning about customers.* The firm must develop skills for acquiring knowledge about customers, sharing such knowledge widely throughout the organization, achieving consensus on its meaning, and then taking action to deliver superior customer value.

2. *Commitment to innovation.* In a hypercompetitive environment, competitive advantage is likely to be imitated by competitors. However, a commitment to innovation focused on customer value is essential to sustain competitive advantage. Research shows that innovation contributes greatly to the success of a firm.

3. *Focus on customer value processes.* The firm has to maximize the effectiveness of customer value creation activities. The firm can outsource some processes if doing so supports the delivery of superior customer value. By having good knowledge about customer needs in light of this new environment and then providing innovative products to customers, firms can create the sustainable competitive advantages necessary to ensure organizational success.

### Customer Value Implication

This framework provides guidance to managers who want to create new organizations to cope with changes in the customer value paradigm. Managers need to understand the relationship between the firm and its environment. They must create market-oriented cultures to truly understand customer needs. Finally, they must provide the customers with product innovation; this makes success more likely in highly competitive markets.

# Abstract 15. Breaking Compromises, Breakaway Growth

(Stalk, Jr., G., Pecaut, D.K., and Burnett, B., *Harvard Business Review*, Sept./Oct., pp. 131–139, 1996.)

## Contribution

The authors encourage organizations to discover what is dissatisfying their customers. Then, they can develop a new strategy based on how to solve this dissatisfaction — breaking compromises. They call this strategy a new opportunity in doing business. Finally, a compromise breaker can outperform its industry, which results in breakaway growth. The authors suggest seven ways to find such dissatisfactions and build opportunities in any business.

## Summary

Even though business is in a slow-growth period, the authors are convinced that any firm can outperform its industry by understanding the concept of how to break compromises. A compromise is a concession demanded of consumers by service or product producers. It often becomes visible when customers need to change their behavior to use a company's service or product. A compromise differs from a trade-off. Compromises offer no choice, while trade-offs allow customers to choose their products or services from among several choices. For example, the hotel industry forces customers to compromise by not allowing them to check in before 4 p.m., but customers can trade off luxury for economy by choosing between a Ritz-Carlton and a Best Western. The authors show some examples of how to break compromises and then develop new businesses around these former compromises. Significant examples include the pasta business (Contadina), a car dealer (CarMax), and a financial service (Charles Schwab). In the case of CarMax, traditional used-car dealers force customers to compromise by taking risks on quality, haggling over the price with salespeople, finding financing by themselves, etc. CarMax has broken these compromises and utilizes a new method for selling used cars in the U.S. CarMax sets prices at below the average blue-book value, provides no-haggle pricing and no-hassle guarantees, gives its cars 110-point safety checks, offers reliable financing service and a 5-day return guarantee, etc. As a result, CarMax has outperformed other used-car dealers, even new-car dealers. The authors suggest seven ways in which any firm can find and exploit compromise-breaking opportunities: (1) shop the way the customer shops, (2) pay careful attention to how the customer really uses the product or service, (3) explore customers' latent dissatisfactions, (4) look for uncommon denominators, (5) pay careful attention to anomalies, (6) look for diseconomies in the industry's value chain, and (7) look for analogous solutions to the industry's compromises.

### Customer Value Implication

The authors offer a new way to create customer value by breaking compromises and then building new business strategies around these compromises. Such a strategy truly satisfies customers. Finally, these firms are able to outperform its industry rivals.

# Abstract 16. Managing the Change From Marketing Planning to Customer Relationship Management

(Stone, M., Woodcock, N., and Wilson, M., *Long Range Planning*, Oct., pp. 675–683, 1996.)

### Contribution

The authors urge firms to apply relationship marketing to their traditional marketing planning. The authors suggest stages of managing a customer relationship, the important components of that relationship, and how to use technology in the relationship.

### Summary

According to the authors, firms need to understand the importance of relationship marketing before undertaking marketing planning. The authors state that relationship marketing is important because (p. 676): "Acquiring customers is much more expensive than keeping them." By applying relationship marketing concepts in marketing planning, firms will increase customer retention and loyalty and gain higher profitability. The stages of the customer relationship are explained: (1) recruitment, (2) welcoming, (3) getting to know, (4) account management, (5) intensive care, (6) potential divorce, (7) divorce, and (8) winback. The authors argue that one of the keys to increasing profitability in firms is focusing solely on customers offering high lifetime value, and a matrix for analyzing such customers is proposed. This loyalty-value matrix shows the relationship between total customer value and customer type. After carefully screening customers, firms can start with the suggested framework. This framework is the integration of relationship marketing and traditional marketing planning. Market and competitive analysis changes to become customer needs analysis, marketing strategies change to customer management strategies, and mix-offer development changes to customer management policies. Moreover, firms must understand the relationship components: (1) contacts with company staff (front-line and other), (2) outbound contact management (mail, telephone, etc.), (3) physical service environment, (4) brand image, and (5) transaction (price, value, terms). Customers should be involved in these components, and firms must respond to customer requests. New technology allows customers to participate easily in these areas. For example, the World Wide Web makes it easier for customers to contact firms and effectively deliver their demands.

### Customer Value Implication

This article provides guidance for managers in integrating the relationship marketing concept with traditional marketing planning. Customer relationship management ensures that firms will increase customer retention and loyalty and that they will survive in this value decade.

# Abstract 17. Measuring Values Can Sharpen Segmentation in the Luxury Auto Market

(Sukhdial, A.S., Chakraborty, G., and Steger, E.K., *Journal of Advertising Research*, Jan./Feb., pp. 9–22, 1995.)

### Contribution

The authors try to demonstrate that customers purchase luxury cars based on their values and that measuring values can enhance segmentation decisions in the luxury automobile market. Based on their research, the authors suggest that the ownership of American, German, and Japanese luxury cars can be predicted on the basis of the values owners endorse and the car attributes they desire.

### Summary

The authors state that U.S. car makers need to gain more knowledge about their customers to better segment the market as well as provide effective advertising, and they use the concept of "personal value" to reach such goals. They studied three categories of luxury car purchases in the U.S., Germany, and Japan. The research results reveal that the ownership of these cars can be predicted on the basis of their importance rating of values. The owners of German luxury cars consider the values of fun, enjoyment, and excitement more important than do owners of American or Japanese luxury cars. The owners of German and American luxury cars consider both self-fulfillment and sense of accomplishment more important than do the owners of Japanese luxury cars. The owners of American luxury cars consider comfort to be more important than do German or Japanese luxury car owners. The authors explain how to apply these findings to advertising planning activities. They suggest that after companies search for customers' value preferences they should position themselves to meet those customer needs. By having such values, they can allocate advertising resources effectively and communicate about the customers' major concerns.

### Customer Value Implication

In addition to applying the value segmentation concept to advertising activities, managers should find this article helpful in related endeavors. If companies know what their customers value, they should segment their markets and provide products to serve customers effectively at the lowest cost.

## Abstract 18. The Discipline of Market Leaders: Delivering Unmatched Value Year After Year

(Treacy, M.E., *The Conference Board*, pp. 9–13, 1995.)

## Contribution

Treacy contributes to the customer value literature by urging firms to adopt one of three value disciplines: product leadership, operational excellence, or customer intimacy. These disciplines will provide best product, best total cost, or best total solution, respectively. Firms which adopt one of these disciplines can make sure that they will survive in this value era. However, they must design their organizations' processes and structures to match with such disciplines.

## Summary

The author raises a serious question as to why companies have difficulty sustaining their leadership in the marketplace. He states that there are these three rules: (1) put the best deal on the market, (2) make it better every year, and (3) nothing else matters. To be a leader, companies must appreciate the meaning of "value" and then find a discipline that meets this value requirement. Treacy suggests that value is recognized as time, price, or best product features. Ultimately, value falls into three categories for which a company can claim it stands: (1) *best product* — having the best goods or products for customers; (2) *best total cost* — a company can offer a product with the lowest cost, the most reliability, and hassle-free service; and (3) *best total solution* — having neither the best product nor the best cost but having valuable advice. Each of these requires a different discipline: (1) *product leadership* — companies claiming the best product need to demonstrate more than product differentiation; (2) *operational excellence* — companies claiming to have the best total cost must be more operationally competent; and (3) *customer intimacy* — companies claiming to have the best total solution must commit themselves to the customers' success and make sure that they have enough knowledge to solve customers' problems. Companies must choose one of these three disciplines. Also, once the companies choose one, they must drive such a discipline as fast as they can, frequently reassessing the other two disciplines and remembering that operational incompetence is unacceptable. Companies need to think about their processes and structures, which means that an operationally excellent company has to focus on the end-to-end product delivery process as a primary process, while product leaders take this as a secondary process. A customer-intimate company must structure itself so that it has the most empowered account teams which can support the customers the best. Treacy warns us that becoming a value leader does not guarantee that a company will continue to be a leader forever. One should consider these three common traps that make companies lose their spots: (1) complacency, (2) combining a high price with relatively low value, and (3) permitting their value to stagnate. The other thing that a prospective leader needs to take in account is the "wall". The wall is considered a barrier that might take a value leader from its position. For example, the wall for an operationally excellent company is higher fixed cost.

### Customer Value Implication

By adopting one of these three value disciplines and avoiding the suggested pitfalls, managers can ensure that their companies find sustainable competitive advantages.

## Abstract 19. Customer Value: A New Paradigm for Marketing Management

(Weinstein, A. and Pohlman, R.A., *Advances in Business Studies*, 6(10), pp. 89–97, 1998.)

### Contribution

The authors suggest a new key concept for understanding how to maximize economic value in the next millennium — customer value. They identify the concept of customer value, propose a conceptual basis for developing a value-based managerial marketing framework, and offer a four-stage value funnel model.

### Summary

Customer value is an old concept but a new imperative. Customer value is utilized by many firms to differentiate themselves from the pack. The customer value concept is applied by several researchers in many aspects; however, it is always defined by the customers. Customers define value as a relationship between the benefits received vs. the price paid. There is no doubt that customer value has a major impact on business performance. Firms need to find ways to discern how customers perceive value and then provide such value to them. The authors review some research done on customer value. For example, customer value consists of three key ingredients: value-based pricing, product quality, and service quality. Customer value is the total experience and includes such aspects as product assortment, respect for customers, time and energy savings, fun, and fair pricing. Sustainable competitive advantage also requires superior customer value. Supply chain management is studied in terms of a virtual value chain to best serve customers. Segmentation and the marketing mix are also focal points for value creation research. Based on the research done, the authors emphasize that customer value is a much richer construct than low price, great quality, or superb service. Value is a multi-dimensional attribute. The authors provide six value creation assumptions: (1) creating or adding value is good, (2) value is subjective, (3) unique value philosophies must be formulated by each organization, (4) knowledge creation leads to value creation, (5) whatever customers value should drive action programs, and (6) value tradeoffs exist in the marketspace. Then, they propose that business performance should be built on a dual foundation of paramount value concepts: (1) anticipating and responding to the relevant values of all constituencies (e.g., customers, stakeholders, employees, or society), and (2) maximizing economic value and knowledge throughout an organization. The four-stage value funnel model is developed based on this dual foundation: (1) global business community (e.g., society, politics, or technology), (2) market (e.g., suppliers or regulators), (3) organization (e.g., stakeholders or business culture), and (4) customers. Then, a realistic assessment of value creation opportunities throughout the funnel is conducted. Increased business performance is the ultimate goal of this model. If the delivered value of employees exceeds the perceived value of customers, business performance is positive. The value funnel is a downward flow but has upward feedback loops from each level.

## Customer Value Implication

The value funnel model provides a significant tool to create customer-focused business strategies. It effectively responds to customers' demands in the value decade. In sum, the creation of superior customer value by an organization leads to competitive advantage and enhances shareholder/financial value.

# Abstract 20. An Integrated Model of Buyer-Seller Relationships

(Wilson, D.T., *Journal of the Academy of Marketing Science*, 23(4), pp. 335–345, 1995.)

## Contribution

Wilson contributes to the customer value literature by proposing a model of buyer-seller relationships. This model is built on the integration of 12 relationship variables. Such variables consist of commitment, trust, cooperation, mutual goals, interdependence and power, performance satisfaction, structural bonds, comparison level of the alternatives, adaptation, nonretrievable investments, shared technology, and social bonds. The process model is based on five stages: (1) partner selection, (2) defining purpose, (3) setting relationship boundaries, (4) creating relationship value, and (5) relationship maintenance.

## Summary

The author explains that relationships between buyers and sellers have become more strategic and increasingly more important in companies' grand strategies. In business markets, businesses seek buyer-seller alliances to achieve their goals. An extended list of twelve relationship variables models different types of buyer-seller relationship situations. Such variables are based on both theoretical and empirical studies: (1) *commitment* — a desire to continue the relationship into the future so the relationship will bring value to the partners; (2) *trust* — a fundamental building block based on each member acting in the best interest of the other partners; (3) *cooperation* — the coordinated actions of both firms to gain mutual benefits; (4) *mutual goals* — the level of benefit goals gained from the joint action of the relationship; (5) *interdependence and power* — the power which one partner has over the other partner; (6) *performance satisfaction* — the level to which the business transaction meets the business performance expected by the other partner; (7) *structural bonds* — the vector of forces that tie the parties involved in the relationship; (8) *comparison level of the alternatives* — the quality of the outcome available from the best available relationship partner; (9) *adaptation* — the process by which one party adjusts its processes or items to accommodate the other party; (10) *nonretrievable investments* — any resources committed to the relationship which cannot be recovered if the relationship aborts; (11) *shared technology* — the value of technology which one partner contributes to the relationship; and (12) *social bonds* — the social interaction which the parties contribute to the relationship.

## Customer Value Implication

This framework provides managers guidance in building buyer-seller relationships. Furthermore, if managers thoroughly understand the buyer-seller relationship, such profitable relationships can be created to yield sustainable competitive advantages.

# Part 5. Customer Value Assessment Tool (CVAT™)

# Customer Value Assessment Tool[*]

## Overview

In today's competitive business environment, offering superior customer service is no longer the exception; it's the rule! Customers expect it, and businesses are relentlessly trying to provide it. Unfortunately, relatively few organizations are able to provide truly memorable service to their customers.

Two words seem to capture exceptional service: "customer value". It is easy to interpret a successful response to the moments of truth. Such companies go the extra mile and add value in order to delight their customers. The bottom line is that we know customer value when we see it or experience it.

## Purpose

The Customer Value Assessment Tool (CVAT) has been created as an instrument tool to help product and service providers evaluate and improve their value delivery to their customers. Supplying outstanding service and value must be a dynamic process; therefore, this tool has been designed to be utilized on a regular basis. This helps to evaluate the extent of any changes and improvements that may need to be initiated.

---

The four components used to appraise customer value in this tool are perceived image, perceived service quality, perceived product quality, and perceived value-based price. The survey focuses on each component as an individual indicator of customer service and value. Collectively, the four components will help companies achieve excellence in managing customer value.

# Guidelines for Using the Customer Value Assessment Tool

The purpose of the CVAT is to rate your current employer based on the four components used to appraise customer value. Rank how well your company matches the statement given.

1    Means it happens all of the time.
2    Means it happens most of the time
3    Means it happens some of the time
4    Means it never happens

The results obtained via the CVAT can be organized into a report that will help identify the strengths and opportunities for improving customer value in your organization.

## Perceived Image

*Image definition:* The company is viewed as having a commitment to the customer, top management, continuous improvement, and the firm as a whole.

1.  The company treats its internal customers with the same care and respect as it treats its external customers.
    1        2        3        4
2.  The company conducts focus groups with customers to determine what they view as strengths and weaknesses in regard to the company's image.
    1        2        3        4
3.  The management style exhibited by the leaders of the company is that of a facilitator, coach, and enabler.
    1        2        3        4

4. Employees are viewed as positive representatives of the company's ideals.

   1        2        3        4

5. The company uses "systems thinking" to solve its internal and external challenges (e.g., the company understands that all events within the corporation are interrelated and each has an influence on the other).

   1        2        3        4

6. The company encourages its employees to seek a good balance between their work and family lives.

   1        2        3        4

7. The company eliminates obvious examples of excess.

   1        2        3        4

Comments on the above section: _____

_____

## Perceived Service Quality

*Service quality definition:* The service given is viewed to be timely and appropriate by the customer. This service may also anticipate the future needs or wants of the customer.

1. The company conducts focus groups with customers to determine what they view as strengths and weaknesses about the customer service the company provides.

   1        2        3        4

2. The company continually conducts customer satisfaction surveys and utilizes the results in order to improve services provided.

   1        2        3        4

3. The company provides special training for all employees on customer service, including ways to handle difficult customers.

   1        2        3        4

4. The company has a monthly "best practices" newsletter that details innovative ways to provide customer service.

   1        2        3        4

5. The company provides its customers with a range of professional and technical assistance.

   1        2        3        4

6. The company commits to and exhibits empathy when dealing with customers.

    1       2       3       4

7. The company constantly seeks ways to enhance its relationship with customers.

    1       2       3       4

8. The company provides a means for customers who wish to comment or complain.

    1       2       3       4

9. The company provides its customers with complete, easy-to-understand information concerning its products or services.

    1       2       3       4

10. The company ensures that complaints and problems are resolved to the complete satisfaction of the customer.

    1       2       3       4

11. The company regularly compares its customer satisfaction levels with those of the competition.

    1       2       3       4

12. The company rewards employees for innovative actions/ideas concerning customer service, regardless of sales outcome.

    1       2       3       4

13. The company regularly reviews progress on customer service goals and objectives.

    1       2       3       4

14. Policies and procedures for serving customers are consistent across departments.

    1       2       3       4

Comments on the above section: _____

_____

## Perceived Product Quality

*Product quality definition:* The product is viewed as being dependable (zero defects) and meets or exceeds the consumer's expectations.

1. The company conducts focus groups with customers to determine what they view as strengths and weaknesses of the company's products.

    1       2       3       4

2. The company forms strategic alliances with vendors, suppliers, and distributors.

   1   2   3   4

3. The company selects vendors on the basis of quality, not just price.

   1   2   3   4

4. The company uses quality function deployment (i.e., builds customer expectations into its products).

   1   2   3   4

5. The company is committed to design quality: "Do it right the first time."

   1   2   3   4

6. The company uses external benchmarking to determine the strengths and weaknesses of its own products.

   1   2   3   4

7. The company has a system for analyzing product performance data (i.e., quality control data) and translating the results into continuous product improvements.

   1   2   3   4

8. The company monitors supplier/vendor performance to ensure that the company's quality requirements are met.

   1   2   3   4

9. The company views corporate setbacks as an opportunity to develop a new approach to solving the problem.

   1   2   3   4

10. The company's marketing programs, methods, and strategies add value to the firm's offerings.

    1   2   3   4

11. The company demonstrates through thought, word, and deed that low quality is expensive and that high quality has a high return on investment.

    1   2   3   4

12. The company is viewed as having a commitment to continuous improvement, or *kaizen*.

    1   2   3   4

Comments on the above section: _____

_____

## Perceived Value-Based Price

*Value-based price definition:* The price level that a customer is willing to pay to receive a given level of product and/or service performance.

1. When establishing a price for a product or service, the company starts with the customer first, considers the competition, and then determines the appropriate price, as opposed to setting price only according to costs.

   1      2      3      4

2. The company's product or service is viewed by the customer as exceeding the expected benefits of a competitive product.

   1      2      3      4

3. The company meets customer expectations without hindering financial performance.

   1      2      3      4

4. The company offers as many convenient payment methods and terms as possible in order to better satisfy its customers.

   1      2      3      4

5. The company looks for ways to cut back on costs and still deliver products or services that meet customer expectations.

   1      2      3      4

6. The company utilizes new technologies that allow them to lower prices and increase profits.

   1      2      3      4

7. The company creates innovations that allow them to offer more for less than the competition.

   1      2      3      4

8. The company raises both quality and service to new levels.

   1      2      3      4

9. The company is viewed as value-adding with respect to the price it charges for its product or service.

   1      2      3      4

Comments on the above section: _____

_____

# References

1. Anderson, K. and Zemke, R. (1991) *Delivering Knock Your Socks Off Service,* New York: AMACOM.
2. Batemen, T.S. and Snell, S.A. (1996) *Management: Building Competitive Advantage,* Chicago: Irwin.
3. Davis, B.L., Hellervik, L.W., Skube, C.J., Gebelein, S.H., and Sheard, J.L., Eds. (1992) *Successful Manager's Handbook: Development Suggestions for Today's Managers,* New York: Personnel Decision International.
4. Gables, W. and Ellig, J. (1993) Introduction to Market-Based Management, Center for Market Processes.
5. Gibson, J.L., Ivancevich, J.M., and Donnelly, Jr., J.H. (1994) *Organizations,* Chicago: Irwin.
6. Melnyk, S.A. and Denzler, D.R. (1996) *Operations Management: A Value-Driven Approach,* Boston: Irwin.
7. Naumann, E. (1995) *Creating Customer Value: The Path to Sustainable Competitive Advantage,* Cincinnati, OH: Thomson Executive Press.
8. Noe, R.A., Hollenback, J.R., Gerhart, B., and Wright, P.M. (1997) *Human Resource Management,* Chicago: Irwin.
9. Tucker, R.B. (1997) *Customer Service for the New Millennium: Winning and Keeping Value-Driven Buyers,* Franklin Lakes, NJ: Career Press.
10. Zeithaml, V.A., Parasuraman, A., and Berry, L.L. (1990) *Delivering Quality Service: Balancing Customer Perceptions and Expectations,* New York: The Free Press.

# Index

# Index